BEAUTIFUL
HERO

HOW WE SURVIVED
THE KHMER ROUGE

D0890499

JENNIFER H. LAU

COPYRIGHT

BEAUTIFUL HERO: HOW WE SURVIVED THE KHMER ROUGE
© 2016 by Jennifer H. Lau
Cover art and design by Palaparthi
Maps by KAI Architecture

ISBN 978-0-9980798-9-9 (pbk.)

LOTUS BOOK GROUP

CONTENTS

REVIEWS

From Midwest Book Review:

"Beautiful Hero: How We Survived the Khmer Rouge tells how a family of eight with six children (ranging in age from six months to thirteen years old) made it through hell and back again and narrows survival skills down to the most basic of needs: water and food. There have been other autobiographical accounts of life under the Khmer Rouge; but *Beautiful Hero* departs from most in its focus on one woman's courage (the author's mother) and how this literally made the difference between life and death for her entire family.

Sagas of family survival are typically thought-provoking, evocative, and compelling. In this case, they also assume a gritty, close examination of the life of a woman whose name translates to 'beautiful hero' in Chinese, and whose destiny seemed predetermined. . . . Few lives can claim to hold such a clear purpose: Meiyeng's ability to solve problems and survive under impossible circumstances came from a steely fortitude developed in early childhood and fostered by life's slings and arrows as an adult.

Readers shouldn't expect just psychological inspection, but should anticipate a read that pulls no punches: Lau's writing paints vivid pictures as it documents the trials and challenges of staying alive under these conditions. . . . And thus, *Beautiful Hero* becomes not one matriarch's biography, but a record of the entire family's experiences and how each family member reacted to and survived these soul- and body-wrenching encounters.

Not everyone emerges a survivor—and those left behind are also left to struggle with their reasons for going on. . . .

Every American should read this saga, which documents an ultimate journey to America and the costs involved in getting there. It's a story that is evocative, gripping, and challenging, all at once; and it's one that leads the reader to better understand the promises and delivery of a kind of freedom that many countries never experience."

From the Broome Street Review:

"Imagine a man who, out of desperation, eats his own children and feels justified in doing so. Imagine an island composed entirely of corpses—decaying bodies piling higher and higher by the day. Imagine having to eat feces and drink urine for nourishment. Imagine the killing fields, walking one foot in front of the other to avoid land mines. Imagine living constantly in fear, treated no better than a beast of burden. Can you imagine being left for dead, forgotten and ignored by the whole world?

Such were the circumstances for those captured and abused by Cambodia's Khmer Rouge. Jennifer Lau, a survivor of the Khmer Rouge, recounts the atrocities of this genocide with startling clarity. In the miracle that her memory, her language, and her spirit remain unbroken, we learn how she and her family survived. *Beautiful Hero* is a story of profound love during chaos. A story of hope out of unfathomable despair. The story of Meiyeng, Lau's heart-of-stone mother—the eponymous Beautiful Hero, whose courage is enough to free an entire family from the depths of hell itself.

Not only is this a paean for a mother whose fortitude kept together a family in the midst of chaos. This is also a tribute to those who lived and suffered through the regime—and a memorial for those who lost their lives. The lives captured in *Beautiful Hero* are each presented with dignity, despite circumstances of unthinkable abjection.

Beautiful Hero stands as a testament to resilience in the face of trauma. This, above all, is a reminder that the heroes in our lives, through their silent sacrifices, preserve for us our psychic continuity and well-being.

We are here now. We have survived and continue to thrive. For this we should all be grateful. Perhaps we each have a beautiful hero to thank for this."

From Kirkus Reviews:

"In this death-defying family saga . . . Lau describes her parents' upbringing, their arranged marriage, and her own childhood in a claustrophobic neighborhood. Lau was still a young girl when the Khmer Rouge took over Cambodia, and she maintains the perspective of a child throughout, as when her passenger train was raided by death squads. "Those captured were on their hands and knees at gunpoint," she says. "As time dragged on, the chaos and the delay seemed an eternity. My bladder was at the point of rupture, so I held and held and even used my hands to stop the dam from bursting."

Each chapter brings some new horror: massacres, midnight firefights, laborers worked to death, a harrowing march through land mine–infested mountains. In one scene, a starving man ate too much food and died. The book . . . documents these tragedies, with Lau's honesty and attention to detail bringing that appalling era into focus. . ..

The story has its share of symbolism, too: Lau's father ran a camera shop, and when the family was forced into a labor camp, he retained his cameras; the useless equipment became a metaphor for the stable life they lost. Later, Meiyeng maintained a verdant garden. Passing soldiers conclude that Meiyeng would never contemplate escape after putting so much work into her vegetable beds. Through it all, Lau's mother remained stern and strong. Her name, Meiyeng, translates to "beautiful hero," and Lau credits the unflappable matron with the family's survival.

The sickening suspense will haunt readers to the end.

Celebrates survival but also provides a street-level view of Khmer atrocities in a powerful reminder of what can happen when revolutionaries turn tyrannical."

DEDICATION

To my parents, for their ultimate love and sacrifice.

EDMUND BURKE

"All that is necessary for the triumph of evil is that good men do nothing."

Map 1: Cambodia

PROLOGUE

Our day began with less than half a canteen of water.

The line moved at a snail's pace. We progressed at the exact speed of the person in front of us. When the person in front lifted his foot off the ground, the person behind immediately planted his toes in that exact spot. This was how we navigated the mine-rigged mountains. At times, we forgot to breathe. Occasionally someone misplaced his foot and, without warning, an explosion would rock the earth. That misstep destroyed not only him but also strangers, friends, and nearby family members. Every correct step led us closer to the bottom of the mountains. The front led blindly; the back followed cautiously.

My family of eight (with six children, ages ranging from six months old to thirteen years old) was in the back. The path required our absolute concentration, and we painstakingly marched in each other's footsteps for days. Along a path paved by the blood of others, we worried about our own survival. How much longer could we last with hardly any water? Luckily, Uncle Jo found us then, after we had moved only ten yards from where we had camped the night before.

As we tentatively made our way down, my three uncles (Mama's younger brothers) carefully moved up against the flow of forty-five thousand discarded refugees to find us. Upon discovering us on the verge of tears and filled with hopelessness, Uncle Jo's eyes misted over.

Uncle Jo possessed vast knowledge: he knew how the politics of our world had landed us in this hell and how the Khmer Rouge had multiplied and risen to power. It was due to four years of bombing, ordered by Washington, D.C. to destroy the cargo route linking Cambodia to North Vietnam. Countless civilians died from 1969 to 1973. Farmers and their children dropped their hoes and spades to pick up AK-47s and side with the Khmer Rouge in their retaliation against the United States.

It was a combination of bad ideology and bad politics that had thrust us into this long journey. Now we were trapped and surrounded by explosives and flying bullets.

To see us utterly distraught and destitute was enough for Uncle Jo to want to end our suffering: "Let's all just jump onto these mines and end it all!" He cursed the world for its shortsighted and reckless politics. He was a man who had long ago reached the end of his tether. Back then, I was a child suspended in a bottomless void, with a soundless cry. The void stretched and expanded, and with each passing hour my throat felt drier and scratchier than sandpaper. In my own way, I had already given up. I wasn't afraid anymore, and I shed no tears at the thought of being blown away.

As a man who already felt dead inside, Uncle Jo felt he had nothing left to lose. He went alone to search for water. Before he left, he told Mama: "If I don't come back, please look after my son." He took the empty containers and headed south, disappearing within the masses: at times moving with them, at times against them, and at times randomly discovering his own path.

He left around nine in the morning, laboriously navigating his way through the mines lying flush to the ground and always mindful not to step on anything that looked remotely like a scrap of metal. Successful navigation required both good judgment and sheer luck. The trick was to be unerringly cautious and light in movement: to go slow and steadily, one step at a time, with eyes wide open and mind focused.

After a mile of navigating the minefield, he heard water rushing behind the trees and boulders. He wanted to run to it, plunging himself into the excitement of such a discovery, but he stayed the course, trying with all his might to control his mind and focus his gaze on the ground. He had unknowingly quickened his pace and arrived at the water in a blank stupor.

His eyes locked in on the glare reflecting off the stream. This spring runoff trickled here from the north. The mist lured him in. The water tasted cool and sweet. He drank hungrily and heartily. He splashed the water onto his face. He could not wait to carry this miracle back to the rest of us.

He filled his containers. Just as he was about to leave, he saw several dead bodies strewn along the edge of the stream. He became paralyzed with fear. His knees buckled and his body and limbs shook violently, spilling water from the containers.

To his left and right, he saw nearly invisible threads. They were trip lines threaded through the trees, bushes, boulders, and even into the water—with corresponding grenades hung from the trees and suspended in the bushes. If only he could remember the way he came! He frantically searched for a way out. Clearly fortunate to have arrived at the water in the first place, he thanked his lucky stars as he desperately begged his ancestors for protection.

He stepped gingerly over the threads to steer his way out through the maze, determined to take the water back at all costs. It took twice as long for him to return. Upon his return, everyone's eyes widened at the precious commodity in his hands.

Some onlookers immediately left to refill their own canteens. They must have tripped the grenades in their haste, for they never made it back.

By the time Uncle Jo reached us, it was already sunset: an all-day ordeal. He had donated half of the water to helpless elderly people and children along the way and shared the rest with us.

Our canteen was full once again.

Uncle Jo came through for us with water on that one fateful day, but it was Meiyeng who was the constant and formidable force in all our stories of survival. I am only alive today because of one woman's courage: my mother, Meiyeng.

Family Tree: Maternal

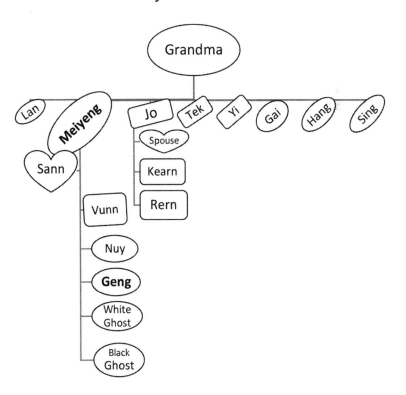

Family Tree: Paternal

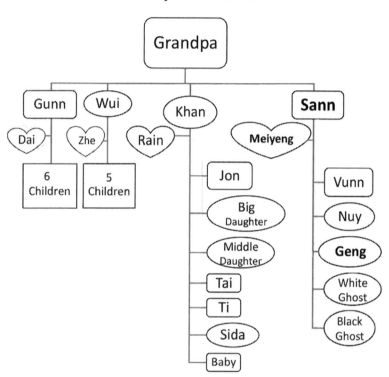

1. THE COUNTDOWN

Meiyeng Chau was nineteen and completely ignorant of her own marriage when her mother (my grandmother) accepted a matchmaker's proposal. The simple reason that Grandma approved of Sann Hong, my father-to-be, as her son-in-law was because his mother was already dead and was therefore not a threat to her daughter's happiness. Papa never remembered his mother: she passed away before he turned one. His father and maternal aunt raised him and his three older siblings.

Grandma was sold at the word "motherless" because the word "mother-in-law" frightened her. She failed to investigate Sann's background to learn about his personality and physical limitations—his stubborn characteristics, his poor eyesight, and his dull business (and, at times, common) sense. She didn't know he was quiet and uncommunicative, born with the genes of an introvert who preferred solitude over society.

Grandma cared deeply about her daughters' independence and happiness. She had five daughters and three sons, and she truly believed she'd made the right decision about Mama's future. She didn't want her second daughter, her clever and strong-willed child, to suffer in the same manner as her eldest daughter.

The firstborn Lan had married into a family whose mother-in-law behaved like a slave driver. Lan became an indentured servant in her husband's family. Her only future freedom lay in her mother-in-law's mortality; she even needed permission to visit her own parents and siblings. Grandma was unhappy and bitter about her firstborn's predicament, and she vowed never to again marry her daughters to men with mothers.

Grandma kept her oath with Meiyeng, her secondborn. She believed that by marrying Mama to a man with no mother to breathe down her neck, her daughter would stand a better chance of living a good life—a life governed by her own free will. The marriage transpired immediately, and it didn't matter if the bride consented to the nuptials, because tradition (within the Chinese culture and community) at the time allowed parents full autonomy over selecting spouses for their children.

My parents were fortunate enough to meet twice before their wedding day. Papa was five years older than Mama and certainly a lucky man, for some higher forces were certainly at play to pair him up with her in preparation for their difficult future ahead. He was immediately attracted to her beauty and her larger-than-life reputation. She had a smooth complexion, big smiling eyes, and well-defined lips, all of which helped to draw attention away from her slightly prominent nose. Her name means Beautiful (*Mei*) Hero (*Yeng*).

Unfortunately, Mama couldn't say the same about Papa when she first met him. "My heart sank to the floor," she said. "He wore glasses as thick as my thumb, although without them he could be handsome. He was so quiet and a little awkward: I knew oxen with more personality. Prince Charming, he was not."

Papa was, indeed, a quiet man: a tinkerer and a dreamer who easily got lost inside his own mind and emerged only when someone called for his attention. He was, ironically, the yin to Mama's yang. And like Mama said, he was somewhat handsome in an austere and occasionally tender way. What Papa seemed to lack in personality and common sense, he made up for with his spiritual acuity. Time and again, Papa proved that in some way, for some reason, he was favored by the spirits and ancestors.

So, Mama was caught, as they would say, between a rock and a hard place. She had dazzled many older women and their sons for years. She could have had any bachelor of her heart's desire, but unfortunately, they all had mothers, so none passed Grandma's muster. Many eligible mothers-in-law had envisioned Meiyeng as their daughter-in-law ever since she was little. People knew she was the main provider in her family.

Meiyeng was loved and admired by the townspeople in Moung. In the almost exclusively and ethnically Chinese community, everyone knew her by name and respected her for her capabilities. She gained her reputation at the age of five, when she improvised a contraption to fend off the thieving crows by tying one end of a rope to the clothesline in the back yard and the other end to a crib swaying inside the house. This caused the shirts and pants to perform a ghostly, macabre dance in the breeze. Many townspeople mimicked her ingenuity in keeping birds from eating the meat that cured outdoors under the sun.

When Meiyeng was ten, she assumed her father's role in the family as he drank himself into oblivion before succumbing to alcoholism within a decade. Her father (my grandfather) had always prided himself on being a debt-free man, but when debts piled up from the cost of building the family home, he faced a new reality. His anxiety intensified. It took only one comment to bring him down and, along with it, his world. Someone blatantly said to him: "If you don't have the money, you shouldn't have purchased the land, let alone built a house on it!" This remark pained him, and he turned to drinking to calm his nerves.

While her father became incapacitated in providing for the family, Meiyeng worked overtime and attended school less than part-time to pay for the construction of their home. Her younger brothers wanted to quit school to help alleviate the family's financial burden, but she forbade them. Through stubborn willpower alone, she saw that they attended school full-time and helped part-time only. After three years of waking up before dawn to feed and slaughter the pigs, haul water, and sell breakfast stew, their house was built and paid off: not a penny was owed. She was only fourteen.

Because she was busy running the household and family business, everyone assumed Grandma wasn't ready to part with Meiyeng through betrothal. So suitors waited on the sidelines until it was too late to compete for her hand in marriage: rumor reached them one day that an out-of-town matchmaker had snatched her away. Once the news of Meiyeng's engagement spread through the community, many of Grandma's lifelong friends were outraged. Many couldn't sleep that night, and some even went so far, the following morning, as to sever all ties with Grandma.

In line with the teachings of Buddha, Mama understood that this life was a repayment of debt from a previous life—a retribution of sorts—and one she must endure. She discontentedly resigned her life to her fate: to Papa.

I was born in January of 1970 at the tail end of the rooster year, and I entered life in the year that Washington D.C. backed Prime Minister Lon Nol in a coup to oust Prince Sihanouk, leaving Cambodia to rapidly spiral into an uncontrollable political hell.

I was a morning chicken, by Chinese astrological standards. My parents believed a morning fowl would work harder and have better business sense than an evening chicken. "Dawn" translated to an eagerness to start the day and roam for food, and "dusk" meant being tired, needing sleep and lacking ambition.

They named me *Geng* ("Graceful Girl" in our old village's Chinese dialect). When I was born, they penned my name after Vunn and Nuy's. They wrote all our birthdays on a special red cloth with indelible ink. By 1975, there were five children in my family: five dates all folded and tucked away in a wooden box in the false bottom of a dresser along with their other treasures.

I was a fighter too, they said, because I struggled to breathe. When I was an infant, the doctor told my parents that I had less than a 25% chance of survival. I had contracted pneumonia caused by an upper respiratory infection. Against all odds, my parents nurtured me back to life. As my weak body lay in the hospital with some IV dripping nutrients into my veins, Papa often sealed my tiny nose with his mouth and sucked out the mucous that blocked the oxygen to my lungs. They spent every second by my side, making sure I didn't miss one breath. Slowly but surely their selfless acts pulled me back to life.

At various times Papa had sucked all our noses when we were sick. Mama said his unconditional love and selfless acts were what kept their marriage together, but his lack of business acumen caused her much anxiety.

After they got married, Mama redirected Papa's business from one that was labor-intensive, risky, and not lucrative to one that was passive and profitable. Papa used to be an auto mechanic, but the job didn't pay well, perhaps because he was slow at it. He later abandoned fixing cars to enter the middleman business, selling fake gold teeth to dentists and transporting heavy rice and metal in oxcarts from sellers to buyers. He'd attempted many business ventures but lacked the wits to make them successful. At Mama's direction and vision, he later became a landowner and performed property inspections on the land that we owned.

♦ ♦ ♦

When I was only one, a boy clawed my face. The scars were heinous, and these marks could be traced back to the Khmer Rouge.

While we lived in the rural town of Sadao in the northwest part of Cambodia, a couple with a three-year-old boy knocked on our door, begging for food, shelter, and work. They told my parents how the Khmer Rouge had pillaged their town, burned their home, and killed their relatives and friends. In haste, they fled north to our town and arrived penniless, dirty, and hungry.

Upon hearing their pleas for help, my parents offered the man a job on the farm and the woman a position in Mama's hair salon. They lived and dined with us temporarily; but after their boy attacked me, we severed all agreements and niceties.

Aunt Gai, my babysitter who was one of Mama's younger sisters, had to pry the boy off of me when, for no apparent reason, he assaulted and scratched me with animalistic rage. My aunt felt horrible about what the boy did to my face, finding comfort only in the fact that he didn't gouge out my eyes. For the next few weeks she tended my wounds with utmost care, clipping my nails to prevent me from scratching at the scabs when they itched. She did everything in her power to mitigate the damage, but I was still scarred by deep scratches.

Fortunately, I was too young to remember the pain. We were all oblivious to the fact that this event was a foreshadowing of the Khmer Rouge eventually taking over our country and scarring us all.

We lived on a busy street in Sadao until I turned three. Our house practically adjoined the neighbors' houses. Mama operated her hair salon downstairs and we lived upstairs. There was a shed in the back of the house where my parents stored tools and empty soda bottles left over from Mama serving her customers, relatives, and friends.

Like many children, I was drawn to the sugary beverages, and since my parents reserved them for guests, they were stored out of my reach. Occasionally they would indulge me with half a glass of soda with a few chunks of ice floating in the delicious drink. After relishing it to the last drop, I would beg for a refill, but my parents wouldn't allow me any more.

One day my little feet brought me into the shed where I stumbled upon a crate of empty, open bottles. To my amazement and delight, each bottle still had a few drops of the sweet nectar. Although orange was my favorite, I soon acquired a taste for cola and lime. Thereafter, I would sneak into the dark shed and work my way through the dregs of the bottles. When someone called for me, I would sneak out briefly to make my appearance before disappearing again into the shed. It became my home away from home.

As fate would have it, my secret habit wouldn't last long. One day I opened my mouth to drink some cola, only to receive a heap of cigarette butts and ash down my throat. I choked and coughed to near suffocation. I learned never to sneak the last drops of soda again.

♦♦♦

It took an army to raise me and my siblings. That army was comprised of Mama's three younger brothers, three younger sisters, and my grandmother; they were in our lives and in our hearts. Mama's elder sister Lan was married and lived with her husband's family elsewhere, popping in and out of my peripheral consciousness.

Before Mama gave birth to her first child, a palm reader told her that she would have nine children in total. She dismissed the fortuneteller as a fraud and went about her busy life making a household with Papa. Four births and two miscarriages later, the exact prediction resurfaced through a different fortuneteller. At the time, her pregnancies included my older brother Vunn and my older sister Nuy. I came next, but my existence was sandwiched between two miscarriages until baby Yook's arrival.

Now Mama panicked. She only wanted three to four children at most—not nine. She came from a big family and had almost single-handedly raised her younger siblings: she was not about to do all that child-rearing and dirty diapers again.

She turned to birth control pills to prevent conception, determined to limit her children to four and no more. She had the right idea but lacked the knowledge and discipline to take the tablets in a timely manner. As a result, four soon became five. The latest addition to our family was a baby girl named Ling.

Ling, the fifth child, came to our world with huge birthmarks: her arms and thighs had white streaks. They were especially noticeable against her darker-than-usual complexion. Because she was dark, she was nicknamed *Haygui* ("Black Ghost"). With her porcelain skin, the fourth child, Yook, naturally assumed the title *Baigui* (or "White Ghost"). These two girls completed the opposite (yet complementary) yin-yang contrast in our family.

Mama believed the birth control pills had caused Black Ghost's discolorations. After she found out she was pregnant, she had swallowed them in huge dosage in a desperate attempt at an abortion, but the fetus had refused to surrender its delicate hold on life. Black Ghost entered our world five months before the Khmer Rouge forced us out of our home.

Mama was plagued with guilt. If she could turn back time, she would have thrown away those pills. Now she cradled baby Black Ghost in the folds of her arms and loved her as much as she did her firstborn.

After she gave birth to five children, she opted to have her fallopian tubes tied, determined to decommission herself for good. Five was all she needed; five was only one more than four, she reasoned.

After the procedure, Mama became deathly ill, contracting a severe infection in her uterus and enduring a few months of excruciating pain as the infections nearly ended her life.

♦ ♦ ♦

Upon approaching my third birthday (two years before the Khmer Rouge took control over Cambodia), I went to our family farm with Mama's younger brothers Uncle Tek and Uncle Yi (ages nineteen and seventeen, respectively). We stayed in our wooden cabin. Papa had often taken me with him to our family farm to collect rent money from the local farmers. My parents weren't wealthy, but they did manage to amass six plots of land (mostly with the earnings from Mama's hair salon). Some of the tenant farmers leased our land and paid cash while others paid a portion of their harvest output.

As prudent investors, my parents often went to the farm and performed due diligence to ensure that the land was being optimally used, and to account for the profits. It was a risky undertaking to visit our farmland because the Khmer Rouge had infiltrated the area. They often frisked Papa and held a gun to his head, demanding money to advance their cause. At night, in those early days, they trespassed on our land and stole fruit from our trees. In retrospect, I wish that I could say these were the worst of their offenses.

My two teenage uncles helped with the farm because my parents were overwhelmed with their fourth child, the latest addition to our family at the time. As the third child, I was the youngest for about two years until my sister Yook came along. She was born a "China Doll": her skin was porcelain white, her eyes were big and pearly, and her nose was a button. This doll coaxed cheek-pinching from doting aunts, uncles, and even passers-by. She was a delight to others, but not to me. With this new China Doll in our family there surged within me a strange and unfamiliar feeling: I was bitter and unhappy—I was jealous.

I didn't know that I was an unsightly child with deep scars all over my face, but I recall feeling cast aside to one corner of my parents' busy lives when China Doll arrived. The jealousy deepened and, perhaps, may help explain why I hid away in the shed. After I recovered from ingesting the cigarette butts and ashes, I continued to go back to the shed just to be alone.

Things started to turn around when Uncle Yi and Uncle Tek took me with them on excursions. I often rode on the back of their motorcycle to go picnic on a wild, grassy knoll at the outskirts of town. I loved every second of my time with them. This was in no small part due to the generally cool attitude of my uncles: they were young, hip, and free-spirited, and I had the good fortune of sharing in their boyish activities. I chased colorful butterflies and dragonflies while my uncles wooed girls and wore fashionable bell-bottom pants to parties. I picked unique flowers and tasted new foods at various eateries. I smiled so hard and had so much fun that the feeling of being rejected (since China Doll's arrival) started to fade away. In a way, my young uncles made me feel special again.

Even so, my uncles were single, inexperienced, and had never cooked a decent meal in their lives. I will never forget the bland food they fed me when they had to live off the land. At the farm, in our hut, they cooked plain rice porridge and added soy sauce for taste, which nearly rivaled the thrill of drinking water. That was all I ate for a week.

During the fateful trip around my third birthday, I woke up from a nap and found myself alone and hungry. I climbed down from the wooden hut to look for my uncles. I spotted a pig milling around the front of the hut, sniffing for feed. Farther out, a yellow cow was chewing and roaming. The two creatures seemed unthreatening.

Everything seemed harmonious for the moment—until I heard the cow charge the pig. Immediately I turned to look, only to see the cow ram its horns into the pig and thrust it high into the air. It landed with a muted thud on the grassy earth no more than ten feet from where I stood. The pig had a terrible gash in its stomach, and blood and intestines gushed out. It was the most shocking and frightening moment in my life, thus far: I had witnessed gore and death for the first time.

Suddenly I realized that my own safety was in jeopardy. I panicked, and adrenaline spurred my legs forward. Before I knew what I was doing, I bolted up the stairs to the hut. All I could think of for the rest of the day was that I could have been that pig.

Later that night, terror shrouded our hut. The Khmer Rouge had been waging small-scale battles nearby and our farm became a part of the battleground. We heard a barrage of gunfire, voices shouting, and wounded men groaning. It was so loud that I imagined them to be just outside where the pig and cow had had their confrontation.

Eventually I succumbed to weariness and fell asleep despite gunfire ringing in my ears. When I awoke, I found myself back at home. My uncles had brought me safely home while I slept.

◆ ◆ ◆

In its infancy, the Khmer Rouge was a small guerrilla faction spawned by the communist Vietnamese during the war with the United States. This faction grew in number when, purportedly, King Sihanouk (the monarch who ruled Cambodia at the time) did nothing to prevent the Americans from bombing the Northern Vietnamese cargo route in eastern Cambodia from 1969 to 1973. Nearly three million tons of ordnance rained down on this once-gentle land. More bombs fell in Cambodia during that era than all the bombs dropped in Europe and Japan during World War II.

The air raids caused immense casualties, and the collateral damage was estimated to be a half-million people. The death toll enraged the souls of many and it compelled citizens who were politically neutral to side with the Khmer Rouge. Even my uncles, who lived near us in the western part of Cambodia (which was removed and distant from the bombing), had thought of joining the Khmer Rouge; but they resisted.

The turmoil and uncertainty intensified when Washington, D.C. supported a bloodless coup to oust King Sihanouk and replace him with the puppet Lon Nol. Lon Nol was incompetent and his leadership lent itself to more corruption, poverty, and chaos. Weapons provided by the Americans to fortify Lon Nol's army ended up in hands of the Khmer Rouge.

My parents and grandparents were not supporters of the king nor of the puppet. Neither man could lead or rule selflessly or effectively, and neither man thought of corruption as a serious crime. As malfeasance and political repression worsened, the hearts of the commoners became jaded and fractured. With most citizens impoverished and discontent with the current government, taking up arms with the Khmer Rouge seemed a natural choice. It didn't take much for the Khmer Rouge to charm people with communist ideology, and it danced straight into my paternal grandfather's soul.

During Mama's first pregnancy with my brother Vunn in 1967 in Sadao, the monarchist government targeted Papa's father (Grandpa). One year his cotton harvest doubled, and the local officials came knocking—their palms outstretched for Grandpa to grease. When he refused, they handcuffed him, accused him of theft, arrested him, and jailed him for six months. There was no trial, no jury, no judge, and not a shred of evidence against him. This was how the corrupt government worked: it spat in the faces of righteous and principled men.

Grandpa's once-unflappable spirit was slowly being beaten down by corruption. Malfeasance ruined an entire country by degrading good souls. It didn't take much for the Khmer Rouge to convince people that our misery was caused by capitalist greed and corruption, and that real salvation could only come in the form of communism—an egalitarian doctrine promising social justice by employing a one-class state.

My parents visited Grandpa and brought him hot meals during those long months. Each visit cost them dearly. They brought cigarettes for the guards and pre-rolled cash as "admission" fees. As each month lapsed, the guards demanded more money. They paid monthly fees for a chair and a cot in Grandpa's cell, and when they missed a payment, Grandpa had to sit and sleep on the floor. My parents paid for a blanket so the cold wouldn't claim him, but the guards continued to squeeze my parents in other ways, including soliciting money to repair their broken bicycles and motorcycles. This exploitation continued until they released Grandpa six months later. Grandpa was never the same again: the experience broke his spirit and he lost faith in the current system.

At this point in Grandpa's life, communism appeared to be the lesser of the two evils. He was intimately familiar with Chinese communism: he had escaped China in his late teens in the early twentieth century to seek new opportunities in Cambodia. He shunned communism like the plague, but he later warmed up to it after serving time in prison: now communism seemed to have returned to him and he couldn't run away from it anymore. He had no choice but to embrace it. When people asked what his thoughts were on communism, he told them it was probably better than what most people feared. He stated that China offered good health clinics, great education for young minds, no corruption, and no homeless people.

Grandpa was not an advocate for the Khmer Rouge; it was just that he loathed the rampant corruption in the current government even more.

When I was three, my family relocated to Poipet town in Ou Chrov district, the closest Cambodian city to Thailand. We abandoned the land, the farm, the house, the shed, and the hair salon in Sadao. It was a strategic move for my family and our extended family, because if the infighting grew, or if the Khmer Rouge seized power, we could always escape to Thailand.

We lived in one of Grandpa's condominiums in downtown Poipet next door to Papa's sister Wui and her family of seven. Papa had one older brother and two older sisters. Grandpa lived with his oldest son Gunn and his family of eight a block from us. Aunt Khan, the younger of Papa's sisters, and her family of nine lived outside the city. Our place was the central point of convergence for family gatherings. I had barely enough toes and fingers to count my cousins with.

Our home was single-story, long and narrow, and was sandwiched between other units with a similar layout. Everything we needed was practically outside our doorstep, from restaurants and movie theaters to clothing stores and currency exchanges. These were my carefree days: playing with my cousins and siblings, visiting each other's homes, and sharing each other's popsicles.

Our humble abode doubled as my parents' storefront shop. They partitioned off the front half of the unit for Papa's photography shop and Mama's hair salon. The other half was a play area by day and sleeping quarters by night. To accommodate the close quarters, we shoved furniture into a corner every night and laid straw and vinyl mats on the floor. Our parents slept on two separate beds against the back wall; Mama took the larger one with baby Black Ghost and Papa slept on the smaller one. Every night we rolled onto one another and woke up huddled with an unwilling sibling in the morning.

There were five of us, then. Black Ghost and White Ghost were babies, and the rest of us were quite mischievous. My parents said I was, by far, the most mischievous and feisty of the children. They called my behavior "middle child syndrome." I overcompensated in my actions to garner their attention and I challenged and rivaled my elders (who were more than two and three years older than me) like they were my equals.

My assertiveness forced Vunn and Nuy to form an alliance to defeat me. We often played pranks on each other just for the thrill of it. One morning, I woke up to find my older sister and brother giggling with their hands over their mouths. They had done it again: poured water on my mat while I was asleep to make it look like I had had an accident. There was a puddle in my spot and I saw them hiding the bowl as I opened my eyes in the morning. When they teased me, I was determined to get them back.

I could never get up as early as my older siblings because they had school to attend and I had dreams to catch. So I plotted my revenge for a different time. I was hoping to exact it when they fell unwittingly to sleep. As I bided my time to even the score with my siblings, the Khmer Rouge advanced from the countryside into the city.

Another time, Vunn and Nuy challenged me to lick something on the floor that resembled baby poop. In exchange for the dare, I would receive a coin. They couldn't keep a straight face when they dangled the money in front of my face. I hadn't fully grasped the insignificant value of the coin, but I knew a thing or two about poop. What lay on the floor was not poop, but a tiny piece of orange peel that smelled citrusy—but I was not about to divulge that tidbit of information. So I licked it and the coin was mine; stashed safely in my piggy bank on a mantel. We always played ridiculous pranks on each other: I could proclaim my courage and strength over their pact and it gave me a sense of pride that I could hold my own ground.

◆◆◆

Although my parents had a photo shop and a hair salon business, their main source of income came from an importing and exporting enterprise. They had finally found a profitable niche with hardly any applied effort. Except for one competitor in Phnom Penh (who developed color film in-house), my parents practically monopolized the color photography industry throughout Cambodia. The money was rolling in faster than they were able to count, but because inflation was rampant, my parents unloaded the currency in exchange for rubies, sapphires, diamonds, gold, and land.

Every morning an intoxicating aroma of culinary delights permeated our front door as restaurant chefs and food vendors prepared their daily menus across the street. Around noon, a man would push his ice cream cart, hollering: "Popsicles! Ice cream! Shaved ice!" Our street was always busy, teeming with cars, motorcycles, oxcarts, and pedestrians alike. Bicycle bells would ring nonstop as their riders attempted to maneuver through the usual maniacal traffic.

As far as a business location went, we were in the perfect place. When people came through our front door from the hustle and bustle outside, I could usually tell what they came for. If a lady came in by herself, I knew she wanted a haircut or a perm—the same went for a man with unkempt hair—but when a couple or family arrived all decked out in nice clothes, they had come for portraits.

Occasionally Mama would feel guilty for neglecting me and, when she had a moment to spare, she would take me for a treat. A small shop across from us sold drinks and desserts. Mama had a sweet tooth. She could forgo all her food, but not the desserts. She would take me by the hand and guide me across the bustling traffic.

We would take up two stools and eat delicious white-and-pink sesame and peanut balls drowned in coconut milk. As we ate, her eyes would be glued to our storefront, watching for business traffic. When there was a line, she would immediately rush back, grabbing me with one hand and carrying a bag filled with iced coffee for employees and her younger siblings, who worked for her.

Aunt Gai was Mama's right-hand person. She was our surrogate mother in the house and Mama's commandant in the hair salon. Uncle Tek became our second father, and he mastered photography lighting and camera angles in the studio. They had, on multiple occasions, mediated the quarrels I had with my two older siblings. They encouraged harmony and love among us children.

I remember the train clearly, and it still haunts me. I'd just turned five when I traveled with my parents and baby Black Ghost to Battambang, the second largest city in Cambodia. Mama, suffering from the tubal ligation infection, had to see a physician. For these follow up visits, someone had referred her to a doctor in Battambang. We were on our way there when our train abruptly halted in the middle of nowhere.

Anxiety swept over us when the Lon Nol soldiers stormed in with their rifles. They barged up and down the aisle, ordering passengers not to move as they commanded several others to get up. I watched, dumbfounded, as they held these passengers at gunpoint before escorting them off the train with their hands tied behind their heads. Their possessions were confiscated, tossed out of the cars, and ransacked.

Everyone on the train seemed distant with worry and a deepening unease hung in the atmosphere. Even Black Ghost felt anxious, for she cried. Mama was quick to silence her with a bottle.

Those captured were outside on their hands and knees at gunpoint.

I was frightened. What sort of crime did they commit? They didn't look like bad people. What was in the bags? Would we be next?

What locked this event even more securely in my mind was that I eventually wet myself. During the search and seizure, we were instructed to stay put: not one of us could leave our seats. As time dragged on, the chaos and the delay seemed to last an eternity. My bladder was at the point of rupture. So I held and I held and I even used my hands to stop the dam from bursting. Mama heard me complaining and saw me fidgeting but gave me a stern look.

All at once, I could not hold back any longer. The dam burst against my will, but all I felt was relief. As I let myself go, my anxiety washed away only to encounter a new one: how I would disappoint my parents with the filth. I sought their faces for signs of anger, only to see their continued distress.

Apparently other things were on my parents' minds; likely having to do with names such as "Norodom Sihanouk," "Mao Zedong," and "Lon Nol" and the names of faraway places such as "France," "Soviet Union," and "America," and other words tainted with latent significance such as "Vietnam," "Khmer Rouge," and "Communism."

War and politics still lay well beyond my childish comprehension; yet these topics were constantly discussed at the dinner table, in Papa's photography shop, and in Mama's hair salon. Change was inevitable. Few had the foresight to anticipate the approaching tidal wave.

◆◆◆

There were people who tried their best to continue living normally amidst the uncertainties, as if this Cambodian New Year (April 15 of 1975) was the same as any before it. People flooded the streets in celebration, dumping water on each other in playfulness and smiling and dancing as though the Khmer Rouge soldiers were their long-lost brothers and sisters. Some even prepared food for the advancing troops. My parents were no exception.

The city was getting ready; hundreds of people had volunteered to prepare a big feast for the Khmer Rouge by contributing their best, cooking everything from tasty stews to entire roasted piglets. Even folks who didn't have much were giving it their all, as if making offerings to their gods.

My brother Vunn rushed into the house. "Quick, come outside! Choppers are everywhere!" We followed him and saw, sure enough, buzzing helicopters in the sky. Hovering above rooftops like giant dragonflies, they seemed to be filming and taking pictures of us below. They were observing and, presumably, waiting to witness political changes as well.

Rumors had reached us that the people of Svay Sisophon, a larger city roughly twenty-five miles to the east, had already encountered the Khmer Rouge's advancing troops, teeming with foot soldiers, jeep convoy and army tanks. In return for the bowls of stew and cheers of joy offered by the townspeople, the Khmer Rouge aimed their guns at them. The city had allegedly experienced a massive, forced evacuation of every man, woman, and child from their homes, workplaces, and hospitals.

The instant those rumors reached Aunt Wui, Papa's oldest sister who lived next door, she packed in a rush. She and her five children came to say goodbye. Meanwhile, her husband Zhe was to stay behind to look after their properties and get a feel for the new and much anticipated political regime. If the situation worsened, he could later join the rest of the family in a designated location in Thailand. The plan sounded foolproof.

Hell officially arrived with a hard knock on our front door.

Map 2: Poipet

2. FORCED EVACUATION (APRIL 1975)

I slept the last night in our home, dreaming and plotting of sweet revenge. I fantasized about sneaking up on Vunn and Nuy with two cups of lukewarm water. My older brother and sister had pulled another prank on me. This time, instead of pouring water to stage my wet bed, they tested a theory to satisfy their curiosity. While I was asleep, they placed my hands in bowls of warm water to open the floodgates to my bladder. It worked, much to their surprise: instead of sweet revenge, I awoke with soiled pajamas.

They played me, but I was determined to get the last laugh! I might be younger, but I was nearly as good as they were in everything. When they were studying subtraction and addition, I learned with them. When they sang school songs, I belted out lyrics with them. At night, we entertained our parents with skits, songs, and dancing. When we disagreed and fought for toys and candies, our parents doled out equal punishment. There was never a time when I did not feel equal to either one of them.

So, determined to get even, I waited for Nuy and Vunn to doze off first. I waited for the lights to go out, but my own sleepiness proved too powerful a lure and I soon joined everyone in dreamland.

Our slumber was cut short that night. My five-year-old body woke, groggy and weary, to the sound of gunfire. I tossed and turned in protest. I yearned for silence to return so

I could sleep in peace. Instead, the clamor grew closer and louder. I squeezed my eyes shut tightly to block out the dawn glow, I plugged my fingers into my ears and turned to bury my face deeper into the pillow, and I drifted back to sleep.

Unfortunately, someone soon knocked on the front door and, once again, I was yanked from sleep to the sound of wheelbarrows rolling, feet scampering, and people yelling outside. The sounds of gunfire and shooting grew louder and louder.

I rammed my fingers deeper into my ears to make the noisy world disappear once more.

The knocking was persistent and became more urgent: I could hear it even through my plugged ears. Papa sprang out of bed and rushed over. He accidentally stepped on me as he crossed over us. I screamed in pain, my fingers no longer in my ears. Now I was fully awake.

"Open up!" a familiar voice shouted. Papa quickly unlatched the door, and much to our relief, it was Uncle Jo, the oldest of Mama's three younger brothers, who was now married and had two sons. He stood in the doorway looking unusually frightened.

Before Papa had a chance to ask what was happening, Uncle Jo thrust two plastic bags into Papa's hand: one containing two paper bowls of pork stew from his breakfast stand and the other holding two loaves of freshly baked French bread, still warm and crispy.

"Pack! Everyone is leaving! See for yourself!" Uncle Jo pointed behind him.

Papa lurched outside. Without his eyeglasses, he could only see a blur of movement with no defined shape. He hollered for us to fetch his glasses. I got up and ran to his nightstand to get them.

Through the open door, we could see throngs of people hurrying down our street. The density of the crowd grew with each passing second. There was a sense of urgency and distress in the people who moved past our front door toward the next block. Some were pushing wooden carts stacked with radios, food, and blankets. Another was pulling a television set on a flatbed cart crammed with baskets, bags, and cages which contained frightened hens and roosters. Most people hauled their possessions in huge wicker baskets dangling from each side of a pole balanced on their shoulders with family members, old and young alike, walking next to them. Some carried only a bundle atop their heads, towing a child in hand. The old with bent backs and the sick limped along, trying to keep up. In that moment, my sympathy went out to every one of them.

"Eat fast and get your things together! We must vacate our homes! Hurry! I still have to inform my wife and her family." Uncle Jo took off immediately, running against the flowing masses.

As soon as he left, Mama and Papa urged us to eat, and to do so quickly. During our feeding frenzy, they went next door to see how our neighbors and relatives were reacting to this news. Sure enough, Uncle Jo was right about the forced evacuation. He was always the most reliable source of information. His job as a street vendor routinely put him in the center of the latest gossip: from dawn until dusk, Uncle Jo saw and heard everything.

After seeing our neighbors and relatives hustling to gather their belongings, my parents ran back. Panic set in as they darted from the big room to the kitchen. We had hardly begun eating the hot stew when Mama started barking instructions to each of us. She had the urgency of one trying to find cover from a falling sky. She bolted back to the big room and began rummaging through many drawers, pulling out shirts, pants, medicines, and jewelry.

The gravity of the morning forced me to realize that we were going to join the people in the streets. Suddenly my breakfast tasted bland. I had eaten, at most, two mouthfuls of stew.

My older sister Nuy and I were assigned the task of changing our clothes and watching White Ghost and Black

Ghost. Aunt Gai, then eighteen, began putting perishables into the baskets. Uncle Tek took off on his motorcycle to inform and collect Grandma and her two youngest daughters (Aunt Hang, twelve, and Aunt Sing, ten) who lived in another town. I headed straight to the big room, stepping on blankets, stumbling over pillows, and getting up again only to freeze when gunshots were fired outside our door.

Next came an angry fist pounding on the door and a voice hollering at us to open up.

"Americans are coming!" a voice shouted. We all quickly converged at the door. There, standing in our doorway, was a soldier clutching a long, black rifle. There were more soldiers behind him, knocking on our neighbors' doors. A whole army of Khmer Rouge soldiers stood there, clad in black with red bandanas around their foreheads and caches of ammunition strapped to their chests. The soldier at our door was tall and skinny with unkempt, wavy hair. He didn't smile at all. His eyes were dark and piercing, which made him appear mature and authoritative. He wasn't someone to be trifled with, and I sensed he wouldn't hesitate to shoot any of us.

To my parents, the soldier was a teenager who was fearless and rude and who lacked education and etiquette, but they had probably endured hardship. Now we were at his mercy, at gunpoint, and he was telling us to leave our home.

"Americans are coming!" the teenager said with conviction. "Everyone must leave their homes to be safe from the bombing!"

There must have been doubt written on my parents' faces because he continued, "Bombs will fall from the sky. We're evacuating the town for your own protection! You can come back in three days! Not one grain of rice will go missing from your home. We promise! Hurry! The Americans are coming!"

One grain? Now that's silly, I thought. I kept picturing a mouse crawling into our rice stash and wondering how in the world he'd know when one grain went missing.

The evacuation was already underway and there was a slight measure of comfort knowing that everyone was in the same predicament. As Nuy and I helped White Ghost change her clothes, Mama and Aunt Gai coordinated, as expeditiously as they could, the gathering of food, medicine, and other essentials, including floor mats, clothes, blankets, mosquito nets, and pots and pans. Despite Mama's barked instructions, Papa remained engrossed in a mission of his own. While we scrambled to get ready, he spent many of those precious minutes delicately packing a sizeable portion of his photography shop's inventory into two huge black bags. Mama was overwhelmed, but she still noticed that Papa wasn't making good use of his time.

"What are you doing?" Mama glared at him in dismay.

"These cameras are coming with us," Papa replied without looking at her as he placed them delicately inside the bag.

"Are you planning on taking pictures with them?"

"I'm protecting our investment. People will steal them while we're away," Papa explained as he continued removing them from the shelves and the display counters.

"Brilliant!" Mama said disdainfully. "I hope those cameras of yours taste good." With that comment, she rushed away to attend to us.

Her mood softened a bit when she found us all changed and ready to go. Nuy showed Mama her school backpack, seeking affirmation. Mama quickly checked the contents and told her that she had everything she needed. At that instant, jealousy reared within me. I wanted a schoolbag, too. I reminded Mama that she had yet to get me one for school. "We still have time. We just ordered the school uniforms. Don't worry, you'll get the backpack next," Mama reassured me.

Only recently, my parents had taken me to school for enrollment. A female teacher, younger and thinner than Mama with bangs and neatly-tied hair, took me by the hand

and led me to a table in the center of the room. She pulled out a chair, flanked by two students who were writing some fish symbols on paper, and gestured for me to sit between them. Just as I sat down, the bell rang and the children, in white shirts and blue shorts and skirts, jumped out of their chairs and filed out of the classroom. Mama, Papa, and I remained with the teacher for a moment longer. That was the extent of my formal education for the next seven years, until I turned twelve.

Meanwhile, Papa was still packing the cameras. These bags stood taller than my head, and I couldn't even wrap my arms around them. Papa struggled to hoist them off the ground. The cameras filled two durable, black nylon bags.

No more than thirty minutes after the soldier first appeared in our doorway, we were hustled out of our home into the teeming masses on the streets. During the chaos, my parents piled the bags of essentials and Papa's cameras onto one of Uncle Jo's four-wheeled carts which Papa had borrowed after realizing that a bigger cart was needed.

During the mad rush, my parents forgot our birth certificates, the property deeds, and our sentimental belongings. Although she remembered her everyday costume jewelry, Mama forgot her collection of precious stones, gold bullion, and the other fine jewelry hidden with our birth certificates.

My nine-year-old brother carried nothing but his cherished slingshot and clay balls. My seven-year-old sister strapped on her school backpack. White Ghost and I carried nothing while struggling to keep our hands on the rolling cart. Aunt Gai shoulder-poled two baskets filled with more essentials. Black Ghost lay hammocked in the crook of Mama's arm, wrapped in a long, thin towel. We children, ages ranging from five months to nine years, were embarking on a journey—an odd and estranging journey; one that felt as though the ground had cracked open and our world had fallen in.

After we walked a block from our house, Mama instructed us to stick together. Thousands of people swirled in madness like a beehive set alight, buzzing and swarming with anxiety while hauling their belongings. Some asked around for family members. Parents urged their children to keep up. Babies cried. Old people moaned and complained. Mama and Papa argued about streets and which direction to go.

Most of our immediate relatives lived near us. I had spent most of every day for the past two years playing with a dozen cousins, running in the streets, and visiting their homes. Now, as we were being driven out, we did our best to communicate with one another and stick together. Except for Uncle Yi (who lived far away with other relatives who were his adoptive parents), the rest of Mama's siblings and Grandma found us in the throngs of people. Papa's brother and two sisters were all married, each with several children, and they remained with their spouses' families.

Soldiers blared into bullhorns and fired guns into the air. We were as frightened as sheep surrounded by wolves. Dust flew into our noses. People emptied provisions from the carts so they could carry their loved ones instead. Everyone walked with an unspeakable heaviness, as if our loved ones had died. "Move along!" a soldier shouted behind us, waving his rifle.

"Follow the crowd!" another soldier hollered a octave higher. "Don't stop!" He pointed at an old couple with their grandson. "Move along, now!"

I became more alarmed. I cringed at the thought of being shot.

A gun went off right behind us. People shrieked and screamed, "He's been shot!" We couldn't see the cause for the pandemonium and we were too frightened to find out. In fact, we raced forward. "Just walk and don't stop! Don't look!" was all the comfort my parents could offer us.

♦♦♦

By early noon, we ran into Papa's sister, Wui, and her family of seven. Theirs were not the faces we had expected to see, because by now they should have been in Thailand. Their failure to reach safety shocked us all. The adults now realized the gravity of our predicament: the probability of a dire and bleak future under the Khmer Rouge had just become more certain.

We dared not slow down to rest. Our feet shuffled onward. To pass the time, Nuy started singing a song she'd learned at school. I'd since picked up the silly tune. I understood every word in the song. That morning, less than a few hours after being tossed out of our home, Nuy started singing it softly: first to herself, then loud enough for me to hear—and I couldn't help but join in. We had no way of knowing, then, that the Khmer Rouge could construe our singing as an act of defiance. So we sang in ignorance.

The song went something like this:

We have a road,
But no one walks on it.
We don't buy with money,
But we trade with leaves.
We have a house,
But no one lives in it.
In haste we live in chicken coops,
And get shit on.

Before our ordeal was over, we would come to envy those who simply got shit on. As we entered the countryside, we sensed the mood had changed. Nuy and I abruptly stopped singing.

The process of extermination had already begun.

3. THE DEATH MARCH (APRIL 1975)

The Khmer Rouge escorted away people of importance as refugees rolled through the landscape like a plague of locusts.

"It was stupid of us not to run to Thailand when we had the chance!" lamented Uncle Jo between breaths.

"No use," said Papa, tugging at the cart holding his cherished cameras. "Remember our chief of police? He must've known. He left with his family a week ago. They even made it to Thailand, but the Thai soldiers robbed them at gunpoint and sent them back."

"Well, I heard that some families made it across," countered Uncle Jo. "They received help from Thai-Chinese citizens on the other side."

"There are no guarantees," said Papa, wiping beads of sweat from his forehead. The temperature soared to well over a hundred degrees. "Mrs. Sum and her family packed and left a couple of days ago. In hindsight, we should've taken the risk with them. My big sis Wui and her children left yesterday morning, but it was already too late." Aunt Wui and her five children never made it to Thailand. When they arrived at the edge of the border, just before venturing into Thai territory, they found that Khmer Rouge lay in wait and were killing everyone who took one step farther away from Cambodia. After seeing so many people slaughtered, she and her children ran back to join the forced march.

"Shut up, both of you!" Mama snapped, irritated by their conversation. "We've got plenty of problems right now! You're wasting time with your 'should-have/could-have' nonsense!"

We routinely witnessed the weak fall behind. Two girls around my age were separated from their family. They were beyond distraught and cried for their parents until their voices were hoarse. Sadness settled within me as we moved past them. In their faces, I saw my own. I shuddered at the thought of losing my family. I was determined to cling to my parents like a button to its shirt.

A young couple stopped to help the distressed children. They asked the girls to join them until they found their parents. They shook and shrieked even louder at the thought of losing their parents permanently. A soldier quickly rushed over to shoo the couple away, admonishing them to mind their own business. The couple had no choice but to abandon their compassion. The girls continued to cry, but that soldier trailed us instead of tending to them.

◆ ◆ ◆

On the side of the road in Nimit, several miles from our home, we came upon street vendors who hawked their wares. It was early afternoon and the Khmer Rouge were no longer vigilant about keeping us in constant motion—perhaps they too were tired and needed a break themselves. Mama stopped our procession, handed Black Ghost to Aunt Gai, and ran toward the vendors. She knew she had to spend all her Cambodian money before it became worthless. What surprised her most was that the people in this outlying town seemed unaffected by the forced march. Their world remained intact.

Mama competed fiercely with hundreds of other evacuees for the same goods. She was, surprisingly, able to unload all the Cambodian currency and secure more clothes, towels, food, and other necessities which she carried back to our cart.

She rushed back to the street vendors to see what else she could obtain. By the time she returned, most of the merchants had already sold their wares. Undaunted, Mama continued searching the area for other sellers. Eventually she came upon a few people who still had some inventory, but they now refused to sell to her. They must have figured out that they would soon be forced to join us in the march. Their time did quickly run out.

Mama came back empty-handed, and before she sat to rest, a dark shadow crossed her face. It had just dawned on her that her precious stones and gold had been left behind. She told us to wait under a big tree until her return, and she disappeared among the crowds of frantic evacuees. No more than fifteen minutes later she walked back, expressionless and dazed.

They had blocked the road back into the city. When she asked a soldier if she could go back home to retrieve our forgotten essentials, he smirked, rubbed his gun barrel, and said: "Sure—go right ahead, if you want a bullet in your head!"

Mama had forgotten the bag of rubies which she had accumulated during those years of owning the hair salon. She was a contrarian at heart; her intuition served her well. A blue sapphire, comparable in cut, size, and quality, was worth at least five to ten times more than a red ruby. As the blue stones continued to appreciate and the red stones remained flat, her customers begged Mama to buy their rubies. Mama carefully selected the best-quality rubies from the town ladies.

She often compared the brilliance of the red gems to the blue ones in a dimly-lit room. The blue looked almost black and devoid of excitement. The red emitted fires, which captured her soul. A few years later, the price of rubies caught up and even surpassed that of the sapphires. Rare rubies could command even higher prices than quality diamonds. Mama had a bag full of the beautiful red gemstones. She could have easily built six huge houses with them. There was one jewel she loved most: a thumb-sized ruby with great clarity and hardly any inclusions. That one jewel alone was worth more than Papa's entire collection of cameras. I could only imagine her anguish.

◆◆◆

After a full day of marching, we were exhausted. We settled down for the night on the side of a road. Our possessions lay on the ground next to us. Having packed food and fresh water for only a few days, and with no idea how long this journey would last, we conserved our resources as best we could. I had my first real meal since the evacuation, which left me wanting more. I could have eaten at least another bowl of rice, some fish, and side dishes like those I was used to back at home. Knowing we had to start rationing our provisions (and not knowing when we would have another opportunity to obtain more food), I retired to a mat in a corner inside the mosquito net to sleep.

Before dozing off to the sounds of clanging pots and pans, I looked at the twinkling stars above and started counting. Although I had never been in school, I had learned how to count from my older siblings.

As I was counting the stars and slowly drifting off to sleep, the adults gathered by our fire pit to discuss the uncertainties. They were struck by the inconsistencies of the reasons used to evacuate us. Some were told the Americans were on their way to bomb our houses; some were told our homes would have to be searched for bombs; some were told we would be gone for only three days; and others were told it would be as long as two weeks.

With so much conflicting information, the adults weren't alone in their concerns, and they soon quieted down to sleep.

♦♦♦

The next day we ran into Grandpa and his elder son Gunn. Uncle Gunn's family of eight—and Grandpa—were relieved to see us. My parents didn't realize that Grandpa had shoved his valise into our cart during the forced evacuation. He had intended on coming with us without our knowledge. He dropped his trunk in our cart before going back to his place for more belongings; however, we had already left the house at gunpoint before his return.

Regardless of who we found and who was still missing, we had to keep moving. My tired feet shuffled onward. Sometimes I chased my shadow and sometimes it chased me. Fatigue dragged us down like a ball and chain. Often I would recognize faces in the teeming crowds: a neighbor, a friend of my brother, or my parents' customers.

We again stopped to set up camp for the night. The same song rose in my head. Nuy and I sang to improve morale. After we finished singing, Mama asked us to repeat the song in front of others. She told them to pay attention to the lyrics. We felt honored and graced them with an encore.

We have a road,
But no one walks on it.
We don't spend money,
But we trade with leaves.
We have a house,
But no one lives in it.
In haste we live in chicken coops—
And get shit on.

An old female relative quickly reprimanded us after we finished singing. "If you value your life, don't ever sing that song again! You hear?" The terror projected on her face instantly made me realize for the first time that this song, if heard by the Khmer Rouge, would be the end of us all.

We nodded. That was the last time we sang.

The adults stood speechless, as if needing a moment to digest the words. They'd heard these lyrics many times before, but had chosen to ignore them. What was believed to be a playful song—one poking fun at peasants—was now about us.

Marched into lines and questioned, people divulged their names, family details, and occupations. Depending on their responses, they were then sorted and selected; whole families were sent for "re-education" based solely on their work and social status. Before our turn arrived, my parents did a mock interview with us. "Never say we had people working for us. Only family members. Never admit we owned land. Never mention we can read and write. Better yet, just don't say anything!"

We stood with hundreds of families in an open field that morning, waiting to be processed and questioned.

"What's your name and occupation?" a soldier holding a clipboard asked a distinguished-looking older man.

He stated his name, then his job. "I'm a doctor," he declared with pride, bowing low. "And I'm honored to be at the country's service."

The soldier expressionlessly noted the information and nodded to his subordinates. The doctor and his family gathered their things before being escorted away.

"Your name and occupation?" the soldier asked another man who was disheveled and shoddily dressed.

He, too, said his name; but he was a street sweeper. The soldier smiled, noted his information, and instructed the man and his family to file behind another group. Apparently street sweepers already had all the patriotic training they needed.

Our turn was next. "Name and occupation?"

"Jo Chau, street vendor," said Uncle Jo.

"Sann Hong, sell cameras and take pictures," said Papa.

"Yeng Chau," interjected Mama. "I cut and perm hair."

The soldier raised an eyebrow and did a double take on us before jotting down the information. "We've fought bravely and many of us sacrificed our lives." His eyes drifted to our cart; to our bags and baskets. "We expect everyone to provide according to their means."

Without hesitation, Papa recognized what the soldier meant and handed him a roll of Thai money (since we had already spent the Cambodian riels), already prepared as though he had foreseen the need for such a gesture. The soldier immediately pointed to Papa's watch on his wrist. Papa took it off and handed it over. The Khmer Rouge then allowed us through the checkpoint, where we regrouped.

Even though I was surrounded by cousins, I hardly exchanged a word with them: I was too distraught and confused. The life that I was becoming familiar with had abruptly ended, and I had yet to know why.

A few days after the forced march, I stepped on Papa's eyeglasses in the dark and broke them. When it happened, I felt wretched. In the morning when Papa asked who broke his glasses, I kept quiet. He asked again, this time directing his question at me. I shook my head, knowing it was better to deny it than get smacked. He stooped down to pick up the biggest shard (about the size of his thumb), brought it up to his eye to look through, sighed, and dropped it. My insides were knotted with guilt.

My conscience had a life of its own. It came alive at night when I looked at the moon and stars. The night sky was vast, like a blanket over my head with tiny holes pierced through for the light to peek out. I wondered what it must be like for Papa. Those sharp specks and the well-defined shape of the moon were a blur for him. Often I raised my palm to cover one eye while squinting with the other to see what only one eye alone could see.

For days, we marched. At each registration point they repeated the same drill, and our savings of Thai currency reduced as Papa gave the soldiers a bribe of money or an item of value. The crowd thinned out around us as the intellectuals, the professionals, the artists, the elites, and the civil servants vanished, leaving behind frightened family members. The criteria for selection became increasingly strange and arbitrary as one woman described to Mama the bizarre questions asked of her.

"When was the last time you ate ice cream or noodles?"

"Can you count to one hundred?"

It was only then that I realized, obliquely, what a blessing in disguise it was that I had ruined Papa's glasses.

Fat people and people with glasses were selected, as well as people with soft hands.

"I'm afraid it's only a matter of time before we find ourselves on their list," Uncle Jo whispered to my parents.

"We're people with assets," Mama murmured back in agreement. "If they find out how much money we were making, they'd list us for sure."

That was when we ran into our neighbor, Mrs. Sum. She was the wife of a local businessperson who had regularly converted our Cambodian riels into the more stable Thai bahts. She and her family had much to lose, so they decided to leave the country even before the communists declared their victory. They almost made it across the Thai border when the Khmer Rouge opened fire on their traveling group.

Mr. and Mrs. Sum each had a child on their back, plus three older children. Her husband and all five children had died when bullets riddled their bodies. She was the only one alive out of thirty people in her group. Somehow spared from their bullets, she was forced to endure the worst fate of watching them being slaughtered. She passed out from shock. Hours later she regained consciousness; but as she looked around and saw her family's ravaged remains, she collapsed once more.

Falling in and out of consciousness, Mrs. Sum eventually found the will to leave. She stumbled back to the city while every living soul was being forced out.

Hearing her story, my family and others gathered in silence, wondering about our own fate. We realized how fortunate we were not to have joined their traveling group. My family had at first agreed to leave with them, but Papa had abruptly changed his mind when he came down with the stomach flu. At that time, he lacked the energy to do much of anything other than to visit the toilet, so he postponed the escape plan. I shuddered to think of the alternative, had he been well.

"Why did you come back to Cambodia?" someone asked Mrs. Sum.

"I don't know," she said. "I really don't know. I had nothing, so I just wanted to come home to something familiar."

Now she didn't even have that.

If we had any doubts before, they were laid to rest with the shattered bodies of Mrs. Sum's husband and her children.

Time was running out.

4. BACKTRACKING (MAY 1975)

They herded us into yet another processing point, but the selections weren't the only factor thinning out the ranks of the city dwellers. I noticed children as young as my brother, boys and girls alike, being gathered and marched off in formation. They were still in civilian clothes, visibly disoriented and traumatized by the unexpected separation from their families. The new regime had recruited them for the revolution and they had little choice but to join the ranks of our oppressors. Will they come for my siblings and me? I didn't understand why the Khmer Rouge had skipped over us. Maybe it was because we were Chinese and not native Khmer. Perhaps they believed we were so corrupt in our way of thinking that they walked past us to the next peasant-looking family.

As we slowly trudged past numerous small roadside villages, country dwellers gazed at us. Their expressions suggested they were half-worried that thousands of homeless would wind up camping in their back yards. After only a week or two, our communist liberators seemed to have accomplished that goal: we were all equally displaced, starving, filthy, and miserable.

While the soldiers openly spoke of re-education, the phrase "whack and dump" traveled from ear to ear. Those who came back from "re-education" recounted tales of the interrogation they had undergone. Those who didn't come back, we assumed, had been whacked and dumped.

Unbeknownst to us children, Papa's other sister and her family were in danger. Aunt Khan's husband (whom I called Uncle Rain) had served as a government official from 1971 to 1973. He had campaigned for the incumbent Lon Nol party that had the political support of Washington, D.C. The reason he resigned work after two years was to maintain a low profile. He predicted the Khmer Rouge would be the victor at the end of the civil war because America had since lost its will to fight and was no longer committed to winning the war. He positioned himself to appear neutral by relinquishing the post. Now his name was on the kill list.

At each registration stop, Uncle Rain's family lied and was able to pass through. When asked if he farmed with tractors or cows, he said cows. How many? He answered two. They continued to drill him. "How could you possibly support seven children and a wife with just two cows?" Relying on the grace of relatives and friends was his steady answer.

A relative whispered to Uncle Rain that someone powerful and high in the Khmer Rouge hierarchy was hell-bent on finding him. Uncle Rain racked his brain, trying to remember if he had made enemies while working under the Lon Nol regime. Not a single name or face came to mind. His conscience was clear. Nevertheless, he and his family wouldn't risk capture. Hastily, his family of nine left before sunrise.

I awoke to find half of our relatives gone; not just the fugitive Uncle Rain and his family. News of the manhunt had prompted my paternal family to go our separate ways to blend in. The thinking was that smaller groups meant better chance of survival from ease of movement. At that moment, Grandpa was torn between staying with his younger son and going with his eldest. He chose the latter; probably because he didn't want to burden my parents further, knowing how difficult it already was to care for the young ones.

Everyone on Papa's side was gone: only Mama's side remained.

Papa was in poor health. He'd suffered a bad case of stomach flu before the Khmer Rouge had banged on our door. The maladies had since magnified.

After two weeks as evacuees, Papa's health required drastic action.

My parents decided to head back in the direction from which we came. We had been steadily heading towards the rising sun; to go back meant to walk toward the sunset. I remember the temporary relief I felt: going back meant going home—back to warm bread and to my clean clothes in the dresser. Going back meant fleeing to Thailand in a last-ditch effort to escape Cambodia.

With few resources and a delusional hope for the best, we rolled up our filthy floor mats one sunny morning. We managed to evade a few checkpoints simply because there were not enough soldiers to guard the sea of frenzied people who were in constant flux. Little did we know that the Khmer Rouge had one eye on us the whole time. Our ignorance of their knowledge emboldened us and other groups and families to march northwest. After a couple of days, we arrived at a small hamlet to rest. We were only a few miles from the jungles separating us from Thailand. We camped out at a fruit farm with other families. At first the country folks chased us away with brooms, but soon greed changed their hearts as their rice and livestock commanded a hefty chunk of gold or a precious piece of jewelry.

A few days later, the chief mandated that one able-bodied person per family work for the collective. Papa, Uncle Jo, and Uncle Tek signed up from our group.

Roughly one hundred families were haphazardly tossed together and doing their best to regain health and energy. The desire to escape swept through us first like a gentle breeze, then grew into a raging tornado as people left for the jungle. There must have been twenty families that disappeared from the farms. With so many small children in our group, we weren't feasible candidates for the treacherous journey. Nonetheless, we longed for and dreamed of our escape. Mama was determined to find someone willing to lead us.

Meanwhile, we took advantage of the calm. Mama traded jewelry for an entire pig. Uncle Jo slaughtered the pig and roasted it over an open fire. The meat was tender and juicy; a slice of paradise drenched in garlic and fish sauce. I savored every whiff and every bite and licked all my fingers until I could eat no more.

Papa was forced to work and, as a result, it worsened his ailments. He had a lethal combination of vomiting and diarrhea with constant shivering and difficulty breathing: all symptoms of malaria or diphtheria. Each day after work, he mustered every ounce of energy to make a shelter to ward against the impending monsoon season. The project, which required a day of commitment, ended up taking him close to ten days to complete.

Unfortunately, many around us succumbed to the same maladies; including Uncle Tek, who exhibited symptoms similar to Papa's.

Nearby, an old man screamed in pain throughout the night. He had fallen and fractured his hip. He died the next morning. His family cried over his sudden departure, but the Khmer Rouge ordered them to immediately get rid of his body.

Everyone worried that Papa would soon die. Uncle Jo felt compelled to do something to help us. He left in haste, leaving behind his wife and children under the care of his in-laws. He headed for Lvea, a rural village, in hopes of finding one of our relatives—one he thought might be able to help Papa.

Uncle Jo's sudden departure infuriated his wife; for his loyalty lay not with her, but with Mama.

By this point, Uncle Jo's wife had irreparably offended Mama. We were short on bowls and utensils, but her sister-in-law had plenty. When Mama sent Aunt Gai over to borrow some, Uncle Jo's wife denied the request and she relayed a message back: "Tell Big Sis that she's more than welcome to go back to my house to get them, but out here she can't have any!"

Mama was livid. Steam seemed to rise from her head and smoke to puff out of her ears. "What an ingrate! Did she forget how many times I saved her? The many times I loaned her money and have yet to receive a penny back? The few times I took her sons to the emergency doctors and paid for their hospital bills? They would've died if it hadn't been for me. I own her!"

Adding insult to injury, the sister-in-law took Grandma's only blanket. Uncle Jo was never told of these incidents. Mama didn't want to be the cause of a chasm in their relationship: instead, she gave one of our much-needed blankets to Grandma.

The sister-in-law's snide remarks and greedy conduct offended Mama. She compartmentalized these grudges deep within her mind. She remembered facts. She kept tally of those who came to her for aid and rescue and then simply turned their backs on her when they had the means to help.

Uncle Jo managed to reach his aunt in that rural village. She gave him a bottle of Hennessy and some western remedies for malaria to take back to Papa and Uncle Tek. While he was there, Uncle Jo learned that Grandpa had settled nearby. He visited him there and informed him of our whereabouts and of Papa's feeble health.

Grandpa packed his bags and was ready to return with Uncle Jo when Mother Nature unleashed a vengeful monsoon rain. Uncle Jo told Grandpa how time was of the essence. The rain would only slow them both down, and the journey back would be too taxing on his old bones.

Reluctantly, Grandpa set his bags down.

We never saw him again. (A year into this wicked regime, Grandpa, Papa's father, died from starvation.)

♦ ♦ ♦

Upon Uncle Jo's return, Papa slowly recovered with the new abundance of food, the proper remedies, and shots of Hennessy.

After camping two weeks on the farm, our family of sixteen people (which included my family of seven, Grandma's family of five, and Uncle Jo's family of four) consumed an entire pig, half a cow, other livestock, and bags of rice, knowing such gluttony might well be our last chance to eat for some time. The food and rest had worked their magic as we prepared ourselves to push west straight into Thai territory. Mama almost found a villager to lead the way; she was in the middle of negotiating the final payment. We were quite certain freedom was finally within grasp.

While we daydreamed, the Khmer Rouge approached the village chief for a list of names. The chief jotted down our daily activities, including what hometown we came from. He even jotted a special note of those who had bought or killed any livestock. Before we could even count our blessings, the pig and cow that had revived us became our death sentence. Because the Khmer Rouge were already on to us, we wondered if any of those twenty families had successfully escaped to Thailand. We began to suspect that the Khmer Rouge had killed them all in ambush. Even if we managed to cross safely over the border, we heard the Thai government would deny amnesty. Handing us back over to the Khmer Rouge would seal our fate. Surely, they then would not hesitate to terminate us.

With no hope for escape, we stayed put. Soon some large flatbed trucks came for us. Approximately eighty families were jammed into ten military vehicles and transported to a holding place. The ride was bumpy. People, belongings, and animals in cages crammed together uncomfortably. My stomach churned with each bump on the road. Papa reached into his breast pocket for Tiger Balm and smeared a dab of the menthol ointment on my nose. The balm helped, but I was still miserable.

It took several hours to arrive at Svay Sisophon because our trucks had to navigate a labyrinth of cars abandoned in the mayhem of the forced evacuation. They eventually dumped us in an area not far from the city's soulless downtown. I was happy to finally get off the truck. Here we were left alone and free to roam around the now-empty buildings. I experienced a sense of wonder and amazement when my siblings and I snuck through the doors of these abandoned homes: we picked money off the ground with no one there to claim it.

There was an overwhelming eeriness as we wandered through the once-teeming thoroughfares, picking unspoiled food off vendors' carts and gathering clothes, blankets, and toys—anything and everything we could take. Dogs stuck their heads out to see if we were their masters. Roosters pecked Papa's hands as he chased them for dinner. White Ghost giggled with delight because she found a tiny mortar and pestle toy. We were lost in the moment: we played hide-and-seek and considered the city our playground.

Two days later, the Khmer Rouge came for us.

5. MARKED FOR DEATH (JUNE 1975)

The same trucks came for us. We abruptly left behind some of the food and supplies which we had so excitedly gathered the day before. White Ghost still clutched the mortar and pestle, and Vunn his slingshot and clay balls. Papa's cameras made it, too. This revelation came after we settled down to take inventory the next day. Mama was furious when she realized that he, yet again, had saved his cameras in lieu of the essentials.

"When will it hit you that these cameras aren't worth a grain of rice?"

I wondered who tormented Mama more: Papa or the Khmer Rouge. Those cameras were too much of a burden and about as useful as an umbrella in a hurricane, but he clung to them like he was clinging on to hope.

Once again we bounced around in the back of the same trucks. I wrestled with the food in my stomach until we reached our destination. A few hours later, we arrived in a small village at a pagoda surrounded by huts propped up on stilts. The roofs of the sanctuary curved upward dramatically. The temple was abandoned with a weighty silence hung over it. Here, the Khmer Rouge ordered us to get off the truck and settle down. As soon as we cleared out of the trucks, we ran to stake claims at this sacred place.

Thanks to Mama's swiftness (even despite the persistent pain in her stomach), our family was one of the lucky ones to find refuge indoors in what used to be one of the monks' rooms. Many camped outside.

We settled in and cooked dinner on makeshift hearths. Some squatted, while others stood and socialized with people they hardly knew. Many speculated that the monks had been disrobed or murdered when the Khmer Rouge invaded this territory.

It was dark when we finished dinner. Nuy and I brought all the dirty dishes to Mama's younger sisters for cleaning. The sounds of spoons and bowls banging and scraping were comforting to me as people tidied up for the night. Despite a few roaming flashlights, paraffin lamps dangling from trees and eaves, and fires in hearths throughout the compound, darkness slowly overtook the skies.

As Nuy and I handed the dishes to our aunts, someone yelled: "Look over there! More people are heading here." The news spread fast. Everyone turned to look at the black shapes shuffling toward us. The conversations and cleaning ceased, which only dared the cicadas to chatter and the crickets to chirp louder. People stared out into the night, not sure what to make of the moving silhouettes. We children rushed to where our parents stood. I grabbed Papa's hand to let him know I was there. We banded together to greet the throng of newcomers.

The newcomers ignored us as they walked past us. They followed each other in a single line. A few of us used flashlights to signal our attempts at introduction, but not a sound came from their group.

Their detachment alarmed us. Their lack of curiosity and indifference felt out of place. We knew something horrible must have happened to them.

♦ ♦ ♦

After an uneventful night, we woke the next morning to roosters crowing and birds chirping. We noticed that the newcomers from the night before could freely roam the countryside while the Khmer Rouge guarded us with disdain.

Our group continued to try to engage them in some form of friendly communication, only to get the same chilling blank stare in return. They treated us as though we were invisible.

Not far from the temple was a man-made dike, designed to collect rainwater for the monks and nearby inhabitants. During our stay, Papa took us there to bathe.

"It's like we're living in a village of deaf mutes," Uncle Jo said. "Their silence gives me the creeps."

"Not only that." Mama pointed to several small figures in the distance shoulder-poling buckets of water. "They actually go out of their way to avoid us. Instead of fetching water from here," (pointing to the reservoir near us), "they trek ten times the distance to get water from somewhere else just to stay clear."

"They apparently talk. Just not to us," Papa chimed in.

Nothing added up.

Eventually the mystery unraveled. One of the mute farmers was a relative of someone in our group. He broke his silence just long enough for us to learn the rumors about our fate. We were condemned, already banished from the realm of the living. We were among those to be "whacked and dumped." The Khmer Rouge had marked all eighty families for termination.

I was fraught with terror upon learning we would all be bludgeoned to death. This marked the start of my intrusive nightmares. I visualized our throats being slit and skulls cracked open. I didn't know what else could be more terrifying than knowing this.

Word spread that these villagers had left their homes of their own accord. They pledged loyalty by imploring the Khmer Rouge to take their properties for the cause. In turn, they were branded as people who willingly "surrendered their bodies and assets." Impressed by their devotion and sacrifice, the Khmer Rouge eventually allowed them to return to their own homes. This would never be allowed for the hopelessly corrupt urbanites, we who greedily clung to our possessions.

As our insufferable wait continued, our worries grew. The vacant looks on the villagers' faces and their awkward silence drew our death sentence into focus, acting as constant reminders of our impending demise.

We didn't have to wait long.

On the fifth morning, the Khmer Rouge surrounded us. "You've been spared!" one of them smugly blurted through the bullhorn. "Although you've betrayed the cause, you're to be given a second chance!" Our relief at hearing this news was short-lived, however: without warning, they fired their guns. Rounds of shots ripped through the sky, shattering our eardrums. We screamed, believing they were shooting at us.

We hurried to get our things. I thought that at any moment, a bullet would fly through me. The throngs of people ran out and stampeded over each other to the road. This was where Mama swore under her breath: "Those cameras of yours will be our undoing!"

Papa must have realized his mistake, for he dropped the cameras to rush back in hopes of salvaging our remaining possessions. However, he abruptly stopped after seeing a dozen or more soldiers scurry around the temple loading goods onto trucks and oxcarts. Even a blind man could see that he was being robbed.

In the panic caused by the Khmer Rouge's duplicity, we fled without taking the basket that contained our family's small photo album and medicine. Our relics of the past were lost forever: not even one family portrait survived. Mama was seething when she saw those bags of cameras.

Again, two dozen soldiers herded us away with their rifles. Guns blasted through the dark clouds, thunder clapped, and onward my little feet shuffled with an urgency that could only have been commanded by the army. Lightning pierced the sky and rain poured down on us. I was more terrified than confused.

I glanced behind me to see if anyone had been shot, but I couldn't tell. What I saw was a herd of people charging behind me with the same frantic speed as that of antelopes being chased by cheetahs. Many tripped and tumbled down as they desperately lugged their possessions through knee-deep water created by the downpour. I fell, scraping my knees on something hard. Luckily Grandma rushed over just in time to save me from drowning in waist-deep water.

6. THE CHICKEN COOPS (CIRCA JULY 1975)

We came upon a site that was nothing but an open cabana surrounded by loosely-scattered palms, and the Khmer Rouge soldiers ordered us to settle in.

"Make no mistake! All of you are dispensable! None of you, not even ten of you, are worth the price of one cow!" a Khmer Rouge member yelled at all of us.

Humans were now the beasts of burden. Four people could do the work of one cow. Men and beasts were now the same beasts of burden in common. Only when the animals rested could the humans drink.

I often saw four men and an ox strapped to an agricultural implement with huge spikes. Together they pushed and pulled the harrow to loosen the soil. Not all men had cattle as their assistants. To supplement the deficit in animals, they shackled eight condemned men to one implement. The Khmer Rouge would stand on both sides, cracking their whips. When a human complained of exhaustion, their responses were the same: "Is the cow next to you tired? Is it thirsty? Is it resting? Work!" The beasts of burden had no choice but to endure just to live another day, or until they drowned face-first in the mud. This latter scenario was all too common.

In horror, I asked Papa and Uncle Jo if they had ever been yoked to the harrow with the cows. They said no, because there were always others who had committed worse crimes than being a street vendor and camera salesperson. Those who were doctors, lawyers, accountants, and engineers suffered worse injustices than the toilet cleaners and street sweepers. My uncles and Papa built dikes and chopped trees for firewood. Mama transplanted the rice seedlings into muddy water prepped by beasts of burden and their colleagues, the oxen.

Once the field was finished, we would dismantle the tents, pack our belongings, and walk to another nameless barren field. Our group of eighty families, which equaled about five hundred people, was a mobile workforce, but our numbers were reducing by the day. The Khmer Rouge shot many who tried to escape.

When we arrived at an uncultivated section of land, Vunn and Papa would pitch the tent next to other families. Nuy, Grandma and I would look after our little siblings while Mama stood in line for food rations. My aunts and uncles tried their best to lend a helping hand. They, however, carried their own loads and worries.

Grandma cared for us in our parents' absence. She would feed us and wash our clothes. My parents would come back when the sun was red and setting at the edge of the earth.

Black Ghost's supply of baby formula had run out weeks earlier. Since Mama was barely lactating, she filled the bottle with liquid from the watery rice gruel, which had minimal nutrients. Mama often searched for women who had a baby in their arms. She looked for the healthiest mothers whose milk let down, and she would appeal to their kindness. Those with empathy would bear Black Ghost's hungry mouth to their breasts.

◆◆◆

It had been raining all night. Water rose to my ankles when I stormed out of the tent. I left because there was too much friction and heat cooped up in there. Everyone was off that day—occasionally the beasts of burden didn't have to work.

That morning my brother and I quarreled with each other, which was more than enough to set Mama in a foul mood. We fought because we were children. Sometimes we aggravated each other with words and, occasionally, with fists. To shut us up, Mama struck our heads with her knuckles—two heads, different ages, but the same punishment. It was unfair of her never to question who started the fight or to give us a warning before striking us. I felt her injustice and left the tent despite the rain.

I sought refuge under the open cabana along with many other people. There I found Papa. He was holding a bowl and extending his arm out into the downpour while trying to shield his body from getting wet. It was bizarre to see him catching rainwater, because it seemed like something one would do out of boredom. He collected and mixed this water with penicillin to make eye drops. We had all contracted eye infections and there was no cure for conjunctivitis.

Papa had traded a pair of his pants for one tiny tablet of penicillin. It never occurred to him to trade the cameras instead; but then again, there was no demand for such useless toys. The tiny penicillin was precious: I could tell this by the way he unfolded its blue wrapping paper to expose the pill.

He sliced it in half with a razor and dropped half into the water he'd collected from the sky. The other half he carefully tucked into his breast pocket. He swirled the bowl until the medicine dissolved completely and then pulled out an empty eyedropper from his pants pocket. Steadily he squeezed out the air in the dropper before refilling it with the water in the bowl. He continued the process until the tiny bottle was full.

He instructed me to tilt my head and open my infected eyes. I did as told, and he delicately dripped the mixture into them. He applied the drops to his eyes as well before squeezing the air out of the dropper to suck in the rest of the solution.

I lingered under the cabana long after Papa left, staring out into the rain, still harboring resentment from what happened earlier in the tent.

About a week later, we were back on the road again. This time Papa emptied one basket so he could carry White Ghost when she became ill. Papa was still holding onto his precious cameras as if he would still open his photo business someday. He went to extreme lengths to transport our belongings.

He created a staggered pattern for hauling his sick child and the cameras. Papa shoulder-poled White Ghost and our essentials for a few hundred feet before setting them down, with one of us standing guard. He then returned for the cameras. With the two camera bags dangling off his shoulders, he ran past White Ghost before coming back for her and the necessities. This went on for a few days until she was able to walk again. It took a toll on him—but not enough for him to abandon either the child or the cameras.

Mama looped a sarong diagonally across her shoulder and around her waist to cradle Black Ghost. She couldn't carry much else; only a light bundle. During the forced march, she walked in constant pain, limping behind us while biting her lips to endure the pain in her stomach. Her womb hadn't fully recovered from the botched tubal ligation and its ensuing infection.

It was hard to imagine that it had been only six months ago that Mama had given birth to Black Ghost. After her discharge from the Thai hospital, she endured a severe internal infection. Back then, I watched her stuff a spool of cotton gauze into her stomach. When she pulled the cotton out it was soaked with yellow pus, which looked like chicken fat.

She cried throughout the entire ordeal. We were all sleeping next to her, listening to her moan, and I was witnessing something I couldn't fathom. She repeated the process until it came out free and clear of pus. Unfortunately, the infection would come back the next day. This went on for several weeks. She sought medical help, but her body was resistant to antibiotics. All day and night she wallowed in pain with baby Black Ghost crying next to her. It was a trying time. She could easily have not recovered, leaving us motherless.

Now on the road with a baby in her arms, Mama struggled to keep up. Her gait reminded me of an injured duck wobbling on webbed feet. Even though Papa was staggering with his loads, Mama lagged behind.

Finally we settled in a temporary shelter with rows of blue tarp tents. We called them "chicken coops" because after a day of forced labor (for my parents), we crawled into them, exhausted, only to wake up the next morning and be subjected to the same routine much like a brood of chickens roaming the farm, pecking at feed, laying eggs during the day, and caged in at night.

One night Mama woke Nuy and me to empty our bladders. Drowsily we squatted in a nearby bush and stumbled back into what we thought was our tent. In the dark, we crawled over warm bodies to get back to our corner and fell back to sleep. In the morning strangers chuckled because we had slept in their tent. For the next few days, everyone laughed at our mishap. These moments of laughter were rare. People seldom smiled or laughed anymore. The flowers no longer bloomed, it seemed, and rainbows no longer appeared after stormy rain. The sky seemed perpetually dark and gloomy.

Map 3: Phnum Sress

THAILAND

DANGREK
MOUNTAINS

LAOS

• PHNUM SRESS

• POIPET

• SVAY SISOPHON

• BATTAMBANG

SADAO •

• MOUNG

• PAILIN

CAMBODIA

7. PHNUM SRESS (CIRCA JULY 1975)

Our sin of attempted escape had long been whispered before we arrived in the small village of Phnum Sress, nestled in District Five of the Northwest Zone. The Khmer Rouge renamed the country to "Democratic Kampuchea." Only recently had the word "Angka" entered my consciousness. Angka was the official name for the Khmer Rouge's Communist Party of Kampuchea, the supreme organization. The Angka informed the natives of Phnum Sress to watch our every move. They knew of our failed escape to Thailand, and that we were here to repent. To live, we must prove our worth to the regime. They assigned a dozen condemned families to settle here.

Our hamlet was lush with flora. Roads were unpaved. Mountains splayed as the backdrop to the north. Green floodplains, water, and rice paddies lay to the south. Water buffaloes, horses, and cows roamed and grazed as if they didn't have a care in the world. Roughly ninety families had resided here before our arrival. They were called the "old-people"—old in many ways other than in years. They were what the Angka revered as the dwellers from ancient times with skills and labor no different than those of their ancestors.

The old-people were the model citizens.

Their children, as young as ten, were the eyes in the trees, the noses in the air, and the ears to the ground. They were to the regime what tentacles are to the octopus. These little informants were to be feared just as much as a Khmer Rouge with a rifle. They were so deeply indoctrinated that they couldn't see the forest for the trees, or parents from strangers. They snitched on their families and friends because the Angka was now their only parent. No reward was more effective than food when one was perpetually hungry.

In contrast to the existing inhabitants, they called us "new-people"—new with our ties to western influences and our capitalistic ways. The regime viewed our minds as dangerous and our souls as polluted. They wanted our spirits broken, and they knew exactly how to achieve it.

Several days after arriving in Phnum Sress, four men helped Papa build our shelter. It was finished in one morning, and I stood there watching its transformation. They chopped trees down to clear the land and used their trunks to frame the hut. They gathered hay and used palm leaves as the materials for the roof and walls.

Our hut faced south, a stone's throw from the main dirt road. It was just one rectangular room raised about three feet off the ground. It was no more than fifteen feet wide and twenty-five feet long: under approximately four hundred square feet of living space for seven people. There were huge gaps in the floorboards and they widened even more from weather and time. We often fell in, wedging our legs in the holes and twisting our ankles.

Behind our hut were endless fields of communal corn and cassavas. These fields were strictly off-limits. If anyone was caught stealing, the punishment would be severe. A serpentine road lay west of the back yard to the base of the mountains. Soldiers guarded this road. It was also the road which allowed them to spy on us.

As I idly observed the men erecting the structure, my left foot accidentally kicked a fist-sized rock. Immediately pain seared through my body: my middle toenail had broken open. I gritted my teeth and cursed the rock as blood oozed out over the dirt. I yanked off the nail, held together only by a sliver of flesh. I was petrified the damage was permanent and that my toe would be deformed forever.

Close to a month later, a new nail sprouted. This new growth fascinated me. It was like watching the dead rise again. The mysteries of the universe unraveled before my eyes, boggling my mind.

More amazing than this new growth was how content I felt when we settled in that village. Our hut always leaked and the floorboards were uncomfortable, but I was happy. For the moment, our march had ended, and I basked in our newfound stability.

Once we settled into the new hut, Mama and I walked to the lake in the moonlight. She carried two metal buckets for hauling water. The moon was almost full and the air smelled of backwater and turned earth. The wind gently swayed the trees; they seemed to whisper in the night.

When we waded through reeds and grass, Mama instructed me to take off my clothes and start washing myself first while she filled the buckets. In no time I became one with the water, unaware that danger lurked beneath the surface.

Suddenly I screamed with the intensity of one hundred bullhorns: I might have awakened the dead! Mama dropped the buckets and ran to me. Leeches clung to my body. Hysterical, I tried to pry them off. Their huge, slug-like bodies were fatter than my big toe. It was impossible to get a firm grip on them and even more impossible to pull them off from their two suctioned ends. I soon realized I was fighting a losing battle, and my anxiety escalated. I scrambled toward Mama's approaching form.

Mama raced to me in knee-deep water as my hysteria continued. By the light of the moon, I could see my body was black from the neck down. Mama pulled a handful of stringy plants and used them to scrape off the bloodsuckers. My screams didn't cease until all the leeches were pried off. I was shaken and exhausted. My body was full of tiny puncture wounds with drops of blood seeping out of them.

That night Mama declined her own bath.

The neighbors had all heard my distressed cry, but none had come to my aid. It wasn't until they saw Mama in the field the next morning that they asked her if it was one of her children who had screamed last night.

After that incident, I bathed during the day, picking a clear spot to quickly dip my body so I could scurry out of the water the second I caught sight of anything wiggling toward me.

8. "THOSE DAMN CAMERAS" (CIRCA JULY 1975)

About one week after moving into our new hut, a handful of Khmer Rouge came early one morning and rummaged through our possessions. Luckily, Mama had hidden what was left of her jewelry. She had sewn a handful of the pieces into the bottom hems of our clothes on the day we moved in. Embedded into the bottom of my pants were a diamond shamrock pendant and a ruby ring. Gold bracelets were hidden in the shirt. Only Nuy and I had valuables on our persons. None were entrusted to White Ghost and Black Ghost. They were too young to know danger and might play with them, drawing deadly attention. Mama instructed Papa to hide the few remaining jewelry pieces in the back yard.

After we hid the jewelry, Papa wanted to bury all his cameras in the garden too, but Mama advised against it because they were too bulky. Heeding her advice, he left the cameras in the hut—all but one. Papa insisted on taking that one to bury it in the garden, but Mama pointed to a spot above the ceiling beam. Like an obedient child, he set it overhead. The camera was neither discreet nor conspicuous, perched there as if no effort nor thought had been applied. From a certain angle, especially at the base of the hut, no one could tell that it was there.

The Khmer Rouge swarmed all over the hut and garden. They pried and poked at spots that appeared to have been dug. Since the day we moved in, we had labored in our garden as if our lives depended on it—which they did. There were two rows of cassavas and yams, which we had recently planted in the center of the garden, and a few tomato plants to the side. One of the soldiers randomly dug up a couple of plants, undoing our hard work to see if there was anything hidden underneath. He found nothing.

We watched the search operation unfold before our eyes as they turned the place upside-down. Immediately, they came upon the two huge bags of cameras. After inspecting the contents, they mumbled something to each other and proceeded to interrogate my parents.

"Mother Yeng, Father Sann, why are there so many cameras in your possession?" Before either of my parents could respond, they continued interrogating: "You must be spies; for why else would you have so many cameras? Tell me who you work for, the Soviets or the Americans?" While they were spitting out their questions at my parents, they were searching our faces to see how we would react to their accusations.

Finally, Mama had a chance to explain: "We're not spies. We're commoners in the photo business. These cameras were our livelihood. They put food on the table, clothes on our backs, and a roof over our heads. So much of our tears and sweat went into those cameras. We carried them around like they were one of our children. Please forgive us for not knowing that we should've had them turned in. Please take them now."

Papa stood there, tongue-tied. He was probably flashing back to how much he had labored to save them, and now these cameras were endangering us all.

"For your own sake," retorted a Khmer Rouge, "and your children's sake, you better be telling the truth!"

Another Khmer Rouge joined in on the threats. "The Angka knows everything! Rest assured we'll be back if your story has holes!"

It took four people to haul those cameras away.

After the Khmer Rouge left, Mama threw a stick at Papa and shouted at him, "Those damn cameras almost got us killed. Your stubbornness will be the death of us!"

For now that one camera, perched alone on the ceiling beam, was invisible to those on the ground.

Three days later, the same crew came back for a second sweep.

My parents had gone for work in the fields about two hours earlier. Our brother had already left for hunting with two native boys whom he had befriended. The world was one big adventure to him, at this point. The rest of us huddled under the hut, playing and caring for each other while the Khmer Rouge stuck their hands into the water barrel, poked the yard, and flipped over the floor mats before they looked up to see the camera.

Immediately, two soldiers were ordered to get my parents.

The floorboards were rattling above our heads as the remaining soldiers continued their search operation, poking, prying, and inspecting every nook and cranny. Nuy and I tried our best to act untroubled. Meanwhile, our auditory senses honed in on their conversations.

We heard the two infamous words "whack and dump" uttered throughout their discussions. We were overwhelmed and fraught with concern.

One of the soldiers voiced his authority: "Let's wait and see what they have to say for themselves."

To reduce our stress, Nuy and I took our siblings to the back yard so we all could relieve ourselves. When we returned, Mama and Papa had arrived with the soldiers.

"Hmh! Mother Yeng, Father Sann, did you store this camera at someone's place the last time we were here?"

"What?" Mama asked. Then realizing the implication, she quickly added, "No! It's always been here. I thought you didn't want it, so I let my kids play with it. Please take it now." Mama gestured an inviting palm at them. "My kids dropped it while playing outside. It's probably broken."

I couldn't tell if they were satisfied with Mama's response or not, but the positioning of the camera made it hard to repudiate her claims. The search party quickly left with the camera.

The gravity of the situation with Papa's remaining camera wasn't felt until later. Certainly, if it hadn't been for Mama, we could have been marching to our deaths. Instead, my parents returned to work. Upon reaching the fields, they parted ways. Mama retuned to the leech-infested water to plant rice seedlings and Papa went to dig trenches and build embankments.

What Mama didn't know was that everyone had already assumed the worst when the Khmer Rouge had summoned her earlier. Seeing Mama return to work unscathed, they were shocked and enthralled. Everyone wanted to know how she had managed to resurrect herself from the dead. It was lunchtime and everyone converged on Mama like ants on sugar.

"Mother Yeng, when the soldiers approached you, I thought it was over. I peed in my pants. It happens every time I see them coming for someone. I can't imagine your small children without their mother." The old lady dabbed away her tears.

"We've yet to see anyone come back once summoned. You're the first!" said another.

"For sure I thought you would get whacked and dumped!"

"Why were you summoned?" asked the lady with the sensitive bladder.

Mama's face blanched with consternation after realizing the enormity of this morning. Her safe return from the interrogation became the foundation of our survival at the village. Initially, the natives refused to associate with my parents; but today they were different. They welcomed her into their circle, into the old-people's clique, and into their world.

Mama's sewing and haircutting skills worked to her advantage. Because of the demand, they created a new position for her to become a tailor, working out of a small hut with only one treadle sewing machine, which was located on the west side, close to Uncle Jo. People came to Mama to have their clothes altered or patched. The head chief himself would drop off a roll of black fabric for her to make new uniforms.

After work, women came to Mama for a haircut, and sometimes they invited her into their homes. Despite the same ear-length, bob-cut style we all had to wear, her free time was booked almost daily. In return, she received plants, seeds, rice, and meat.

The seeds, vegetable plants, and saplings thrived in our garden. There was a wall of wild millet dividing our garden from the collective cornfield to the right of the back yard. Next to this wild millet was a tree with bitter fruits the size of my fist. We ate these fruits out of necessity during famine, when we wouldn't eat them otherwise. For protein, we would eat maggots found in wasp nests, hornet nests, and beehives on this tree and any others.

Meanwhile, our garden thrived. The plants grew and multiplied. We propagated and shared them with relatives and friends.

Mama told us the land where our hut stood had once belonged to the lady with a sensitive bladder. She used to own acres of land until the Khmer Rouge took over. She handed all her assets over to them and moved into a small, flimsy hut in the middle of a rice paddy. The Angka gladly granted her and her family the status of "old-people."

Native families surrounded our hut. On the right was Mother Len's family, with her lame husband, who walked around with a cane, and their three children. Her son Cern worked as an informant, and her two daughters were around Nuy's and my age. From the start, Mama told us to keep our distance. She sensed that their entire family was calculating and conniving.

To the left was Mother Yearn's family. Her son Rort was also an informant.

Mother Lei, who lived southwest of us by the granary next to a barn holding haystacks and the giant stone grinder, was the most likable of all the old-people. She was a ray of sunshine and a flower in Mother's soul. She had three young children whose ages ranged from four to nine years old. Although no one in her family was a Khmer Rouge or an informant, her family had been in this village for many generations, so she was privy to information from her trusted friends. She had a gentle soul and was a devout Buddhist at heart.

Mother Lei went to Mama for a haircut. What Mama got in return, in addition to a can of rice, was priceless advice: "Tell your brother Jo to keep his distance from his friend. They've been onto Hak for some time now. Abandon your Chinese heritage and traditions. Speak only Khmer. It can be construed as conspiratorial and counter-revolutionary if you speak anything else. They perceive it to be an act of defiance."

When Mama came home that night, she told us never to again utter a word in Chinese. She instructed us to speak

Khmer and to use generic and informal peasant words. We dropped *"Mama"* to *"Mae"* or *"Mother"* and *"Papa"* to *"Pok"* or *"Father."* She sounded frightened, but her demeanor frightened me even more as she ran to Grandma, who lived less than a half mile east of us. Curious, I went after her.

Mother emphasized that every one of us should renounce our Chinese heritage. She then told her siblings to sever all ties with their friend Hak. "He has a big mouth. He always speaks Chinese and rubs them the wrong way. He'll drag us down with him."

My uncles protested, stating it was impossible not to interact with Hak since they worked together in the fields. It wasn't for the lack of effort, though: they did tell him to keep quiet on many occasions. He failed to take the advice to heart.

That night and the next couple days, we practiced saying *"Mother and Father"* in Khmer, and no longer uttered the Chinese words, *"Mama and Papa."*

At night, while lying down in our hut, we had the uneasy feeling that someone was eavesdropping on our conversations. The Angka dispatched spies throughout the village under cover of darkness. Except for sparks flickering off the hearthstone to the front of the hut, the rest of the area was black. Although we had a paraffin lamp, we used it sparingly. Only when the moon refused to reveal itself would we light the lamp.

In the moonlight, we saw shadows crouching behind the trees and bushes surrounding our hut. Like cockroaches, the spies stealthily crept beneath our floorboards. They listened for voices of discontentment. We became paranoid and found it difficult to even sing a silly song or hum a happy tune. We seldom whispered among ourselves, even if the topics were non-incriminating in nature.

Although our parents had taught us simple math, we only counted from one to one hundred. We never recited the multiplication table; for it would send the wrong message to our illiterate oppressors: that we were educated (even though my parents had no more than rudimentary education). It didn't help knowing that the village chief and his brother were practically living next door to us and directly across from Grandma.

◆◆◆

My uncles' advice to Hak, to shun his Chinese language and to keep his mouth shut, was ignored. About a week later, the Khmer Rouge came for him at night. My parents told us they killed him because he spoke Chinese. After hearing this, we felt more compelled than ever to abandon our knowledge and culture of all things Chinese. We stopped using chopsticks and ate with our fingers. We picked leaves off trees and boiled them in batches to make dye. We soaked our floral clothes in the pot to dull any vibrancy in the fabric.

After they killed Hak, I experienced nightmares every time I went to sleep. It wasn't because I knew or cared about him: it was sheer paranoia eating away at my innocence—all that I had fantasized, heard, and witnessed since the forced evacuation was manifesting before me. In my dreams, my family and I would fall to our knees, our hands tied behind our backs, as a Khmer Rouge wielding a sickle cut through our heads one at a time.

While my parents worked their way into the natives' circle, Uncle Jo warmed his way into Veern and Chuam's hearts. Uncle Jo lived next to Veern, who headed the informant team. Veern would often approach him to chat and invite him to join his group for lunch. Tempted by food and lured by their cliquish power, Uncle Jo willingly joined them.

There was also another powerful man that my uncle worked closely with in the fields. In his earlier years, Chief Chuam was a devout Buddhist monk. He had a wife and two children. Uncle Jo worked harder and faster than anyone did, and all his efforts were not lost on Chuam. The two developed a mutual respect.

While Uncle Jo gave it his all to gain the Khmer Rouge's trust, his wife habitually complained about his absence from home. He needed only look at the disappearances of his two friends—first Hak, and later Gok—to know he couldn't put family time before collectivism if he wanted to protect his family.

Indeed, it was only Uncle Jo's relationship with Informant Veern that saved Uncle Tek and Aunt Gai from Gok's fate.

Gok and his sister were "new-people" like us. We had come to know them since our stay at the blue-tarp "chicken coop." Informant Veern unwittingly told Uncle Jo about his current investigation into fake marriages. The Angka had long suspected that Gok's marriage was phony and that he was claiming his sister as his wife. Gok didn't heed Uncle Jo's advice to stop fooling around.

Gok would often joke with the Khmer Rouge as though they were his brothers. He talked about his wife in front of them. He was so deeply immersed in his own lies that he cornered himself and left no room to wiggle his way out. When he was interrogated about his marriage, Gok had no choice but to continue claiming that he and his wife were a loving couple and shared the same warm bed; but the Angka knew of his deceit, for they never once saw him sleep in the same corner as his wife. Shortly after, the Khmer Rouge came in the dark for him and his sister.

Then they came for two sets of siblings: Uncle Tek, Aunt Gai, and their respective spouses. No doubt the Angka were already suspicious of their living arrangements. Uncle Tek and Aunt Gai both lived with Grandma on the east side, and their spouses resided on the west side. Uncle Jo had alerted them to the investigations and all four parties had time to formulate and agree on one convincing answer: "Our parents had intended for us to get married, so we got engaged. At first the relationship was fine; but toward the end we didn't get along. We got into a fight and we all called it off." They even worked out the details of the fight.

The next day, my aunt and uncle were told to pack their belongings. They joined a moving brigade and didn't return until many months later. Had they woven a different story, their fate would lie in the grave instead.

9. THE BEST OF TIMES (CIRCA AUGUST 1975)

After we moved into our hut, we labored relentlessly in the back yard. We chopped down the overgrown thickets and removed tree stumps to make room for a vegetable garden. This garden was the main source of food for us. The toughest work was leveling the land and digging the dirt. No one suffered as much as Mother did. In the process of clearing out the wilderness, she stepped on mounds of fire ants and tolerated their bites. I was always amazed at her high tolerance for pain.

In addition to the ant bites, mosquitoes were a constant threat. Bees and wasps added another hellish dimension to gardening; for we often intruded upon their hives. I lost track of how many times their stingers attacked my face, arms, and legs. Snakes, scorpions, centipedes, and millipedes crawled out of the woodwork to add more anxiety to my already-frail nerves.

Many times, we found snakes coiled in the corners of our hut. Some graced us with their acrobatic skills by dangling from the ceiling beams. We threw sticks and stones in attempts to chase them away.

Our neighbors scared us out of our wits. They told us to always remain in our hamlet and never to venture into the forests; especially the mountains behind the village. They said that monsters resided in there and children had disappeared without a trace.

"What do the monsters look like?" I asked Father Pea, our cat-owning neighbor, whose sons taught Vunn how to catch birds.

"Well, monsters are ugly and mean. They've big mouths, big eyes, big heads, and long bodies with legs!" he said with an exaggerated expression of fright. "Big enough to swallow children whole! Just ask everyone here about the two missing children. They disappeared without a trace."

"Is the monster as big as the giant snake you caught recently?" I asked.

"Yes, something like that; but with legs. The main thing is not to go beyond our area!" His voice held a hint of irritation.

Almost six, I couldn't distinguish fact from fiction. Nuy was of no help; she was just as gullible. Since I was responsible for firewood, these monsters weighed heavily on my mind. Every time I ventured alone to collect twigs, the hairs on my neck sprang up. The fear of a monster eating me alive consumed my every step. My ears were tuned to the slightest of noises. Even as I bent down for the twigs, my heart raced and my legs shook because I imagined a monster was sneaking up from behind to attack me. There was never a time when I felt at ease.

At one point I saw a giant python caught by Father Pea and other village men. It took roughly ten men to haul it home. Father and I went over to see the commotion and saw the men hacking away at the snake. It was a monstrosity and could indeed have easily swallowed me and two other children whole.

After seeing this python, the world became much more frightening. Thus, when told of the monsters living in the forests, I was already a believer.

♦♦♦

After a few weeks of gardening and taming the wilderness in our back yard, my tiny hands were bruised and callused and my nails were destroyed. At barely six, I knew how to sharpen knives with a rock.

I was entrusted with a rusty spade to loosen the soil. I became careless one day and my foot slid off the top of the spade, cutting my pinky toe. It turned into an infection and it bubbled with blood and pus.

Our lame neighbor, who limped around with one leg shorter than the other, advised me on how to cure the infection. "Get a big fat leech and have it suck on the wound to cure it."

His advice sounded insincere, so I ignored him.

"If you don't, you'll lose your leg and become a cripple like me!"

Now he had my undivided attention. "But I'm scared of them," I pleaded.

"Which one are you more afraid of: losing your foot, or a spineless creature?"

Of course I wanted to be whole. So I hobbled to the lake carrying a bucket. The memory of those leeches feasting on me on that fateful night came rushing back with each step. At the edge of the backwater, I splashed the water to call the bloodsuckers to me. Because the pail was heavy, I only managed to scoop a little water; but just like that, there were a thumb-sized leech and a few tiny ones. Slowly I emptied the bucket and left the bigger leech inside.

I fished it out with a stick to put it on my toe. The leech was stubborn and refused to adhere to me. I used the stick to hinder its mobility and eventually succeeded in guiding it to the intended target. I could feel its prickling and tightening sensation and see its body moving over the wound methodically like a slow wave—forward, backward, and up and down—while it was fattening up.

To kill time, I concentrated on my surroundings. Two shirtless boys about my age were fishing on the other side of the water. I saw Grandma fetching water as I strained my neck to observe. A tiny green frog leaped from lily pad to lily pad and never missed a landing. Finally, I pried the engorged bloodsucker off me.

For the next few days, I revisited the lake for the same therapy. To my shock and amazement, the infection was going away. I gained some semblance of respect for leeches, but my general aversion to them remained alive and well.

◆◆◆

To prevent us from drowning in our new habitat, Father taught us, one by one, how to swim. He led me to the southern edge of the village to swim in a huge lake. Surveying my surroundings, I noticed the water was glistening and vibrant. The body of water mesmerized me. Its surface looked like a beautiful painting made of living colors where the glassy waters released their silver streaks upward to the blue sky. Behind me, the sun was setting, and the intensity of the orange color seeped into the water to blend heaven and earth into one perfect landscape. To the left, a huge tree branched out majestically over the water's edge.

I saw children stretched out lazily on the tree branches. They were tanned from exposure to the sun. They climbed the trunk and crawled to the edge of a branch to dive into the water, then they swam back to repeat the thrill. Their laughter sounded so pure and innocent that I was aware that I was on the outside looking in. I realized then how much I missed my former life with my cousins and siblings. I missed their faces, the ice cream, the playfulness, and the beef noodles. I wondered if I would ever experience any of that again. I kept wishing that the forced evacuation had never happened. How I wished for the Khmer Rouge's first knock to have never occurred!

My gaze shifted from the tree to the rest of the lake. It was so vast that I couldn't see the far edge of the banks. The shimmering reflection hurt my eyes and eclipsed my vision.

Carrying me in his arms, Father slowly walked into the water. He stopped when the water reached his chest. I felt anxious and recoiled tightly into his arms, seeking his reassurance that I would be fine.

He assured me that both Vunn and Nuy had felt equally frightened by the water at first; but after a few days, they could swim. That did it for me. Father needn't say more, and he knew how to push my buttons. If they could do it, so could I, with ease—I was sure of it. His encouragement compelled me to paddle away from the comfort of his arms, yet he was always within reach should I need rescue. The water was deeper than my head. I was fearless, and after two days of kicking, wading, and swallowing water, I could float freely and dive to the bottom to grab his feet.

When Vunn, Nuy, and I swam together, I was pleasantly surprised that I could swim as well as any of them. Father later told me that I was the fastest learner of all three. It took him only half the amount of time to teach me.

One day we had surprise visitors. After living one month in Phnum Sress, Uncle Rain and his family strolled down our walkway into our back yard. We were busy gardening in the late afternoon sun. They knew of our whereabouts because Uncle Rain and Uncle Jo happened to work in the same field one day. They settled in Tapan a few miles northeast of us, also in District Five. Aunt Khan, Uncle Rain, and my six cousins (Jon, Big Daughter, Middle Daughter, Tai, Ti, and Sida) all looked different. They seemed gaunt and feeble. I kept staring at their faces.

They had since lost their youngest family member. Their infant would drink only formula and had refused breast milk and rice soup. He subsequently died of hunger. The news of the baby's death swept in and lingered like humidity on a hot day, but we were so happy to have found one another that our sorrow eventually dissipated. We children chased and tagged each other and played kick-the-can. Our time together was ordinary by any standards: it was neither subdued nor excessive in giggles and laughter, but it felt as if we had all met in heaven.

While the children played outside, the adults were inside confiding their worries to each other. Uncle Rain remained horror-struck that someone was still searching for him for elimination. My aunt talked about their meager daily rations being not enough to fill a child's stomach. My parents knew the depths of their suffering. We packaged almost all of our food for them to take back: dried fish, a couple of cans of rice, a chunk of palm sugar, and a half jar of salt. Salt was a precious commodity, so Mother had it dissolved in fish sauce to elude detection at checkpoints.

The children's merriment suddenly turned to shrieks. The adults ran over to find Jon, their first-born, riddled with rashes on his face and neck. He had climbed an unknown tree. On contact with the tree, he had experienced a severe allergic reaction. Now a wave of panic ran through all of us. His neck and face ballooned and his eyes were swollen shut.

We had nothing to ease his pain.

It was not in his nature to inconvenience others, so he lied. He told us it was only a rash and that it was not itchy, all the while scratching at his neck and hands. His rashes made me uneasy. I wished there were a salve in my palm to soothe his pain.

The sun was setting, but Jon was the most reluctant to leave. We walked them to the main road to send them home. The sky was beautiful, radiating an iridescent mural to honor our farewell. We waved at each other. They turned their backs to us and headed toward the sunset. I watched the silhouette of a boy scratching himself before he turned the bend, heading north.

10. THE GARDEN OF LIFE (CIRCA SEPTEMBER 1975)

A group of Khmer Rouge and informants strolled through our back yard. Mother was in the thick groves chopping big bamboo stalks to make trellises for the garden. Their boisterousness alerted her to remain still and undetected. She listened in on their conversation as they walked through our garden to get to the main road.

"This is one heck of an impressive garden! How in the world did she find time for this?" exclaimed a voice, in awe.

"Who said Mother Yeng's family is a flight risk?" asked another.

"That can't be so. No one in her right mind would invest this much energy if she plans on running away," opined a third.

"I agree. They're not a flight risk. The garden says it all!" said a fourth.

Meanwhile, Mother remained frozen: too frightened to even breathe. She stepped on a mound of fire ants and had no choice but to suffer their pain silently. Their bites turned to tiny needle injections filled with lighter fluid. What she heard made her more uneasy than the bites.

After eavesdropping on their conversation, she became obsessed. She considered the garden as our road to salvation, tending to its expansion.

The cool monsoon season could fall below 60º F: not terribly cold by any means, but chilly enough to warrant extra layers. The few possessions we managed to take with us since the forced march slowly disappeared between involuntary confiscation and willful bartering for the essentials.

Without much to wear, cold swept through us during winter. At night I curled into a fetal position with my hands tucked tightly between my thighs to conserve their warmth. We paired up for the blankets. We often tossed and turned from the uncomfortable floorboards. By morning, one of us usually ended up hogging the blanket while the other shivered.

Father sacrificed his own warmth for our food. He pulled the sweater off his body to trade with a villager for a fishing net. The villager soon exchanged the sweater with a new-person for gold. A month later, Father saw a Khmer Rouge wearing his black sweater with red stripes. Upon inquiring around, Father discovered the new-person, who had been escorted away one night, disappeared without a trace. The killer loved the red and black ensemble—red (or Rouge) being the color for their cause and a word of their name. The soldier coveted the article and he killed for it for his personal gain. Had Father still possessed the sweater, no doubt he would have been eliminated, too.

With the fishing net, Father fed us. He sacrificed his sleep and risked his own life to ensure our survival. In the dead of night he strung the net against a running river to catch fish. He would wait a few hours before gathering and pulling it back. He often trekked the same path and he was always careful not to get caught. Fishing was strictly for collectivism and not allowed for private use; but for some reason, native children about my age were seen with long sticks and worms standing by the lake.

Father snuck out to the water once or twice a week. I often begged him to wake me so I could help, but he never did. If he had known that I had broken his glasses, he would have understood my intention: a daughter wanting to lead her blind father.

◆◆◆

Unlike Father, who leveraged and exchanged his sweater for a fishing net, Mother flat out gave it away. She pulled the sweater off Black Ghost's body and headed out.

On a clear morning a couple of days later, a native woman visited our hut. She had not once bothered coming to see us after we'd moved in. Today she trekked over with her chubby baby to say hello. Immediately, I recognized the sweater on her baby boy. She came empty-handed, not even bearing a chunk of palm sugar nor a squash to reciprocate the gift. It was a one-sided exchange. She acted as if she were a god demanding our sacrifice to be in her good graces. I felt the rawness and sting of the injustice done to my little sister.

The sweater had sweetened the woman's demeanor and sugared her voice. Today it was especially soothing and melodic. It bounced gently up and down like her breasts, each bigger than my head. She didn't practice modesty. When her baby cried, she lifted her shirt in plain sight so the infant could suckle.

She was a close relative to the head chief: his sister-in-law.

♦♦♦

The winter season meant less work in the back yard. I now had more free time than I knew what to do with. If the weather permitted and the ground was not flooded, I would leisurely tag along with Vunn to loop snares for birds. We zigzagged our way to the south before reaching the lake where Father taught us to swim, and then veered to the right to marshland and mangroves where wildlife thrived.

While Vunn continued to set traps, I gathered dead twigs. I developed a strong sense of responsibility, dutifully replenishing the firewood stockpile. I couldn't step over a stick without seeing it and picking it up. On a few occasions, when the supply was depleted, I paid the price. Utterly consumed with her worry over keeping the household running, Mother punished me swiftly and severely, chasing me with a bamboo stick as thick as my thumb. My head, back, arms, and legs would bruise and bleed. It hurt just as much, if not more, than when my toe had split open on the rock. I begged and cried for mercy, but I received no pity nor clemency.

"You'll get it ten times worse if this happens again." The stick swished and hissed against my skin.

Pain kept me from becoming a repeat offender. I could spot potential firewood and kindling the way an eagle spots prey from the sky.

We saw plenty of birds that day but trapped none. This was how Vunn spent his days; both alone and with company. If he was lucky, he would snare a bird. At times, he returned with other creatures. We ate whatever he brought back. One time it was a big lizard and another time, a toad. With seven stomachs to fill, food was a constant challenge; but all was bearable for now.

When we weren't venturing into the wilderness, we would visit Grandma. Her hut was our second home. She was mostly alone during the daytime because her two youngest daughters Hang (thirteen) and Sing (ten) had to work. When not building roads and dikes at labor camps, my aunts would be collecting cow manure and water buffalo dung in the village to fertilize the communal gardens and paddy fields.

Grandma had her hands full with grandchildren. Her place had a huge front yard surrounded by trees, which included trees bearing tiny clusters of sour fruit. We ate only a small amount: eating any more than could fit in a palm would result in severe diarrhea.

Grandma's house had plenty of space for us to play and shade where we could rest. A swing was suspended from a huge tree on the right side and two hammocks were tied to trees to the left. Nuy and I relished the times when Grandma shared our babysitting responsibility. She spoiled us with so much love and tenderness, she hardly expected us to do anything. She even cooked for us and washed our dishes: chores we would otherwise perform at home.

I was a tree climber and spent most of the time daring my cousins and siblings to catch me. Before anyone could touch me, I swung from the branches and landed on my feet. Then, just as quickly, I climbed another. Like a monkey, I moved with ease.

It had been more than a couple of months since we had last seen Uncle Rain and his family. We had been saving dried fish and dried beans for them, but we dared not cross the border to visit them. We needed permission to leave our hamlet; and my parents did not want to be stigmatized as lazy people. We wanted the Angka to believe we were hard-working folks who obeyed all the rules.

One day, while staying at Grandma's place, I had a premonition that someone was waiting for us at home. This sort of inkling had happened before, and I found our hut devoid of humans but full of snakes coiled in the corners. One time I counted eight snakes: there were more of them than us.

This time, Big Daughter and Tai were there waiting. I could tell they were on a serious mission and hardly in the mood to stay a minute longer.

I immediately reached into our pot and fished out the remaining cooked yams and cassavas for them. They devoured them so fast that the food stuck in their throats. Quickly, I handed them a bowl of water to drink. I could tell they had been starving for days. I gave them the food that had been set aside by Mother to take back.

After they left, I headed back to Grandma's. I could hardly wait to share the news of their visit.

One strange morning, an old man was digging huge holes in our front yard. Our eyes didn't play tricks on us: he plopped down three banana trees and proceeded to fill in the dirt.

We approached the man. He turned around with a big smile. There was a huge gap in his bottom teeth, making him look almost toothless. The red betel juice stained his mouth.

"Excuse me," Mother said. "I think you're working on the wrong house!"

The old man shook. "No! I'm not," he replied as he spat out the red juice. "You don't have bananas, but pretty soon you will."

"What about those houses?" Mother randomly pointed.

He whipped his head again. "Only this house. I like you, Mother Yeng. You're a nice person. And this is your family, so I like them, too. I'm only doing this house. Not theirs." He pointed to four other houses within sight.

"Thank you" was what we each uttered to him while heading back to the hut, leaving the man alone with his mission.

Mother described his mental capacity as "half-water" because he wasn't all there, implying that if his intelligence were to be measured in a cup, it would only fill up half-way; whereas a normal person's would reach the brim.

We later learned more about the old man. He was native to the hamlet. He had a wife, and his son Kong was an informant. Due to his inability to comprehend or follow instructions, the old man was left alone and free to do as he pleased. Today, planting banana trees had tickled his fancy.

At that time, we also encountered a minor health concern: head lice. Inquiring around, we discovered how the natives addressed this problem. We marinated charcoal in water and let it sit a few days until the solution turned from black to yellow and looked and smelled like urine. Then we drenched our hair with it. This helped, but the solution was never strong enough to kill the lice eggs, so the itch would return after a few days. People often sat behind one another to delouse and rummage through each other's heads the way monkeys and chimpanzees do.

Mother found a permanent solution for this health problem. As a pragmatic person, she didn't have the time nor energy to manually search out and destroy the infestation: she would rather channel our energy into the garden as a matter of survival.

Convinced by her logic and in no position to argue, I reluctantly surrendered my hair to the razor. We all did. It was a comical sight when we all stood next to each other like a bunch of Buddhist monks at roll call. Every time our hair grew back an inch or two, the razor grazed our heads all over again.

11. THE WORST OF TIMES (CIRCA APRIL 1976)

The Angka sent Father away to labor camp. During his absence, we had no fish to eat. Mother battled our starvation by bringing bits of food home from cutting people's hair and mending their clothes. Food was always in short supply, and we were constantly hungry. We went to bed thinking and dreaming of food every night. I often imagined the taste of that warm bread and breakfast stew which we left behind on that one fateful morning when the Khmer Rouge burst through our door.

The Angka had control over all aspects of our lives, from what to say to what to wear; but in their zeal, they failed to realize that they had no power over nature. The indigenous rice originally grown here was immune to nature's wrath because of its ability to thrive with the rising water, but the rules had since changed. The Angka detested our rice, calling it inferior even though it was hearty and dependable. They ordered us to switch to new crops.

The adults worried that the new rice crops would not survive the floods. What they feared would eventually become our reality.

Another factor we faced was the impending arrival of twenty thousand families to District Five, of which roughly one hundred families, or five hundred people, would settle in our hamlet in less than one week. This would instantly more than double the population in Phnum Sress. At the meeting, the Angka referred to them as the "twenty thousand families of new brothers and sisters." Their arrival afflicted each of our neighboring villages. Even before the newcomers, Uncle Rain's family was starving: the twenty thousand families had put a death sentence on all of us in District Five.

Mother didn't leave it to chance. She turned to our garden for self-preservation.

Like a drill sergeant, she yanked us out of bed when morning was still night and the roosters were fast asleep.

After gardening, Vunn would set out to catch food with his friends and we wouldn't see him until mealtime. I cleaned the pots and dishes while Nuy banged and bruised her ankles from the metal buckets to refill the water barrel and nourish the plants. Nuy often complained about the pain sawing her neck and shoulders, but Mother could only sigh in pity before saying, "My children know only suffering."

I often made multiple trips for firewood. Physically, I was limited to how much I could carry as well as the size of the branch I could break off. Mother always complained that the twigs I brought back were much like hay used in kindling: they burned too fast. I eagerly agreed and asked to be spared from the responsibility. She smirked and steadfastly said, "No! You just need to gather more of them!" Vunn deserved some credit in this department, too, because he sometimes carried an armload back to contribute to the stockpile.

Within days of the new-people's arrival, they reduced our rice rations. What didn't make sense to any of us was that we were during a successful harvest season. Countless fields of rice stalks overlaid the village. When the rice matured, the stalks turned golden brown and top-heavy, bowing and swaying gently in the winds. Everywhere, people were harvesting with sickles and threshing the stalks to separate rice kernels from hay. Two men rotated an enormous stone grinder clockwise to mill. Women squatted to winnow by tossing the grains up and down in a flat basket to separate rice from husk. I stood there scanning for Mother and observing the busy bodies of workers, all clad in black with straw hats and scarves.

Normally I wouldn't be visiting Mother during work hours, but today Black Ghost was sick. She was about one and a half years old and physically small. Even White Ghost could carry her around. Black Ghost had bouts of diarrhea, and her rectum slid out of her anus half an inch. Her entire face drooped, as if she had no reserve left. She lacked the strength to open her eyes. The bouts took a toll on her already-frail body.

Mother unwrapped the towel to inspect Black Ghost's rectal prolapse. The timing couldn't have been worse, for Black Ghost involuntarily released additional liquid excrement. Mother carried her to the water barrel for a quick rinse. She demonstrated to us the method of cleaning and stuffing the rectum back inside. My stomach convulsed at the sight of it and I let out a gagging sound. Mother glared at me. Nuy, the more mature one, observed in silence, afterward taking the dirty towel and soiled clothes to wash in the lake.

Later that day, Mother bartered a pound of beef to make a strengthening broth. Her attention was now focused on saving her child. She boiled desiccated roots and medicinal leaves to make a concoction to remedy Black Ghost's ailment.

The next morning we woke up to a pot of cooked fish. For a second I thought that Father was back from the slave camp, but Mother had gone fishing with his net in the dead of night.

She shouldered our survival alone. At first her silent sacrifices went unnoticed as we hungrily devoured the pot of fish for breakfast. She sat there with a tender and concerned look on her face, watching us eat. Seeing how we sucked on the fish bones and ate their heads and eyes so ravenously, she uttered: "Eat slowly. Don't choke on the bones. We'll have fish again tomorrow." Her silent sacrifice of another sleepless night struck all of us.

The Angka rotated Mother and Father's time at labor camps. Shortly after his return, she received her orders to leave.

While Mother was away, Uncle Rain visited us. One mid-afternoon when I returned home with firewood, I found Father and Uncle Rain in tears. I was told my twelve-year-old Cousin Jon, who was allergic to a tree in our back yard, had died. He had survived the allergy, but soon passed away from a weakened immune system. He died from malnutrition and lack of proper medical care. He had once been a healthy boy with an alert and strong mind.

Uncle Rain recounted the story to us. At only twelve years old, Jon was mature beyond his youth. He never once caused the family any grievance, was always ready to help, and he never once complained. Daily, he snuck out to forage for food. When in possession of a lizard, snail, frog, grasshopper, or crab, he would take it home to share with his mother and siblings when other kids would have selfishly devoured it.

Uncle Rain had returned home from the camp after having been gone for over a month, so he was with his family the night Jon came home from work. Jon didn't acknowledge anyone: he simply crawled into bed and skipped dinner. His parents knew then that something was seriously wrong. The next morning they told him to stay home and rest, but they didn't know until nighttime that Jon had snuck out to work against their wishes. When asked why he had defied their authority, he responded with teary eyes and a shaky voice that if he didn't go to work, they wouldn't give him food.

His condition worsened. By nightfall, Jon said he was too tired to eat and he just wanted to lie down. The next day Uncle Rain took Jon to the chief for permission to stay home, but the chief diagnosed him as having "Sick-in-the-Head" syndrome and told him to go to work and stop dreaming about the past. Jon was too ill to walk. In the morning, he remained at home, and his health continued to deteriorate. He didn't receive his rice allowance, so food was meagerly shared among the family.

Jon finally died in April 1976, at the age of twelve, exactly one year after the forced evacuation.

The news of my cousin's death numbed me. I couldn't accept it. I didn't know how to grieve his loss. I crept out to the back of the garden, climbed a tree, and cried.

A fire burned nearby, and its smoky tendrils and ashy fumes reached me. While I was still in the tree, my nose sniffed the burnt air. My eyes searched for the fire and traced it all the way to the bamboo forest. I jumped off the tree to investigate and slowly followed a foot trail into the bamboo forest. As I drew near, I saw Uncle Rain and Father, who were on a mission to smoke out bees from their hive. They hollered at me to steer clear: the bees were agitated. Before I turned to run away, I saw the stingers on Father and Uncle Rain's hands and faces.

A bee stung me on the left cheek just before I stepped out of the bamboo, and then, out in the open, another one nabbed me on my upper right arm. By the time I reached the hut, my cheek had swollen to the size of a ping-pong ball and my arm sported another big bump. I would have gladly tolerated a dozen more stings, if not hundreds, if they could only bring back my cousin.

My uncle and father returned with a mutilated mass of honeycomb in a basket lined with banana leaves. I looked at this squirming mass and saw huge white larvae fixing their eyes on me. Uncle Rain said everything was edible, including the wax, and Father told him to take all of it home. My uncle diligently wrapped the honeycomb and the maggots with banana leaves as he emptied the clear honey into a glass jar which was normally used to store fish sauce.

He expressed deep gratitude before he left, carrying with him the honey, dried fish, tomatoes, squash, and yams. I was moved by Father's generosity in Mother's absence. He gave away all the honey without saving a spoon for us to lick. There were sacrifices reflected in all our eyes.

At the first sign of dawn, Father's work brigade footslogged a great distance to work in a labor camp, joining others in digging earth. He worked and slept side by side with hundreds of people, hoeing and shoveling the dirt into baskets to build the elevated causeways. Men directed water from the rivers to the paddy fields and mixed manure as fertilizer.

Mother's face gleamed when she told us that Father would be coming home soon. Lately, she hadn't been sleeping. Those early morning trips to the river had created black rings around her eyes. She told us his work brigade would be attending the communal meeting first, before coming home. I rushed to finish all my chores early in anticipation of his homecoming.

Arriving at the meeting, I immediately found Mother and, as usual, she was busy socializing. This time she was talking to the woman whose baby was naked and no longer wearing Black Ghost's sweater. I approached and asked, "Mother, where's Father?"

"He's on his way back," the other woman answered in her sweet voice. She was cooing for the baby, bouncing him up and down on her lap. She smiled at me and I smiled back.

She continued, "His group should be here any moment now. Don't worry, you'll see him today." She seemed to know everything. It was part of her power and might to be related to the head chief. She tickled her baby and he giggled and laughed in delight—then, for no apparent reason at all, the baby cried. She was quick to roll up her shirt to feed him. Her breasts, the size of a small watermelon, were exposed to all wandering eyes.

The meeting was noticeably crowded with newcomers. I climbed my favorite tree for a better view. There were two boys already in the tree, staking out good spots. The meeting had more than doubled in size. The head chief and his entourage arrived and stood at the center of the meeting circle. Murmurs hushed into absolute silence.

The speech began with the familiar introduction. This much I understood. Mother and Father explained the rest to me later.

"Brothers and sisters, today I have good news for all of us! We were awarded this red flag because our village exceeded the rice quota output to the Angka." The head chief waved the small red flag and gestured the crowd to cheer. Not having a choice, the people applauded. I followed suit, hanging with the boys in the trees.

The head chief cleared his throat and continued. "The Angka expects our output to double next year. We'll make Angka proud! We now have more brothers and sisters to work alongside us. Let's give it our best! Let's work hard so the excess will overflow to our granary, too!" He pointed to the brown barn against the sinking sun.

From the tree I could only see the back of Mother's head.

This same spiel went on and on until I almost fell out of the tree in exhaustion. I climbed down just in time for the meeting to adjourn. The people stretched their arms and backs, which were stiff from standing or sitting too long. No one challenged the unrealistic quota; everyone remained quiet.

After half of the crowd left the meeting, Father's brigade arrived.

I quickly ran to grab his hand, but he flinched as though my hands were hot coals. To comfort me, he showed me his swollen pinky. With his injured hand, I knew a piggyback ride was out of the question.

Mother approached us and together we headed home. Most of the new arrivals trekked westbound, but we trailed east. Once the road was clear, Mother piped up: "Our chief is one stupid man! He gives away all our rice. What good is a flag when we have nothing to eat? Just because we have more people working doesn't mean we don't eat! What a stupid man!"

Father admonished her to lower her voice.

Curious, I asked, "Where did the new-people come from?"

"Most of them were from Phnom Penh. They came here by train." Mother controlled her volume.

The word "train" felt dirty and heavy. It felt much like the weight of a book condemning its reader as an intellectual, or an incriminating photo showing elites draped in jewelry, or speaking Chinese when forbidden. These were all signs of defiance.

The closest remnant of something connecting me to my previous life was a radio. I had seen the head chief walk around holding the radio to his ear, his neck always bent to one side. That radio had once belonged to Grandma. He had ransacked her hut and confiscated it for his personal use.

There were no paved roads in our village. The sky was devoid of planes. I had seen men haul bags of rice on oxcarts, leaving our village. Men riding horses and boys riding cows and water buffaloes were a common sight. I never once saw an automobile, a motorcycle, or even a bicycle in this village.

Mother told me that most of the women were widowed by the time they reached District Five. Since Phnom Penh was the biggest city, it housed the most professionals.

"Mother, what do you know about our new neighbors? Their children always stick their heads into our hut."

"That family has suffered much. Be extra kind to them. Take their older children to forage with you," she instructed me. They were Chinese from Vietnam. The two sisters were widowed: one of the husbands had been a doctor and the other had owned a famous soy sauce factory. Both men were killed within days of the forced evacuation. Their parents didn't want to go on living with their pain and heartache, and disease and hunger eventually claimed their lives.

12. LOVE THY NEIGHBOR (CIRCA MAY 1976)

Of the roughly five hundred new arrivals to our village, two became my friends. I wasn't sure if these two were siblings or cousins. We suffered from a language barrier, since they couldn't speak a word in Khmer and the Chinese dialect they spoke was one I could barely understand.

Gently raising my hand to my chest, I introduced myself: "My name is Geng."

The older girl pointed to her nose and said, "Jie," then she pointed to the younger boy and said, "Didi."

Now I was perplexed. Jie sounded like "older sister" and Didi was "younger brother" in Chinese; yet I didn't understand what they were saying. I was convinced they were siblings, but Mother was adamant that they were cousins. She explained how it was customary for cousins to address each other as siblings, especially if they shared the same surname. Whether they were siblings or cousins didn't matter: I now had friends.

In their household, seven people lived under one roof: two widows, an uncle, and four children.

Their hut was ensconced in trees. They lived almost directly across from us, but if they hadn't stuck their heads into our place, I would never have known they existed.

Jie was Nuy's age, and Didi was mine. Their two youngest siblings were the same ages as White Ghost and Black Ghost. Their faces reminded me of my cousins, Big Daughter, Middle

Daughter, and Sida. They had porcelain complexions with huge almond eyes.

Jie and Didi came to fetch me for our daily foray, and I handed them a few yams and cassavas which Mother had set aside for them. Heading out together, we made a quick stop at their place to drop off the tuberous roots. I saw their two half-starved younger siblings, and I was unable to tell if they were little boys or girls. They ran over, snatched the food, and ate the yams raw. Their hollow eyes fluttered at me, almost as if they were thanking me. I looked around and didn't see anyone else. It was typical for even small children to be unsupervised.

Since we had a language problem, we walked in silence.

We became more daring as we ventured farther south to find crabs and snails, even though it was uncharted territory for us. With Jie and Didi as friends, I no longer felt lonely; however, the frustration of not being able to communicate with them was affecting my ability to truly enjoy their company.

After passing through countless paddy fields, we eventually arrived at the southeastern-most edge of the village. We came upon flooded mangroves where crabs, snails, tiny shrimp, and fish wiggled in clear shallow water. Didi took off his shirt to use as a bag. I had a thin towel that I tied to make a pouch.

Immediately, they chased after fish and crabs. Their feet splashed and muddied up the water, scaring away a potential meal as the crabs scurried into their burrows. Fish vanished, but a few black leeches were swimming our way.

Determined, Didi stretched his back as he positioned himself to reach his arm into a hole where a crab had just crawled in for refuge. Before he stuck his hand in, I let out a frightful squeal: "No! Don't!"

My shriek froze him as he searched my face for the cause of my alarm.

Knowing I wouldn't be able to explain myself to him, I picked up a large twig floating near me.

Seconds later, I placed the stick in his hand. Only then did he understand my intention. He inserted the stick into the hole and out swam a black snake about six feet long, which slithered away in the water. The crab never came out. Whether the serpent was poisonous or not didn't matter: as far as Didi was concerned, I had saved his life.

The snake rattled all of us, but we were still determined to bring food home. Our hope renewed: as the scorching sun cast our shadows at our feet, the water cleared up and the creatures crawled out once more. We managed to catch a few crabs and a bag of snails. To my astonishment, Jie and Didi ate the crabs raw. I, too, had been hungry before; but I'd always manage to have my meals cooked properly.

We lingered out there for another hour or two until we caught enough snails and crabs to make a decent meal. On our way home, they each crunched a couple more crabs.

The first time we foraged together, they found three tiny bird eggs near where Vunn and I set traps. Without hesitation, Didi cracked two eggs and gulped them down before giving one to Jie. What struck me as odd wasn't eating the raw eggs itself: rather, it was their selfishness. They didn't take them home to share with their family the way I would have done. Soon I would be the judge of my own action.

Again the same thing happened with the crabs: they were simply too busy eating them. By the time we arrived home, they had eaten all the crabs and only the snails remained. I emptied my sack into Didi's shirt when we arrived by the front of our huts and parted ways for the day.

Mother occasionally sent me to deliver produce to them. They were always polite and grateful, but most of the time the older widow, Wonhing, would come to our place to speak to my parents. Mother often gave her food from our garden to take back, and each time she bowed her heartfelt thank you.

♦♦♦

The Angka attempted to sell us a vision of a better tomorrow: a perfect utopia where we wouldn't go hungry. Everyone was equal; we were all one big unity. My parents never raised their hands to make suggestions, but there were always a few people who recommended the use of machinery and tractors to increase efficiency and production. The Angka nodded in agreement, then further hooked our souls by mentioning the need to educate young minds. When asked who could teach the classrooms, a few eager hands always waved. All those with their hands up received a sack of rice and their names were jotted down.

At the next meeting, the Angka informed us that they had placed the order for tractors, leveling equipment, and milling machines. The shipment would be arriving within weeks. Those who recommended water irrigation, roads, hospitals, and schools stood up and were each handed a bag of rice. It seemed the Angka was genuinely following the ideas put forth by the people.

The Angka walked the extra mile to identify locations for schools and hospitals. In a follow-up meeting, the leaders again asked for doctors and teachers to run the much-anticipated facilities once they were built. Several people, half-hoping to contribute to the new society and half-expecting to be rewarded with a bag of rice, raised their hands, and the crowd applauded.

Months passed. There were no tractors, no road expansions, no hospitals, and no schools. In the face of famine and oppression, when stomachs chewed on themselves, brains forsook good judgment. Those who possessed the strength and the smarts kept silent and continued to starve. Those who could no longer control their hunger fell headlong into the Khmer Rouge's web of deceit, and the extra bag of rice became their last meal.

♦♦♦

Surrounded by new arrivals, Mother became the village's underground broker. People came to her with gold and jewelry and she would help them barter for rice and poultry. Her fluency in three Chinese dialects and Khmer positioned her as the perfect conduit between the haves and the have-nots. Sellers and buyers never met each other, thus perpetuating the veil of secrecy for both sides. Her function as an intermediary was lucrative, but risky.

For her service, she imposed a ten percent surcharge. If an ounce of gold rendered ten cans of rice, Mother would take one can and the buyer would get nine. It was hard to find suppliers of rice to meet the bottomless demands. Daily, she walked around with someone else's jewelry in search of potential buyers and relayed messages back and forth between the two parties. Once both sides reached an agreement, Mother delivered the jewelry to the exploiters and hauled the perishables to the hungry.

Early one morning, Mother dropped the gardening tool to fulfill a transaction. She removed a log from the side of the hut and took out a gold chain. Hiding the necklace in her bra, she ran to her appointment.

An exchange took place with the supplier and she was now in possession of the rice. While en route to the buyer, she unexpectedly encountered an informant: the young man who lived a few huts down from us.

He yelled at Mother to stop and turn around.

With that bag of rice on her person, she was certainly doomed.

"Hmh Mother Yeng, what's in the bag? Rice? Are you conducting illegal transactions?" Rort asked contemptuously, assuming an authoritative posture like that of an emperor.

Mother took a quick breath to gather her courage. She looked around nervously as if there were other informants nearby before she leaned into him to whisper.

"Shhh, Rort, lower your voice. I obtained this from your mother." They quickly locked eyes. Her steely outward appearance didn't betray her frayed nerves. She commanded his attention now, and she must retain her composure.

Rort blushed at the implication, and he quickly turned around to walk away, vanishing faster than the strike of a cobra.

If Mother's blatant lie were ever found out, it would be the end of us all. She must see to it that it would not be so.

Time was of the essence. She ran home and scrambled to one side of the hut to hide the rice, then rushed to another corner to retrieve a hidden bracelet. In a hurry to cover her tracks, she bolted out of sight.

Her panic alarmed us. I noticed the bag of rice she had brought back sticking out from under a pile of blankets. I walked over to shove it deeper into a corner and pull those layers of blankets over it. That day we safeguarded the rice by staying home. It was not so much our ability to prevent the search and seizure; rather, it was our presence that deterred such conduct.

To turn the lie into reality, Mother took the bracelet and headed straight to Rort's mother. Luckily, she caught Mother Yearn in time, just as she was about to leave for work.

The object was to trade the jewelry for rice. If she was successful, she could feel at ease because if Rort were to crosscheck with his mother, her story would pan out.

"How much?" Mother Yearn inquired.

The bracelet would not be a hard sell, so Mother quoted the fair market value of what it could command: "Ten cans of rice."

Mother Yearn shook to decline the offer, saying: "I don't even have ten cans of rice at hand. How about next time when I have more rice, then come back with the same bracelet?"

"How about five now and the rest later?" Mother countered.

"Until I get my next batch of supplies, I'm afraid to trade even one can, let alone five."

Mother needed this transaction to occur to validate her claim. If Mother Yearn wasn't willing to do the exchange, she was as good as dead.

Mother insisted: "Alright, how about you give me one can today and nine cans later? This bracelet is a beauty. It won't last long."

She must have sensed the desperation in Mother's voice, and she countered: "Two cans today and that's my final offer. I must get going now. We'll have to continue this another time."

Mother accepted the two cans.

13. ONLY A HEART OF STONE (CIRCA JUNE 1976)

Forced labor wrung Uncle Tek dry of his essence. The Angka discharged him when he became too frail to even sit, let alone walk. While he was working, the Angka deprived him of food, medicine, and rest. Even his optimal performance was not worth much. Many propagandist slogans reflecting such labor abuses were drummed into our heads: two of which were "To keep you is no gain. To lose you is no loss" and "Work like a mule: be deaf and dumb."

In his skeletal frame, he mustered every ounce of willpower to journey back to Grandma. He would occasionally hitch a ride on an oxcart; but for the most part, he hobbled slowly on foot, at times on all fours to propel himself forward. His aim was to die at home in the comfort of familiar surroundings and faces. It took him several days to reach us. He encountered many soldiers along the way, but they left the dying man alone.

When he finally returned to us, he stood at death's door. His eyes were yellow and listless. He couldn't remember the last time he had defecated. Urination pained him, as if needles were passing from his bladder through the urethral tube.

Grandma and Mother almost fainted when they inspected his private parts, aghast at the disfiguration.

The infirmary had no real doctors and the imposters prescribed "rabbit dropping" pills and nothing else. It would have been kinder to abandon him out in a field than to leave him in the hands of untrained teenage nurses with rusty syringes and expired penicillin.

I once tasted these rabbit droppings. It was as if they were made of grass, wood, and leaves. They were round like the tip of my pinky finger, light like a rolled leaf, and brown like dry hay. They had a hint of mild sweetness, but for the most part, they were bitter. The taste lingered a few seconds on my tongue before I spit them out.

Death was running at breakneck speed toward Uncle Tek. Without a moment to waste, Mother raced home to harvest spices in hope of creating a remedy for him.

Grandma, Nuy, and I were busy harvesting tiny red chili peppers, spearmint, and basil leaves as instructed by Mother before she rushed home. Several minutes later, Mother came back with ginger, galangal, turmeric and other herbs and spices.

Heaving and gasping for air, she handed the ingredients to Grandma and instructed her to mash them in the mortar and pestle. When Grandma noticed the contents in the bowl, she shook resignedly. "Have you gone mad, Yeng?"

"Ma, desperate times calls for desperate measures. Don't interfere! He's dying. You need to trust me!"

Without saying more, Grandma, in a state of shock, reluctantly prepared the ingredients.

One of the antidotes to Uncle Tek's quivering was the tip of a spoon scraped over his skin: Mother applied the Chinese coining method all over his body to rid him of toxins. He barely moved or moaned, plunging in and out of consciousness throughout the process. Mother intermittently fed him the mushy ingredients and forced him to drink hot water: with or without his consent, he swallowed them.

By the time she finished coining his body, he had eaten over fifty tiny chili peppers along with the other spices and herbs. Each spoonful must have packed a deadly punch to his body. It became clear that the remedy had begun working when he kicked away his blankets.

Mother's theory was simple: the spices and herbs would generate internal heat and would cause him to sweat with the coining of the skin. To speed his perspiration, she covered his body with additional blankets and warned him not to kick them away. He listened to her despite his own discomfort.

A short while later, Uncle Tek was secreting freely from every pore. Drops of sweat formed on his forehead and trickled down the sides of his face and his entire body was drenched as if stranded in a sudden downpour.

He wailed and moaned, tossed and turned, and kicked away the many layers of blankets.

Mother was not to be defied. She returned to pull the blankets over him, adding, "Should you kick it away again, I'll shove another bowl of chili down your throat." Instead of handing him cool water, she gave him a bowl of steamy hot water and told him to drink it all down, and she stood there to make sure he drank to the last drop.

My uncle was no longer himself, but he still obediently consumed whatever was given to him. A few minutes later, she handed him another bowl of hot water.

Time slowly marched on and death's pace slackened. A couple of hours later, his body finally gave in to nature's call: though painful, he released the fluid and impurities through urination and perspiration.

At first Mother helped him up and encouraged him to take small steps to circulate the blood flow; and soon he regained the strength in his legs. A few days later, she added another layer of cruelty: she chased him with a long stick, hitting him the way she hit me. The two ran in a circle in front of Grandma's house.

I watched the entire scene in an awestruck daze. I was too afraid to intrude and didn't want to distract her and risk endangering his life.

Grandma couldn't take it anymore, and she commanded Mother to stop. "Have a heart. He's sick and dying!"

"Only a heart of stone can save him!" Mother yelled back.

Mother didn't come home the first few nights: she stayed with Uncle Tek to keep vigil over his recovery. Sometime in the middle of the first night, he broke wind. They welcomed his foul odor over a freshly picked flower.

When the stick broke in two from excessive force, she replaced it with a pliable stalk from the midrib of a long banana leaf. Though her methods seemed insanely cruel, the results were undeniably effective: Uncle Tek grew healthier with each rising sun and his bowel movements became more regular with each passing moon. Only after he could outrun her was he able to free himself from her wrath.

The adults discussed marriage for Uncle Tek so that he wouldn't be sent to labor camp for another long duration. After his brush with death, he eagerly agreed to take Hing as his bride. Hing was one of the new-people from Phnom Penh. We nicknamed her Skinny Wife because she was unnaturally thin and boyish-looking. She was a learned individual who taught art class before the Khmer Rouge stormed the city. She barely talked to anyone and she was more fluent in Chinese than Khmer.

There was no celebration, no gathering of family members from both sides, and no food preparation to consummate their matrimony. They simply, unceremoniously, became husband and wife.

When Hing moved into Grandma's hut, she came alone. I never saw her family, but I was told she had a younger brother and a widowed mother. The rest had died, although I didn't know how many that included. All she brought with her were a set of clothes, a rotted blanket, and a frayed towel.

Uncle Tek and Skinny Wife respected each other as any two strangers would. She was a walking skeleton and he was not much better. Theirs was a loveless marriage of convenience, to remain unconsummated throughout their lives.

However, they maintained the husband-and-wife facade at all costs. The two lived with Grandma at night but left for the fields at the first crack of dawn. They both benefited from this marriage by working closer to the village and enduring much shorter absences when they were sent away.

14. AN ISLAND OF BONES (CIRCA JUNE 1976)

The forest was eerily silent. Each time I stepped into the woods, I anticipated something heinous springing out at me. It was dense and dank: a perfect refuge for birds. This anxiety was as palpable as the layer of mud coating my body, but dread never stopped me from going in alone. I had to gather firewood, and though this convenient forest was nearby, it still took a heavy toll on me.

Logistically, I didn't have to travel a great distance to haul the wood home. My objective was to go in and get out as fast as possible.

I was always on alert, ready at a moment's notice to bolt. I only roamed the edges of the forest because I assumed that pythons and other monsters resided deep within the heart of this habitat. My ears perked, sensitive to the slightest noise and movement, and I grew as leery of scorpions and poisonous snakes as I was of the unseen and the imagined.

We heard the story of a man who tried to kill a python for dinner; but instead the snake wrapped around him and constricted his bony body. When a group of men went looking for him, they saw an anaconda-sized snake slithering away, abandoning its meal. The man was found dead without any external wounds or cuts on him: just a pale, ghostlike face.

As I bent down to retrieve a big dry branch on the ground, I heard trampling and rustling coming from behind, growing closer and louder. Within a split second, I snapped upright and spun around to brace for an attack with my hand clutched tightly to a big stick. To my surprise and overwhelming relief, I spied three men (not monsters) walking into the forest. All three men sized me up, and I them. My gaze quickly shifted to the ground and I anxiously scurried away.

I couldn't believe my eyes.

Only when I emerged safely out of the forest could I process the sight of the two Khmer Rouge soldiers dressed in black escorting a man with bound hands into the woods.

After that day, I never set foot in there again. The threat of confronting deadly horror became real. The Khmer Rouge were the true monsters.

♦♦♦

Ma Om was a remote hill which turned into an island during the monsoon season. Uncle Jo made multiple trips there to bury the dead when the floodwaters receded. When the newcomers arrived at Phnum Sress, food became scarce and people didn't stand a chance against starvation and death. It was a common occurrence for him to bury a dozen people per day. When the island ran out of space, they had to re-dig the existing graves, forcing new corpses to take up residence with already-interred remains. When the floodwaters rose over ten feet high, the corpses buried in the lower ground floated upward, causing human skulls and bones to ebb and flow and drift aimlessly with the current.

Even when they were over a mile away, their foul stench assaulted our noses.

I often crossed paths with the gravediggers as they made their way to a burial site. A sack dangled in the middle of a long pole as they carried it away. They wove through the marshland with resigned looks, moving like zombies with their eyes glued to their feet. They lost a bit of themselves each time they buried a person.

One time, as I saw Uncle Jo en route to a burial, I called to him. The wind carried his name from my mouth to his ears. He looked around to see me waving at him, but he couldn't quite remember who I was; so completely weighed down with the enormity of his task that he failed to recognize me. I had waved to a stranger, and the corpse dangling from the pole erased my relationship with him.

When color and life seeped from Uncle Jo into the pits he dug, they replaced him with someone new. Only the greenery and muddy water could cleanse and purify his mind and nurse him back to his meager life.

It had been more than a week since Father stole fish from the river. Lately, his body trembled and his legs grew limp. He surrendered to having his skin scraped to red stripes. Mother was the go-to person to perform this ancient remedy. It was supposed to sweat out the ailment in his body. She did it to all of us, including Black Ghost. Hardly a week went by without one of us cringing in pain.

It wasn't until a couple weeks later that Father was able to set the net for fish again. Despite his illness, he continued to show up for work. His quiet fortitude and silent suffering moved us all. He didn't want the Angka to label him as having "Sick-in-the-Head" syndrome, a phrase synonymous with being lazy. Though he was a slow worker, the old-people loved him because he was dependable, and he rarely complained.

Mother woke early to catch crabs when Father was indisposed. Juggling our survival and working for the Angka consumed almost all her hours in a day, leaving her with hardly any time to sleep. It took her, on average, an hour to leave the house and return with a tray of crabs; whereas Father would spend almost an entire night out for a basketful of fish. Her twilight trek to the rivers used to start around five o'clock, one hour before cock's crow; but with so many newcomers secretly making the same trek to the riverbanks, there were simply not enough crabs to go around.

Mother was determined to outsmart everyone, so she woke up earlier. Five o'clock became four. Four o'clock turned to three. Depletion of stock set in and she would come home with only one or two crabs.

When the nearby supply of crabs ran out, Mother faced a dilemma. She asked herself a tough question: should she watch her children die, or face the specters of ghosts? She reasoned: ghosts don't kill, but starvation does. With that mindset, she gathered her courage and ventured out to the island of Ma Om—where Uncle Jo buried countless bodies— alone at night.

As she navigated in the dark through the island of dead bodies formed by the Khmer Rouge, she prayed for the spirits and ghosts to leave her alone. She would surely die of a heart attack if something were to spring up at her.

No one dared to go through the island of corpses; even the gravediggers steered clear.

The realm of the dead, filled with ghosts and the afterworld, was as real to Mother as the pain she experienced during labor. The night air felt thick and heavy on her neck. Goosebumps arose on her skin.

She began to question her sanity and then she remembered us: five reasons to brave the wet depths of her own fear.

When she returned, she yanked her five reasons out of dreamland and greeted us with boiled crustaceans for breakfast.

15. WHEN THE CROWS CAWED (CIRCA JUNE 1976)

As if our outcry could revive the dead, nightly we yelled at the black crows. The blare of words and incantations bounced from hut to hut to wherever the crows flew. When their wings fluttered above us, we yelled, "Murderer!" "Evil!" and "Get lost!" until they flew away. Our loudest competitor, Mother Len's two daughters, hollered in unison, chorusing similar phrases: "Leave us alone!" "Bastard!" and "Don't come back!"

This was a native practice, and I wasn't entirely convinced of its usefulness. Mother Len's daughters told me that these black crows were the messengers of Death. "They can smell people dying many miles away." They roamed the area searching for languishing spirits. Once detected, the crows would usher the souls to the afterlife. To get along with the natives, we nightly joined them to berate the crows. It proved therapeutic.

Never once did I hear any shouting from Jie and Didi's household.

At one point, I found myself strangely looking forward to the nightly cawing. Screaming felt liberating. When we cussed at the birds above, my mind replaced them with the Khmer Rouge soldiers forcing us out of our home at gunpoint. At times the image switched to the head chief hidden in the banana trees. I had long harbored disdain for him. He had taken something that belonged to me.

One day, I walked by a huge hut which had been converted into a school. It was presently empty inside, as the children played outside. Though I had never set foot inside the school, this was the place where young minds received their daily doses of brainwashing. There were trees and hammocks surrounding the perimeter, and people of importance and with strong connections lounged there without a care in the world, as if they were on vacation.

To the far right, beyond some clearings and a meadow, a man chiseled and carved out the inside of a huge tree trunk with hand tools under a large shady tree. He was the canoe master, with his young apprentice working beside him. The canoe was starting to take shape and would soon ply the waters.

I knew the canoe master was a man of valuable skills; one revered as ancient, and one the Angka would preserve at all costs.

I was drawn to both the canoe and the children, happily playing at recess. As I contemplated which direction to take, Mother Len's daughters saw me. They hollered and waved. I felt the weight of everyone's eyes instantly fall on me. My heart thumped faster. I felt like a trespasser, an imposter.

Mother had constantly warned us to distance ourselves from these two sisters. "They have sweet mouths with bitter hearts. Watch out."

Unsurprisingly, when the sisters caught up to me they appeared friendly, but I sensed they were putting on an act. "Geng, come play with us! Don't always work!"

Half of the people there were whispering "Isn't she one of Mother Yeng's daughters?"

I saw several familiar faces. I recognized our head chief and the tall lanky man who had built our hut. The adults took shelter from the heat by sitting anywhere with shade. The chief was busy talking to someone as he glanced at me.

In spite of my discomfort, our game commenced. I played hopscotch with the sisters and four other girls for roughly half an hour. I got so caught up in the game that I failed to notice that the diamond shamrock pendant had come unstitched and fallen from the hem of my pants. One of the girls saw it and picked it up. My heart raced when I saw what was in her hand. My mind projected a rapid succession of catastrophes. They would search our hut again, uproot our plants to discover fish bones and jewelry, tie our hands behind our backs, and lead us away.

The girl who found the diamond pendant gestured for us to come over as she displayed the treasure in her palm. I kept quiet and tried to calm my troubled mind, forcing myself to be unaffected as the girls consulted with us about what to do with the pendant.

We all agreed to hand it over to the head chief. All the children called the head chief and other men with children "Father." The girl headed straight to him, blaring, "Father, look what I found!" She presented the treasure in her palm for his eyes to feast upon.

My eyes moved from the pendant to the chief's astonished face.

"Where did you find it, child?" He extended his palm to receive the diamond.

"By the hopscotch game," replied the girl who found the treasure.

The chief's eyes widened. His lips stretched into an evil smirk.

As the chief sashayed over to the airplane drawn on the ground, he asked: "Which of you dropped this?"

No one answered.

"It's okay. I just want to give it back. Come forward, please."

We all looked at each other flatly while slowly shaking our heads. The chief observed the unanimous denial and perhaps concluded one of us wasn't telling the truth. "Well, since it doesn't belong to any of you, maybe you know to whom it does belong? If you tell me, you can take food home." While saying this, the chief shifted his eyes to mine.

"Aren't you Mother Yeng's daughter?" he asked.

"Yes," I nodded, stealing a moment to blink the guilt away.

"What's your name, child?"

"Geng," I answered.

"How old are you, child?"

"Six. Almost seven." I never knew my exact age, so I rounded up.

The chief moved closer while dangling the shamrock pendant before me.

"Geng, isn't this your mother's? Here, take it back to her." He stretched out his hand to offer it to me. I almost saw the pendant as a bag of rice or a whole chicken. I felt the pang of such a loss, but I refrained from reaching out to take it back.

My hands remained at my sides. I shook my head as if it had no value to me. "What is it?" I asked him instead.

"You can tell me the truth." The chief softened his tone. "I just want to know whose it is so I can have it returned to its rightful owner. Or, if you know who it belongs to, I'll give you rice to take home." He smiled so sweetly when saying this that I almost believed him.

I gathered my courage, determined to best him in this game of pretense. I looked at the treasure in his palm. "What's this?" I asked him again. "It looks like glass." I proceeded to pat the stones. "Do they cut if I touch it?"

He pulled it away from my fingers as though to prevent me from dirtying it. He searched my face, staring deep into my eyes.

"So you've never seen this before?" he asked me again: not so much a question, but the affirmation of his own finding.

"What is it?" I pressed on with feigned ignorance.

While retracing his steps back to the shade, he muttered, "Now, I wonder who dropped this."

I apologized profusely to Mother that night. For sure I thought she would punish me for deviating from my duty to play with dangerous children. I told her how I didn't fall for the trap when the chief handed me the jewelry. She was enormously relieved and said the most comforting words to me. "You did the right thing by denying it. Had you fallen for his trick, you would be admitting to a crime of holding on to a valuable possession: a crime punishable by death. It's a huge loss. It was one of my favorite pieces, too; but we'll be alright. Now give me your pants so I can reinforce the stitches so this won't happen again."

I took a towel to wrap around myself and pulled my pants off. Mother inspected the hem. "This ring is about to fall off, too. I'm just going to remove the jewelry completely because the fabric is too frail to risk another mishap." After the removal, she patched my clothes with mismatched fabric.

Since the diamond pendant incident, I wished for the chief to suffer. I took it out on the crows as if they were the chief himself, flying over my head. The crows were a guise. I could freely shout, "Killers! I hate you! I hope lightning strikes you dead!"

I took so much pleasure in denouncing those black birds that Mother felt uncomfortable and warned me not to overdo it. She did not want the enemies to take offense. It must have been too obvious. I toned down my vulgarity. Sometimes I kept quiet altogether while others continued to chant their curses and phrases. One less voice wasn't going to make a difference, especially when I wasn't in a mood to yell.

Without the incantations, I felt the full weight of frustration again. I wondered if the gods looked upon me with love or with hate, with sympathy, or with a strange detachment—in that way I dispassionately favored butterflies over bees. I wondered if how I perceived the insects was how the gods perceived me.

My mind drifted.

♦♦♦

Following the cawing of the crows one night, a pregnant woman wailed in pain as she went into labor. Mother took off to help Father Pea's wife deliver her baby. The woman made the most unbearable sounds and many of us who lived within earshot couldn't sleep.

Mother, along with a few other native women, spent the entire night delivering the baby. Throughout the ordeal there were commands to "Push! Push!" followed by shouts "Ugh! Ugh!" When the sun was about to come up, the outcry ceased. The baby never made a sound. Only Father Pea and his sons cried.

Mother came home looking tired. The mother and the baby both died during the delivery. They used too much force to get the baby out: almost the same force and weight as someone sitting on her stomach. Both died in the end.

Later that morning, Mother Len's daughters came to our hut. They thanked us for the red-hot chili peppers, which they harvested from our garden. "Mother Yeng, your chili peppers are so sweet. Can we have more?" they said. These tiny chili peppers were hot and deadly. There was nothing sweet about them. They were flattering her to get more produce from our hard labor. Mother was no fool; she knew these girls would harvest all we had if we didn't limit their access to the garden. Since they loved the sweet chili peppers, Mother told them to stay put while instructing me to pick a handful of chili peppers for them.

As I handed the produce to them, the two sisters told me the crows had put a hex on Father Pea's wife and infant.

"Didn't you hear how loudly the crows cried last night?" they asked me.

I asked them about other times the crows came, but no one had died.

"It's simple," they said. "Our collective efforts chased the evil away before it was able to attack any human soul." I saw a big hole in their reasoning, but I knew I should stop arguing and start agreeing. Just play dumb, I thought.

Mother Len's two daughters knew so much about death and spirits, it seemed. They took much pride and pleasure in teaching me and Nuy about their native ways and beliefs. They also said the spirits of the mother and the stillborn infant would linger in a tree nearby, and at night they'd wander around looking to recruit other dying souls.

They told me to beware of trees with no nails hammered into them to prevent the spirits from leaving the tree. Now I was in danger of losing one of my favorite pastimes; I couldn't even climb trees without having to worry about an attack by ghosts. After that, I checked to make sure there were nails in trees before I proceeded to climb them. Often, I would find nails already hammered into the bark.

16. UNCLE JO PLAYED WITH FIRE (CIRCA JUNE 1976)

Uncle Jo's wife manically raced to our hut, looking for Mother. My aunt's hysteria indicated that something disastrous had happened. Upon discovering Mother wasn't home, she went straight to Grandma's place. Whatever the crisis was this morning, it didn't prompt any of us to run after her or to help her locate my parents. We had never felt her warmth, only her silence and distance. Our loyalty lay with Mother; we liked whomever she liked.

A short while after Uncle Jo's wife left our premises, Grandma rushed over to our hut.

Panting and breathless, she said: "Geng and Nuy, if any of you see your mother, tell her Uncle Jo has been taken away to be whacked and dumped!"

The fright on my aunt's face earlier was reflected on Grandma's. Suddenly the air in my lungs turned to stone.

Grandma was frantic. She scurried westward to look for Mother. As her silhouette faded in the distance, I faintly saw her wiping away tears. I hated seeing Grandma feeling helpless and frightened.

I knew she was on a mission to find Mother. A series of questions ran through my head about Uncle Jo. Did they overhear him speaking Chinese? Did they catch him stealing food? Did they want him gone so they could take his possessions? I had so many questions, but no one was there to answer them.

My body had learned to switch on and off between feeling and unfeeling, to survive; but at this moment I felt everything. The weight of the death of a beloved uncle and the pain in Grandma's eyes stabbed me in the heart. The shock was too great to comprehend. Already I keenly felt the angst and the void left by his sudden demise. Tears rolled down my cheeks. Soon numbness took over as I regained control of my breathing.

◆◆◆

Earlier that morning, the soldiers had stormed into Uncle Jo's home and taken his personal belongings.

Not surprisingly, the first person that Uncle Jo's wife turned to for help was Mother, despite their tenuous relationship. It was obvious to us that my aunt and Mother didn't like one another. Mother still harbored resentment toward her for being ungrateful and selfish in our time of need. She could never forgive her sister-in-law for taking away Grandma's only blanket and not letting us borrow her bowls and utensils. It was her sarcasm and disdain that bothered Mother.

Grandma and Uncle Jo's wife finally found Mother at the sewing station.

Mother, of course, dropped everything to help her brother.

After frantic inquiry, Mother learned Uncle Jo was still alive and imprisoned, awaiting execution. She ran home to dig out a gold necklace buried by the big tree in our back yard. Without a second thought, she set out to save him.

Mother ran to Chuam, the second chief in the village, and told him about Uncle Jo's impending death. She knew him to be a kind person. He had been a devout monk in his teens; but later in life he'd married and had children.

With much earnestness, she begged Chuam to save Uncle Jo. Mother discreetly handed him the piece of jewelry and thanked him as if he had already rescued her brother.

Meanwhile, in the prison, the guard tossed the last meal to Uncle Jo. "Here! Enjoy it while you can!" the Khmer Rouge said sarcastically as they leered at him.

As he stared at the food, his tears came unbidden. His nose was running and dripping. It was then that he retched and wet his pants.

◆◆◆

Uncle Jo knew why they came for him. Veern, the leader of the informant squad, had accused him of planning to run away. While he was out plowing the muddy field, the Khmer Rouge unexpectedly summoned him. They told him to leave for an education camp to retool for collectivism. His face turned white at the all-too-familiar phrase. Everyone knew people seldom came back once they left for "additional schooling."

The Khmer Rouge pointed the guns at Uncle Jo's back when they led him away. He walked away in a trance.

He didn't deny the accusation. It would be useless. If anything, it would hasten his death.

In the beginning, Veern and Uncle Jo had become fast friends. However, their friendship took a drastic turn when Uncle Jo's younger sister-in-law walked past Veern and he fell instantly in love with her. Veern anticipated Uncle Jo's blessings, including his participation and collaboration in making her his wife, and he asked Uncle Jo to go to his father-in-law for her hand in marriage. Uncle Jo didn't think much of it when he nonchalantly replied, "Ask him yourself. Leave me out of it!"

The seemingly-innocuous remark became Uncle Jo's death sentence. Once the response left his mouth and reached Veern's ears, he became a dead man walking.

Uncle Jo's friendship with Veern was once invaluable to us. Veern had inadvertently slipped us information regarding fake marriage investigations, and Uncle Jo had relayed the message to his siblings to thwart an interrogation.

His connection with the head informant had its downside, too: Uncle Jo brought us horror stories of our family friend, Gnee. Prior to being a slave in dystopia, he used to own a bookstore on our block. My parents often found him behind the counter reading. He loved his books just as much as his wife and two daughters. Now his family of four had been reduced to two. He lived in a nearby village and he often worked in the same fields as Father and Uncle Jo.

The news of Gnee's execution came from Informant Veern.

Gnee was ill and he missed work. The Khmer Rouge soldiers went to check on him. They found him fast asleep in a food-induced coma, having overeaten. They became suspicious and searched for evidence of what he ate. They opened the pot and found what looked like tiny human bones inside.

They then realized his daughter was missing.

When asked if he had murdered her for food, he denied it, saying she had already died. He was too hungry and didn't want her corpse to go to waste.

They dragged Gnee into a nearby forest and dug a hole for him. He wasn't fully awake when they struck him.

The main reason why Uncle Jo was reluctant to set Veern up with his sister-in-law had to do with the wickedness in his heart. Many times, he had proudly showed Uncle Jo the liver of someone he had disemboweled. In his hand, on one occasion, was the liver of another family friend, Lin Shiu.

Veern and his band would roast the livers and eat them.

Uncle Jo hadn't known how to distance himself from such a wicked soul. Now he was sitting in jail awaiting execution.

◆◆◆

Second Chief Chuam arrived at the jail where they were keeping Uncle Jo. He barked questions at the guards. "Why is Jo locked up? What crime is he guilty of?"

The guards replied, "Informant Veern said he wanted to run away."

Chuam roared at the guards, "Nonsense! This man is a hard worker just like us old-people. I vouch for his outstanding character and work ethic. You have my personal guarantee that he is not going anywhere. I demand his release at once!"

Five minutes later, they set Uncle Jo free. One of the guards threatened him with a clenched fist next to Uncle Jo's jaw. "Don't breathe a word to anyone or else we'll come back for you!" Meanwhile, another guard made a quick hissing sound as he raised his index finger and dragged it across his own neck.

For two days following his release, Uncle Jo was in shock. At first, he felt relieved. He thanked the gods and the spirits of our ancestors for watching over him; but then anger replaced his feelings of gratitude and deliverance. He wanted to kill them all. One day, should he ever survive this, he would come after those who had wronged him.

With rage controlling his heart, where the gods and the Khmer Rouge were equally cursed and culpable, he abjectly walked to the muddy brown field to resume his forced labor.

The afternoon sun taunted him with its glaring brightness one minute, then cast ominous shadows the next. Beneath the shifting clouds, he accompanied one cow as he plowed. When moonbeams streamed down to the earth, he and the beast continued working. Day and night lacked distinction; time ceased to matter.

Hunger cried out to him and exhaustion knocked him into the mud, but despite his weak limbs, he got up to plow. He put his hand on the ox, patting it with envy: it would be ideal if they could trade places. Even the leeches he flicked off his feet were much better off than he was.

After having worked nearly two days straight, with body and mind still pulled apart by immutable feelings of revenge and despair, he saw soldiers walking along the causeway in his direction.

Once again, he involuntarily wet his pants.

There simply was no time to shed his last tears.

The soldiers gestured for Uncle Jo and the ox to halt. They spoke to him. "We've seen you work nonstop for two days now. Even the cow needs rest. Go home and sleep! Let us take over. It's an order!"

Sudden relief broke through: this driblet of compassion came so unexpectedly that it touched his heart. Their kindness profoundly invigorated him, as though invisible hands were at work mending the missing pieces of his soul and body back together. Just like that, his head and heart embraced. His humanity rushed back to him, and he returned home to his family—to us, who had mourned for him.

◆◆◆

Mother went back to Chief Chuam and handed him another piece of jewelry, effusively thanking him for saving Uncle Jo.

A few months later, Chuam met his own fate.

Rumor had it that he had fallen in love with a Vietnamese girl whose relatives had died under the Khmer Rouge regime. Chuam fed her and took care of her.

The Angka viewed him as a traitor to his own people and a betrayer to the cause. His crime was not so much one of committing adultery and abandoning his wife and two small children: rather, it was of pitying the Vietnamese girl. They charged him with the crime of copulating with another race—especially one which the Khmer Rouge suddenly despised.

The Khmer Rouge barged into the girl's place and caught them together and he panicked and took off running.

They gave chase on horseback. Not far out on the open rice fields, bullets pierced his body.

They led the girl away with bound hands.

With the second chief gone, we became even more vulnerable.

17. THE HEN THAT LAID THE GOLDEN EGG
(CIRCA JULY 1976)

After Uncle Jo returned from the brink of execution, I witnessed a drastic change in him, his wife, and his two sons. They all had their heads shorn by Mother (except for his wife) in a humble gesture to thank the gods and spirits for their protection and blessings. It also symbolized a new beginning.

Uncle Jo's wife had softened. She brought us field rats and even went the extra length to clean their innards. She helped Grandma water her garden and thanked her for babysitting her children.

We knew Uncle Jo's vulnerability. The evil Veern could concoct yet another excuse to "re-educate" him. He jumped at the shadows of palms, and he paused in mid-sentence when a bird fluttered its wings. He hopped when a frog leaped.

"This life is unbearable!" he told my parents. "I can't go anywhere without feeling the weight of their eyes on me."

"We know. You're not the only one," Father said. "We feel it, too. They are underneath our hut every night."

"Just be careful," Mother told him. "Keep your mouth shut. Plant a tree. Be deaf and dumb like a mule. Work hard."

Despite overwhelming worry, we celebrated Uncle Jo's rebirth. Grandma untied the two hammocks and rolled them neatly, for barter. She came back with roughly ten cans of rice. She cooked all the rice, skewered the rats, and stir-fried a dish of vegetables. She gathered us together. Mother's other siblings were away at labor camps and were clueless about Uncle Jo's recent danger. When they came back, they noticed the missing hammocks before the story revealed itself.

◆◆◆

Death came for Uncle Jo's father-in-law about two weeks after his release. Even at only four years of age, my Cousin Kearn was fond of his grandfather. He was the older of the two grandchildren on his mother's side. The old man's passing darkened the clouds around him even more.

Soon the pendulum of exiting the realm swung to Kearn's mother, Uncle Jo's wife. She became gravely ill shortly after her father's burial. Her skin hung loose and sallow. There were almost no traces of life in her when she dropped off her sons to Grandma.

When Uncle Jo's wife failed to show up for work, her supervisor sent soldiers to hunt her down. They stuck their heads into her hut to make sure she was sick, but it was empty. Naturally, they assumed she was shirking her duties.

Throughout her ailment, she'd stayed home while her children remained with Grandma; but that day of all days, she was determined to visit them. If she was lucky, she would eat some of Father's fish.

Believing she was ditching work, the Khmer Rouge tracked her down. They ran east to Grandma's place. That day Mother returned home from a quick lunch at the communal kitchen to work on the garden. When she heard the high-pitched cry, she snuck out to watch. She saw two soldiers mercilessly beating a woman in front of our place. She soon realized it was her sister-in-law. After they beat her senseless, they dragged her away.

The next morning we saved fish for Uncle Jo's wife. "This meal might be her last, if it's not already too late for her," Mother said. "Do good deeds to others so the spirits will protect us." Her compassion and heart of stone worked in mysterious ways: she was a river with two currents, crisscrossing and moving in various directions.

Mother found Uncle Jo's wife alone with her children. At her own request on the night of her beating, she asked to be with her children. Uncle Jo brought them back from Grandma's place.

Tears pooled in Mother's eyes, upon seeing her mangled and bloodied body. Flies feasted on her wounds. Her eyes were so swollen she could barely open them.

Mother could see that she was in tremendous pain.

The sister-in-law was moved by the unexpected visit. Her jaw twitched slightly to acknowledge Mother. Her throat was dry and swollen into silence.

Mother propped her body up and fed her water. She struggled to swallow it. Her body was feeble: life was slowly fading from her. She mustered a whimper, a weak noise. Mother lowered her head to listen but couldn't understand what she said.

Eventually Mother thought she could hear the words "Sorry" and "Please look after my children."

Upon hearing those words, Mother's heart of stone turned to silky tofu. The pent-up feelings of past grudges and resentments and the issues with the dishes, blanket, and money: all seemed petty and insignificant now. They shared a common pain.

Mother squeezed her sister-in-law's hand, saying, "Save your strength. Try not to talk. Let bygones be bygones. I'll help Jo look after them."

The dying one responded by clasping Mother's hand weakly, an expression of humble apology.

Mother gripped back firmer with another unspoken exchange of each other's forgiveness and acceptance.

Their eyes searched for and locked onto each other. They communicated without words. It was the deepest conversation they'd ever had. Their silence was an understanding of forgiveness born from the constraints of time. Her eyelids drifted downward and closed, surrendering completely to fatigue.

Mother let go of the hand. She turned around to look at her two nephews, who were two and four. The younger one was tugging and pulling at his elder. Melancholy enveloped Mother and tears of sorrow and goodbye blurred her vision.

Uncle Jo's wife passed away two days later.

◆ ◆ ◆

This reality prematurely aged my four-year-old cousin. Nothing could excite Kearn anymore. He cocooned himself in a thick cloud of despair after losing his beloved mother and grandfather. I often found him sitting on the swing, as sedentary as a log stuck in mud.

"Guess what?" I asked him. "The chicken is about to lay an egg today!"

My eyes and mouth were wide open in anticipation of his reaction. Surely the mention of having an egg to eat would cheer anyone up, I thought. His attention remained transfixed on the ground below. The news of the egg should have lit up his eyes like those of a child in a candy store.

I didn't know how to let a ray of light filter into his sorrow. I waved my hand in front of his face. For the longest time, he didn't blink his eyes.

Even the promise of an egg had lost its effect on him. The magic and power of food had ceased. Crushed under the sheer weight of mourning, he soon joined his mother and grandfather.

♦♦♦

Nuy and I became experts in gauging due dates and the size of the eggs. Hunger forced us to perform close examinations on the poor bird, but we had no idea how we were traumatizing it. Like a doctor with a patient, we made house calls to check on the fowl. During our first attempt, we were both nervous and reluctant.

I tiptoed to the hen in the hutch from behind, then pounced. The bird was blindsided and trapped under my strong grip. It cackled and fluttered its wings in protest, shedding a few feathers. The frightened bird pecked my arms ferociously. It tried to squirm away, but I was determined to hold on.

I repositioned the bird so the rear could stare Nuy in the face.

She exhaled a puff as she looked hesitantly at her hand. A look of disgust overcame her. I pleaded: "Hurry, I don't think I can hold it much longer!"

The distress in my voice forced Nuy to speed up. Her index finger pierced the bird's anus. My sister closed her eyes with great discomfort. Moving her finger in circles, she said, "I feel something." Her eyes opened as she described her findings. "Round and soft and the size of a marble—a cluster of them."

Two days had passed, and the hen still did not produce any egg.

"I'm going in," I told her. "It's your turn to grab the chicken!"

Nuy took the hen out of its cage and held it tightly. It struggled, molted feathers, and pecked as incessantly as before. She presented its butt to me. My finger wiggled in as I shut my eyes in revulsion. The inside felt warm and had the texture of wet mud. It smelled atrocious. The bird excreted yellow waste. There was nothing I could do other than to poke in farther. My finger hit something hard. I motioned around the oval object, at the same time panicked that I might break it.

"Well? Egg or not?" Nuy was impatient and demanding.

"Oooh, I feel something!" I smiled with bright eyes. "Round. And big. And hard."

Nuy's eyes mirrored mine in delight. "Here, hold it." She thrust the bird to me. "I want to feel it, too."

We switched around. The hen shed more feathers.

She confirmed my assessment. We released the bird back into its coop. It scurried away, cursing us in its "*bok-bok-bok*" tongue. It ran to the farthest corner of the cage to get away from its tormentors.

Together we skipped and hopped to tell Grandma of the possibility that an egg would be coming out soon.

As predicted, the egg came out in mid-afternoon the next day. It was stained with specks of wet blood and yellowish excrement. The shell was somewhat deformed and translucent. We could see the yellow yolk inside. We immediately took it to Grandma, and we were especially mindful of our steps. She scrambled the egg with shrimp paste, fish sauce, and some vegetables. Once it was braised, all of us converged on this one dish.

We didn't know that we had traumatized the fowl into sterility. So began the vicious cycle. The longer it took the eggs to come out, the more we performed those rectal exams.

Several weeks later, our hen disappeared; perhaps it was running away from two children.

18. THE HUNT FOR UNCLE RAIN (CIRCA OCTOBER 1976)

We encountered one devastating monsoon season. Losing our produce to the flood forced us to chase after green frogs and ugly toads. These amphibians, along with black water beetles, subsidized our diet. Mother struggled to profit from her ten percent charge to broker exchanges of food and jewelry.

The backwater by Father Pea's place had risen by ten feet, and over two feet of floodwater pooled under our hut. Daily we walked over to Grandma's place to pick lily stalks to make soup and stir-fry.

In a nearby village, Uncle Rain suffered the loss of yet another child. Big Daughter, Uncle Rain's second oldest child, eleven at the time, delivered news of their latest casualty when she came to our village to forage. The tragic news crowded our emotions in ways we could never sort out. We managed to send her back only a jar of fish sauce; there were no yams, due to the flood.

Around a month later Uncle Rain came around, urgently looking for my parents. The downpour and wind thrashed our roof and battered the banana leaves outside. My younger siblings and I hovered in one corner as the adults occupied the opposite end of the room and carried out their conversations. It was adult business, so we kept quiet, hypnotized by bellowing winds and the fierce downpour.

Uncle Rain told my parents that the Khmer Rouge trackers were getting close. They were within striking distance, only a village away from capturing him.

"Have you seen this man?" The Khmer Rouge detectives approached many villages with a picture in hand.

Although Uncle Rain had never seen the photograph, he knew beyond a shadow of doubt that they were looking for him.

Before Uncle Rain left our hut in the torrential downpour, he shared with us Ti's death. Ti had been the pickiest eater of all his children. He ate only rice. Since rice was scarce, he picked at his food, searching for the few grains. He refused to eat vegetables or yams, no matter how hard they tried to force them on him.

One night Ti was listless and dying. His mother lifted him on her lap and hugged him tightly. Tears dripped down her face onto his cheek. He had tried his hardest to open his eyes and look at his family one last time.

Uncle Rain looked at his wife with hopelessness as their dying child drew his last breath. At that instant, Uncle Rain cried and said to him, "My child, my beloved child, when your spirit reincarnates, pick a country that's free. Don't come back here, you understand?"

Ti died in October 1976 at the age of six, ten months younger than I was at the time. Uncle Rain and my aunt wheedled their way into the chief's heart for permission to cremate the body.

My friends, Jie and Didi, each with a toad in hand and smiles on their faces, paid us a visit. While holding a toad in one hand, Jie slowly made motions over the creature with her other hand. It didn't take me long to figure out her intention. She wanted to know how to clean the toad. I retrieved a knife to show them the correct way to skin and disembowel the amphibian. It was Vunn who taught me the proper way of cleaning toads, having learned from his native friends.

After I finished with Jie's toad, Didi handed me his and I re-demonstrated the dissection. Once finished, they cautiously stepped on logs laid in our walkway to go back home in the flood.

This monsoon was the most unrelenting. All the plants drowned and perished. It would have been fine had our village planted the native rice seedlings that had adapted to the floodwaters instead of changing them to a more desirable grain, which drowned. It was a hard time for all of us and tested our will to go on another day.

About two months after the big flood, Mother came home one night and announced the news that my friend had died. When Wonhing approached Mother to save her daughter, Jie was lifeless already, dipping in and out of consciousness. Mother tried everything from coining her skin to feeding her a bitter concoction, but she had showed no sign of improvement. That night she died with worms wiggling out of her body through all imaginable holes.

Hearing of my friend's death was naturally upsetting; but then something pulled me into a world of nothingness—a dimension of numbness with no beginning and no end. Having reached my limit, I was no longer saddened by death; it was now a normal course of life. When I saw two gravediggers walk over to haul her body away, I didn't go over to visit her family or see her one last time. It was as if I had simply checked out of the Khmer Rouge hotel and moved into another room, to be free. My head and heart were two separate entities, disjoined to either survive or to die a painless death.

I later encountered Didi while gathering firewood. The water had forced us to cross paths with each other to a few patches of dry ground. Though we didn't exchange words, we roamed together in silence. He mourned Jie's loss while my head could think of nothing but food. My stomach could feel nothing but the colony of parasites twisting violently inside of me.

The search for twigs took twice as long. By this time we were both starving and had searched the surrounding plants for edible fruits, but found none. We noticed ants were gathered in a pool of floodwater: we each scooped up a clump and ate it. It tasted sour and prickly at first, but after the initial shock, it wasn't so bad: like crab with lime.

Photo 1: Uncle Rain and Firstborn Jon

Photo 2: Uncle Rain and Family

L to R: Moy-dut, "Middle Daughter"; Jon-wa, "Jon"; Jon-tai, "Tai";
Sida, "baby"; Aunt Khan; Jon-ti, "Ti"; Moy-tum, "Big Daughter";
and Uncle Rain

19. THE ENTRAPMENT (CIRCA FEBRUARY 1977)

It was pitch black when my parents came home from a meeting. Elation enveloped us that night, filling our hearts with so much yearning and hope. "In about a week, we'll be going to Vietnam." Mother eagerly announced the news. "The Angka allows the Vietnamese citizens to repatriate. Because Chinese and Vietnamese share similar features, we can claim we're Vietnamese: no one will be the wiser."

I was too young to know the geography of Cambodia in relation to Vietnam, or Cambodia in relation to the rest of the world, for that matter. Names of many other countries swam between my ears, but none landed on solid ground. Because there were so many Vietnamese expats living among us, I surmised that Vietnam was nearby and perhaps reachable on foot.

For the next few days, my family dreamed. We fantasized what it would be like to live in a foreign land with an abundance of food. I pictured my family sitting at a big round table filled with laughter. I also envisioned myself clad in a white and blue uniform with a backpack skipping to school. It was like having another chance at redemption. I had mentally left the Khmer Rouge and the misery behind.

Wonhing, Didi's mother, visited us more frequently since the repatriation news. She couldn't wait to help us get settled in Vietnam, which was her former country and her childhood playground. She was well connected. It was, in her own words, her chance to repay us for the good deeds we had done for her family.

◆ ◆ ◆

We packed our belongings a few days before the departure to Vietnam. Mother Len's two daughters came to our hut when they saw me returning with firewood. I always questioned their intentions. There was a saying in the Khmer tongue which Mother often used to describe our neighbors, "Drinking water while scouring for solids in the glass"—meaning that they had ulterior motives.

Those girls sweet-talked me: "Your family will be missed greatly. Now we have no one to help us scare the crows away."

I managed to put on a smile and responded, "I'll miss playing with you, too."

"Can we have your garden when you're gone?" They anxiously blurted out the question.

"Sure, I guess; but wouldn't it be up to the chief to decide? That's what Mother told me," I said. They had no idea how much work we had put in to re-grow the garden after the flood.

They shrugged and then added, "Can we harvest your garden now, since you won't be here much longer?"

"I don't see why not," I stammered in surprise at their boldness.

Before the day was over, the sisters came back for more from our garden. Rain and poor weather didn't inhibit their selfish harvest.

During times of starvation, we all had an implied understanding of the unspoken rule about food. Asking others for a dab of salt or a few tiny chili peppers, let alone food of major sustenance, wasn't acceptable. Anything of value was a bargaining chip. To ask someone for yams and cassavas was akin to removing a crutch from a cripple or drinking someone's precious water in the middle of the desert.

When these sisters asked, their words sounded more like a demand. What could I say? I felt cornered and had no choice but to give in. I had always feared the two sisters because their brother was an informant. After all, we would be leaving for Vietnam in less than a week, I reminded myself. I was glad my time with them would soon end.

The two sisters continued to seek me (and Nuy) out at the most inopportune times, like bullies taunting a lonely child.

"Your garden is amazing. Everything tastes so good. Can we have more?"

I was fuming inside; I could picture my hands throttling their necks. My sleepless nights and my endurance of Mother's afflictions were all for naught. I had sacrificed so much, only to feed those whom I bowed to. The concept was unsettling, but I had to put on a different face when they were near.

I nodded to the girls. They ran to the back. I wouldn't miss this garden one bit.

We were packed and ready.

Mother made her last round, cutting people's hair and visiting people to say her goodbyes. She bid her farewell to the man who planted our banana trees, to the lady with a sensitive bladder, to the big woman and her baby, to Mother Yearn (whose son caught her carrying a bag of rice), to Father Pea who scared me with monsters, to Mother Len, whose daughters taught me everything I knew about ghosts and spirits.

The general farewell from them was: "We wish you and your family a safe journey to Vietnam. You will be missed. When you go, we have no one to turn to for haircutting and sewing."

Each and every one to whom Mother waved had all waved back with untroubled smiles and with no traces of nervousness—all except for Mother Lei.

"Mother Yeng, I'm urging you not to go with the Vietnamese. Angka will eventually let the Chinese go back to China. Just wait until then; trust me," said Mother Lei.

Mother detected the troubled tone and nervousness in her speech.

Sensing that her advice held a hidden message, Mother leaned in for the truth. "Why's going to China better than Vietnam? Are you trying to tell me something?"

Mother Lei leaned in closer to Mother's ear. "You didn't hear this from me. Angka is fraught with lies! All those Vietnamese expats who believe they will safely return home will instead be whacked and dumped. I wrestled with my conscience to tell you this. I have my family's lives at stake. Please don't betray my trust!" She made Mother vow on our lives not to divulge this to anyone.

We shared this knowledge among our family only. I was the youngest one to be privy to such secret. I guarded it with my life in the same way I guarded the jewelry hidden in the folds of my clothes.

We were grateful that Mother Lei was our savior, guiding us away from imminent demise. How was it, then, that she was able to warn us, but we couldn't extend the same courage to Wonhing and Didi?

To understand our frame of mind, one must understand our fear. We feared the Angka the way seals fear killer whales, the way parents fear their children getting kidnapped, and the way a debtor runs from a loan shark. Shapeless, colorless fear lived within us always. One wrong move, one wrong word, and the Khmer Rouge would be at our throats instantly.

We were one of the bottom feeders. Mother Lei belonged to the upper tier. She stood on firmer ground than we did. In addition, she didn't have a phantom enemy spreading rumors about her family being a flight risk. Our faceless enemy cast a shadow so large that we felt it lurking in every bush, following us through every path, and sleeping with us in every corner. I felt it through Mother's behavior and actions, in her pinching and slapping me in the predawn hours to work. I felt its suffocation like a pillow over my face.

♦ ♦ ♦

The departure time had finally come for those leaving for Vietnam. It was a dim and cool night with a light drizzle. Didi's family came over to bid their farewell. They thanked us profusely for being generous to them. Wonhing handed Mother an American bill: one hundred dollars. "Since we'll be in Vietnam soon, you might need the money more than we do."

Mother shook her head to decline the offer, adding, "Money is useless here. Even gold is almost useless. Take the money with you."

"I'm afraid they'll search us and confiscate it," Wonhing insisted as she pushed the money back at Mother. "I have nowhere to hide the money."

"Here, hide it in your bra." Mother rolled the bill and motioned an insertion in Wonhing's chest. "It's much safer there." She grabbed Wonhing's hand and placed the money back in her palm. Knowing it was useless to argue, she stuffed it in her own shirt. Her eyes flitted from Mother to Father and down our individual faces. Her pearly black eyes glistened and gratitude gleamed out of them to thank each of us.

While she and her family felt indebted to us, we felt a burden of guilt.

"If you should later change your mind and end up in Vietnam, please look us up." According to her, it wouldn't be hard to find them in Vietnam.

Mother pleaded again, "Please stay, I beg you. Don't go. Please wait until they let us repatriate to China, then we can all go together."

"I can't wait that long. China is farther than Vietnam, and we don't know anyone there. We'll die if we have to stay here one more day."

We waved our goodbyes. Didi stuck out his head to search for my face. He waved and meekly smiled at me as the moonbeams shone down on us. I waved, but I didn't smile back. I just couldn't. My insides churned, knowing they were heading straight to their deaths. With their possessions in their arms, they left in an optimistic mood. If only they could hear our thoughts.

I was awake that night. I tossed and turned, as did my parents and older siblings. Remorse weighed us down, but none of us dared speak the inner turmoil that raged like a tsunami in our souls.

That night I kept seeing Didi's face staring at me—just before his head was lopped off.

"Jo, are you stupid?" Mother pressed on: "What . . . you still haven't figured out the madness? If the Khmer Rouge can wipe out the infrastructure and kill anyone who can read, you don't think they're also capable of mass murder and genocide?"

"Big Sis, under normal circumstances I would heed your warning. But lately, all of them are out to get me. They spy on me nightly, just waiting for my mouth to slip. In the field, they scrutinize my every move. I can't continue like this. If going to Vietnam means death, so be it! I'm done living in this hell!"

Despite Mother's warning him of the Angka's intention to slaughter the Vietnamese, Uncle Jo was still eager to go to Vietnam.

To risk dying now with the possibility of making it to Vietnam or to die later in Cambodia with absolute certainty— he opted for the former. A potential repatriation to China hadn't been widespread knowledge; it appeared only the old-people had heard of it, as they had with the Vietnamese genocide. China was but a figment of Uncle Jo's imagination, too unattainable for him to feel the ether of its hope.

Mother beseeched him to wait it out. "Death happens once, and it's permanent," she said. "You want to die, go ahead and be my guest! What about your son? Don't be reckless! If they kill the Vietnamese, we know not to line up for China. If they genuinely allow the Vietnamese back, then we can go to China when the opportunity presents itself."

Uncle Jo decided, then, to wait with us. The following day, he changed his mind again. Back and forth he went, torn between leaving and staying. We spent whatever precious hours we had after work debating the pros and cons of leaving. They still couldn't determine the reason behind a possible massacre. The phrases "It's a trap," "They're lying to us," and "We'll be slaughtered" were exchanged almost daily in an undertone among the adults.

We children were on the lookout as they deliberated among themselves whether to go or not. Our ears were attuned to the trees and bushes, and our eyes to the shadows. Should we suspect any movement or any suspicious noise, we were to casually cough or sneeze to signal danger.

During one discussion inside our hut, we children spotted a shadow looming in our fruitless banana orchard. The shifting of the stalks and leaves and a directional sweeping movement toward us alerted us to cough. Mother and Uncle Jo took our cue and changed subjects.

"So, do you know if fish oil will light up the lamp? Ours ran out. Do you have extra to spare?"

"I heard fish oil and rat oil work equally well. Let's see what I can do to get you some."

We all faked our coughs and pretended to sneeze on numerous occasions.

With much convincing, Uncle Jo ultimately decided to wait with us.

About a week after Didi's family left in the night, the Angka announced at the meeting that the Chinese were free to return to China. This time Uncle Jo didn't fall for the trap. Not one single soul raised his hand to leave Cambodia. By then everyone knew of the lies and the ensuing massacre.

Mother learned the details of that unforgivable night from Mother Yearn. Her son was the one who caught Mother with an extra bag of rice, but since she had implicated his own mother as her accomplice, he feigned ignorance and left her alone.

Mother Yearn sealed her lips until knowledge of the killings became widespread.

On the night that Didi and family left for Vietnam, all the informants (including Kong, the son of the old man who planted our banana trees; Cern, the brother of the two girls who taught me how to scold the crows; Rort, Mother Yearn's son) and Khmer Rouge soldiers were summoned from nearby villages in District Five to secure the perimeter. Roughly one hundred fifty men, women, and children showed up. Upon discovering the huge pit before them, they let out a collective gasp. At gunpoint, they stripped naked and tossed their clothes and belongings into one big pile before the Khmer Rouge attacked and mutilated them.

"I'm so relieved your family didn't go that night," Mother Yearn told Mother. It was pure hell. The cries of agony roared in the moonlight. Even the shadows and spirits of the trees and stones couldn't bear to witness. Babies were smashed against tree trunks and boulders. They tossed small children, alive, into a pool of blood and fresh corpses. "Those who tried to escape didn't make it far. My son had his orders to shoot. He didn't have a choice. I hope the dead know that." Her son suffered from depression and couldn't sleep peacefully thereafter.

♦♦♦

After the Vietnamese massacre, we didn't sleep either. Mother became more obsessed with our garden. She would slap me awake. It was Mother's morning wake-up call. Exasperation clawed through every inch of my nerves, causing abnormal palpitations in my chest. Living was less alluring than death. Sleep was the void death lurked within, and now I wanted to be one with the void.

The pinching, poking, and tugging continued. I turned on my side with my back to her, hoping to be left alone. Mother's hand yanked me back to face her as she sank her nails into my flesh. It was useless to ignore her. "Get out there and join Vunn and Nuy! I'm warning you; tomorrow better not be like this!" I finally arose and fumbled down the stairs in frustration and anger.

The hearth was burning brightly and on it boiled a pot of water, a sure sign that food was forthcoming. For once, food was the last thing on my mind. Right now I wanted to lose myself in blissful slumber, nightmares and all.

The chill air numbed my fingers and soothed the pains caused by Mother. A terrible idea invaded my thoughts. *She should be away to labor camp. I don't care if she never comes back!*

Ice encased the night. Even the moon and stars were too afraid to reveal themselves. The roosters had yet to crow. The bamboo and palm trees were whispering in the winds. Nature gently blew and hummed a lullaby for those fortunate enough to sleep. Every fiber in my body envied them, especially the two sisters in the hut next to us. I loathed Mother and, at that moment, I hated her more than I hated the Khmer Rouge.

She must have sensed my anguish, for I could hear softness in her voice: "Your father should be back soon with fish. He's been gone a while, now. I'm boiling water to cook the catch. Get ready. We'll eat soon."

I was instructed to till a new patch of soil next to where Vunn and Nuy were working. Judging from their work, they had been out here awhile. They weren't thrilled to be working, either.

I squatted and began to dig with the shovel. My eyes refused to cooperate no matter how hard I forced them open. My eyelids turned to lead. I saw Mother clearing the bushes to the far end, Vunn planting the cassava plants, and Nuy harvesting the edible leaves. I was busy jabbing the ground to loosen the soil. The next thing I knew, I was happily watering the plants. They were in full bloom with butterflies and bees swarming about.

Mother pinched me by the ear in a swift upward motion which almost uprooted me from the ground.

This time I exploded.

"Ow!" I fought hard to hold back tears. My eyes burned with hate. "This is so hard, so unfair! I bet Mother Len lets her daughters sleep. They hardly do anything! You make us work nonstop. I don't see anyone else digging! It's always garden, garden, garden. I'm sick of—"

Mother slapped me before I could empty my thoughts.

Before my face could register the full sting, she grabbed me by the arms, pulled me to her face, and in a low but forceful tone said, "I've told you already!" She sprayed hot breath in my eyes while twisting and sinking her nails into my flesh. The startling pain was enough to upend me halfway off the ground. "This garden saves our lives. Those who sleep now will die later. You envy Mother Len's daughters, but soon you won't. Mark my words! Don't worry about not getting enough sleep. Once you die, you can sleep all you want! You hear?"

I nodded. She shoved me to the ground, and I fell onto my bottom.

She walked away toward the fire, leaving me in tears. I once again reached for the shovel.

20. LABOR CAMP (CIRCA MAY 1977)

Without warning, they further fragmented my family. They sent my eleven-year-old brother to an all-boy collective workforce in a faraway place. They pulled Father deeper into the jungle to chop timber. As soon as Father and Vunn were away, they ordered us to leave first thing in the morning. Neither Vunn nor Father was aware that the hut would be empty if they were to return home.

The chief told us every family was on a rotation to form a part of something great. They needed us at a remote labor camp.

Our essentials were packed. I was assigned to carry our vinyl floor mat and a small bundle with utensils and blankets. Nuy overlaid one brown straw mat on top of another and rolled them tightly into a big roll before tying it with rope. Mother carried Black Ghost and a small basket of food and water. White Ghost carried a small package of clothes and towels.

As we were about to take our first steps away from our hut which had housed us for almost two years straight, I took mental pictures of my surroundings, only to realize that all of us were now standing at the spot where Didi and his family had stood on the night they left for Vietnam. Hallucinations of bodies piled high in a sunken pit, naked and exposed, raw and covered in blood, emerged before my eyes.

"Mother, what if they kill us the way they killed Didi and his family?"

"If only death were that easy," Mother responded. "Do you know that next to rice, people seek poison more than any other thing? Do you know that if we had poison, we would all drink it? I don't know who's luckier: the dead ones or us."

Mother was mindlessly spilling words from her troubled mind. She continued rambling, but I'd already stopped listening as my mind conjured images of drinking poison from a vial and passing it on to the next person in my family. One by one we would each take a sip. Immediately the effect would kick in and I would seize my stomach before collapsing.

Our legs continued westward, with the sun slowly rising behind us. My mind was not at ease. "Mother, if every family is required to help, then why isn't Mother Len's family coming, too?"

I asked this because I had run into Mother Len earlier when Mother sent me over to Grandma's with essential items for safekeeping. Her unhurried stride and patient demeanor suggested she didn't have to leave the village.

Mother slowed down her pace. Finally she saw the horror carved deeply on my face and realized the severity of my paranoia. She calmly explained, "Mother Len has been promoted to supervisor, so she's needed here in the village. But I do know about other old-people who left recently. I don't think it's a death trap. Let's just save our strength for the journey. Are we clear?" I sensed that her patience had run out. Something else was occupying her mind. I fixed my eyes on the path where Nuy was about twenty steps ahead of me, while White Ghost was about ten steps behind. I looked at Black Ghost's tiny body bouncing on Mother's hip and she smiled meekly at me, almost as if she were self-consciously aware of the burden of her weight.

Breathing in the morning air, I refocused my attention to my shadow on the ground, only to realize it was no longer in front of me, but to the left. Before we could ascend the mountain, a group of soldiers stopped us and Mother showed them our written permission. Most of the Khmer Rouge soldiers were illiterate; almost any note scribbled on a piece of paper would have sufficed. Both Uncle Tek and Uncle Jo had forged their own notes before, but there was always the risk that a soldier who could read would confirm the legitimacy of the note. If caught, the consequence was dire.

Both dread and wonder swelled within me with every step I took. This was my first time setting foot on this path. The dirt road was wide enough for two oxcarts to lumber through side by side. The path was lush with trees, yet at times only sparsely speckled with brush, vines, and rocks.

The path wound to the left as it was about to reach the plateau. It slowly blended into a plain, then spilled downward into a hamlet like pieces of fabric so seamlessly sewn together that beginning and end were indistinguishable. Before we knew it, we had crossed through many villages, and the mountains loomed behind us.

White Ghost looked exhausted and she grimaced. I, too, felt weary. Black Ghost must have grown from a gaunt baby to a boulder in Mother's arms. Mother would put her down to walk, and after several meters she would pick her up again.

The vinyl mat atop my head earlier was now on Nuy's, and I carried her rolled-up mats. When we both felt that our loads were too heavy, we swapped.

About two hours later, we stopped again. This time White Ghost and Black Ghost moaned and groaned because they were hungry. The walk had drained us of our energy. It was lunch hour, and we stopped to rest under the shade of tree branches on the side of a dirt road. We drank more water and ate yams and cassavas.

We encountered a few passers-by. They were all skin and bones, with round bellies like watermelons mounted on broomsticks. They glued their hungry eyes to our food and their mouths parted slightly as they licked their lips. They were salivating like a pack of wolves prowling around a piglet. I felt the weight of their piercing eyes. Their strides seemed slow and their glares burned my face. I swallowed my food fast to avoid their uncomfortable stares.

We were on the road again. An hour or so later, we were stopped again for permit inspection. The soldiers told us we had an hour to go before we would reach our destination. The paths guided us through prairies and snaked through endless neck-high grasses and reeds. One hour for the strong-footed men translated to almost two hours for my family.

When I could see clearly the four identical bunkhouses and smell the rice and fish cooking, my legs turned from cement to cotton.

The four bunkhouses were raised about a meter off the ground. There were only three walls to each hut and each was made of hay and palm branches. The front was open and exposed. There was no privacy from the other three huts and no protection from mosquitoes and rain. A couple of girls no more than fourteen came to clear their corner for us to occupy. They spent less than a minute moving all their belongings.

Approximately twenty-five people were crammed into each unit. At night we could hear our neighbors whispering to each other. Sometimes their hushed conversations turned into sniffles.

I was feeling euphoric. I was simply relieved not to be sharing the same fate as our Vietnamese neighbors.

On our first night, we realized we hadn't packed the mosquito net. Throughout our stay, we woke up daily with at least a dozen bites each.

Black Ghost was one of the youngest and sickest children. Although we had no idea where and when she had contracted it, Black Ghost had a severe case of tuberculosis, a sure promise of death.

At night everyone hated us. They complained about Black Ghost's chronic cries and coughing. Mother told the superintendent about Black Ghost's weak health and asked for Nuy to be her caretaker instead of helping in the fields. The supervisor granted the request, and Nuy babysat.

Each morning Mother and the others left for work before we woke up.

It rained often. There was rarely a day where it was dry enough for us children to go outside. There were ten other children lingering under the four roofs who were too young or too sick to work, waiting for their mothers, sisters, or aunts to return from work.

All day long we children languished on our mats, playing with pebbles as a substitute for a game of jacks. Those children with hair sat in rows delousing each other's heads. Our hair was short and stubby, if not completely shaved off: we didn't have to exhaust any energy killing lice.

When we were bored, we would nap. Sometimes I would take three naps, since there was nothing at all to do.

We had two meals each day: watered-down porridge with salt for lunch and a bowl with thicker porridge and a thumb-sized piece of dried fish for dinner.

After a few monotonous weeks in the work collective, we packed our belongings and headed back home.

The supervisor told us that Black Ghost's nightly ruckus was disruptive to others: she negatively affected the productivity and efficiency of the collective.

What others didn't know was that Mother had stone-hearted herself. She amplified the nightly cries into frightful squeals by stealthily pinching Black Ghost's arms and thighs while others snored.

Nuy and I had both seen her handiwork.

♦♦♦

We returned from labor camp to find that our hut had turned into a wild jungle. As we tamed the wilderness back to a recognizable garden, Uncle Rain visited us to deliver more bad news: there had been two additional casualties since five full moons ago. Middle Daughter was their fourth casualty. Uncle Rain's entire family had succumbed to poison from eating wild tree roots and bark: they all violently vomited and became feeble.

Their village chief gave them sugared water to drink and many were slowly recuperating from the poison, but Middle Daughter had taken a turn for the worse and experienced incurable bouts of diarrhea.

Uncle Rain took a bowl and set it beside her so she didn't have to walk far to perform the messy deed. Having no strength to prop herself up, she instead released her liquid stool on the blanket wrapped around her. Uncle Rain was upset, and his tone sounded harsh and insensitive when he asked her, "My child, why didn't you use the bowl I gave you? I'm too weak to walk to the lake to wash your soiled blankets."

After he finished ranting, she looked up at him with pleading eyes; whereupon he realized the life in her was fleeing, along with her soul.

Middle Daughter squealed, "It hurts!"

Her mother rushed to her. She held on to the warmth of her daughter's body before it turned cold in rigor mortis.

"It hurts!" Middle Daughter gasped in shallow catch-breaths. Their hands quickly came together. Middle Daughter shrieked, "It hurts! I can't breathe! My chest's crushing me!"

Knowing her daughter was only seconds from leaving this realm, Aunt Khan choked on her own phlegm as she instructed her dying beloved child. "Middle Daughter, my dear child," she paused to collect the courage to say the painful parting words. "After you leave us . . . remember to find your siblings. And tell them to reincarnate and reunite in Thailand, where you will be free. You must not come back to this forsaken place! Remember!" Tears stung her eyes and the pain of yet another loss morphed into a vise, clenching her throat and lungs.

Her dying daughter tried to say something; but she struggled to produce audible sounds. Instead, her daughter's listless eyes rolled slightly upward to look at her father one last time and back again to her mother's face. She blinked away the tears gathered in the corners of her eyes. They were the tears of aching separation and of deep sorrow and misery . . . then the end came. She exhaled her last breath, and her head fell as she released her mother's hands.

My aunt, uncle, and cousins wailed together, mourning their fourth death and the same painful aftermath. The air was always short of reaching the lungs. My aunt and uncle wanted to turn back time. She wanted all her children, both the dead ones and the live ones, to crawl back into her womb. She wanted to undo their sufferings—if only she could force time to retreat before this cruel existence!

Uncle Rain was overcome with remorse and self-reproach from having scolded his now-deceased daughter only a short while ago. He begged her for forgiveness, but it was too late. He cried hysterically while wailing words, hoping that somewhere in her spiritual consciousness, she would know how much he loved her and what a good daughter she had been.

Middle Daughter died in December 1976 at the age of eight. Through much begging and pleading again, their chief allowed her cremation, but added one proviso that this time would be their last. It was counterproductive to burn a body rather than to bury it. It required too much wood and too much manpower, whereas a hole in the ground required only one man and one shovel.

After recounting Middle Daughter's passing, Uncle Rain talked about Tai's death; his family's fifth casualty. He died in January 1977 at the age of seven. Tai was by far one of the bravest boys I knew. Several times he would sneak into our village to forage wild water spinach and to beg my parents to come home with him. My parents couldn't make the trek nor the promise to visit, but they did manage to send food back. His enormous hollow, pleading eyes revealed his suffering at home. They were acutely aware that none of us had visited them in Tapan, which lay within walking distance.

How could one leave when one was labeled as a flight risk?

In order not to give anyone a reason to tarnish our reputation as "lazy-city-folks" or an excuse to purge us, we stayed put.

Time and circumstances proved unkind to us all: they pelted us with stones of sickness, hunger, and separation. Our minds turned numb, leaving our hearts with little room for tender feelings.

Tai didn't even have the luxury of dying in his mother's arms.

Aunt Khan was sick and under the care of her mother-in-law. Tai asked his father to take him to his mother at his grandma's place. Both mother and son embraced each other as if they knew this could be their last time together. She stroked his hair tenderly, whispering gentle words of healing to him. She told him to obey his father's order to exercise more by walking around to circulate the blood in his body. Tai nodded in the most obedient way.

Every endearing touch and every gentle embrace between his wife and son pooled tears in Uncle Rain's eyes. His vision of them dying and leaving him forever in this world stirred a pain so indescribable that he wished to reach inside his chest to stop his own heart from aching.

Uncle Rain didn't want to trouble his already-burdened mother, so he carried his son back home to be cared for by him and his two remaining daughters, Big Daughter, eleven, and Sida, who was five.

A few days later Uncle Rain and his two daughters heard the now-familiar cries. "It hurts! It hurts!" screamed Tai as he grabbed his stomach in agony. Uncle Rain rushed to pick him up. Darkness was descending rapidly to envelop his beloved son: at most a minute or two was left to embrace the warmth and consciousness of his own flesh and blood.

"My son, my good son—life has been cruel. You've been shortchanged. Join your siblings, and may your next life be a much better one. Pick a good country for reincarnation!"

Tai's eyes revealed his determination to acknowledge his father's parting words, while his entire body convulsed. His breathing ended when his seizure stopped. His eyes opened wide and his mouth lay agape. Uncle Rain gently shut his eyes. The loss of another beloved child shattered him. He howled in rage and anguish, overwhelmed with helplessness. His two daughters joined in with their fitful cries.

After Tai's death, Uncle Rain brought Aunt Khan back from his mother's place so she could see her son's face for the last time.

She rushed over to her son's lifeless body. The intestinal worms were wiggling through the many exits of their now-dead host. With tears dripping down her face, she pulled a few worms from his mouth, hugged his body, and pecked his cheeks.

She whispered to him, "My child; my obedient son. Your mother won't last much longer. I'll join you soon. I'll be able to take better care of you all in the afterlife. I'll beg the spirits to grant us another life, another do-over: one that'll last longer and be happier." She then chanted a Buddhist mantra: a prayer for the spirit of her dying children to find peace and happiness in the afterlife, in a different lifetime.

Uncle Rain approached the chief to request the cremation of his son. The chief responded with disdain. "No. It requires too much firewood and wastes too much time! Just bury his body and get it over with!"

21. THE SKINNY WIFE (CIRCA JULY 1977)

At the age of nine, the Angka claimed my sister Nuy as a war slave and put her to work in the village. Vunn was still at the all-boys work camp. Grandma often babysat Black Ghost and Rern (Uncle Jo's son), and White Ghost mindlessly followed them everywhere. I was left to shoulder most, if not all, the household chores. The burden of living had never felt heavier to me.

Everyone must eat at a designated area during lunch, based on proximity to his worksite. Right around the time they enforced the communal luncheon, the chief and his gang raided our hut. They carried away for collective use our metal bowls, utensils, and a big pot. Only a few items were left behind for our family of seven to share. We had no choice but to remedy the shortage with coconut bowls and wooden spoons.

Mother took her lunch near where she sewed, Uncle Jo was somewhere else, and the rest of us were by the lake where we'd learned how to swim.

Lunch started with four or five makeshift kitchens to accommodate everyone, over one hundred fifty people in each group. As the island of Ma Om rose higher with human bones, the people consolidated to form fewer groups. I always showed up early to receive my ration. On a few special occasions they doled out solid rice to eat; but those days were too few to count on all fingers.

Dinner was different. Each family would send a representative to line up for food to take home. Before sundown, I would haul an average-size container to collect dinner for the six of us. Six people amounted to six ladles; less than half the kettle.

I had developed a habit of stealing food on my way home. Although I knew it was wrong to eat more than my fair share, hunger blurred the lines of morality.

I'd stop by the side of the road, set the kettle down, and break a leaf off a bamboo tree. I would fold it into a cone and scoop up the porridge to feed the worms in my belly. Each time, I promised it would be the last time.

My feeling of guilt vanished on nights when fish, snake, lizard, or rat subsidized our dinner. It surrounded me and weighed me down when we ate nothing but what was rationed. A handful of times I was able to part with a spoonful from my bowl into Black Ghost's or White Ghost's bowl; but many nights, I looked down and quietly swallowed my food.

♦♦♦

That day wasn't the first time I found a clump of cow dung and dead leeches floating in my soup. My stomach soured.

Father happened to find me before he lined up for his food. He heard my hollow gag and asked if I was feeling okay. I told him of the manure and the leeches. He showed no reaction. They obviously did not faze him. I set my bowl down on the grass and told him I was leaving. He instructed me to wait until his return and not to throw away the soup.

While he went to line up, I fished out the cow dung and the leeches. A tiny silver fish was buried in the soup, but I had lost my appetite and didn't eat it. After Father returned, I said goodbye to him. I didn't have the stomach to watch him eat the filth from my bowl.

After scavenging for dry twigs on the ground and breaking branches from the parched mangroves, I arrived home exhausted, hungry, and thirsty. I stacked the wood to the side of our hut and proceeded to go for a drink of boiled water. Suddenly I heard the panicked cries of a woman running from boisterous men.

The ruckus grew louder and clearer. I froze behind the low wall and peeked out with much dread. I felt oddly out of place; like I shouldn't be home to witness something forbidden, or I shouldn't have eyes to see what I was about to witness.

I peered from the hut like a rat from a hole. I saw my new Aunt Hing, Uncle Tek's wife, being beaten by two Khmer Rouge soldiers.

The air left me. I should've stayed to eat the leech-and-dung soup.

After Skinny Wife married into our family, we often found her sitting or lying in the same corner of Grandma's hut. After work, she sought warmth in the threadbare blankets. Her supervisor allowed her to convalesce at home when she started shivering at work. Mother spoon-scraped her body and fed her an herbal remedy to make her better. She was never well enough to work nor infirm enough to stay put. She visited her mother and stayed over for a few nights. The Angka became vigilant and came down hard on people shirking their duties. They checked on her almost daily to confirm the legitimacy of her ailment.

Since today was her last day of recovery, she went back to Grandma's place to eat and to rest. Grandma's place had a bit more food than her own mother's. She loved to eat not so much the rats or snakes, but Father's fish and Mother's crab, if she was lucky. It was a risky undertaking to come home to rest, especially when her supervisor and the soldiers were already accusing her of being a malingerer. That day, two Khmer Rouge followed Skinny Wife to Grandma's place. Without warning, they attacked her from behind.

Startled, she sprang forward to distance herself from their onslaught.

She didn't get far.

Their whips melted into her flesh like a hot knife on lard. They accused her of being a "lazy-city-folk" who refused to do manual labor.

"If you're sick, why aren't you home resting? How come you have energy to walk?" Endless questions gushed out of their mouths, each phrase matched by the rhythm of their whips. "If you have no strength to work, you should have no strength to walk! And if you claim you're sick, we'll make sure you become just that!"

Her high-pitched sound of torment reached me as I sipped my cup of water. So shrill was her voice that I couldn't tell if it was coming from a human or a cat being skinned alive.

They continued the death knell: "To keep you is no gain! To lose you is no loss!"

The whip kept pace with every syllable of their mindless mottos. Her cries were in sync with their beating. I was petrified, but I couldn't stop watching.

She escaped into the bamboo thickets, only to be chased out to the banana groves. She trembled and was about to pass out from exhaustion and pain. There was no way she could outrun them. They pounced on her and she fell down spread-eagled. She used her arms to buffer their attacks, but that only infuriated them into applying more force to assert their dominance. She crawled on her stomach, her limbs scrambling in all directions, but her body didn't move far.

The soldiers stood opposite each other with their pitiful victim in the middle and took turns hitting her mangled body. With each powerful strike, the back of their heels bounced off the ground. Her body involuntarily jolted upward. She was practically naked; I could see her tiny breasts. They had beaten her almost into unconsciousness. Her brown leaf-dyed shirt was torn. The bottoms of her long grey pants were shredded into unrecognizable tatters, and blood oozed from her skin. She was as helpless as a chicken with its neck at knifepoint. She mewled weakly. It was all she could do, clinging to what little life she had left.

"I'm tired. Let's take a break!" one of the soldiers said.

Both nodded and caught their breaths. They tossed away the broken stalks. Skinny Wife struggled to crawl away. She managed a few feet. Her pants were soaked and stained with urine and feces. The filth slid down her legs as she attempted to prop herself up. Disoriented and blind, she wiped blood from her eyes. She looked both ways frantically, appearing to be lost in despair, before hurriedly gathering herself and trying to head straight to Grandma's place.

She had more will than energy. She took two steps before collapsing down on all fours. At that instant, one of the soldiers charged at her yet again. He struck her back with his foot and smashed her face into the dirt. He pressed down on her so hard her rear end arched upward.

He yelled to the other soldier, "Comrade, get me a new stalk!"

The other soldier walked to our banana orchard. He shifted the long gun from his side to his back as he took a small knife from his calf and proceeded to cut off two big banana leaves. Stripping the midribs of the leaves with his hands, he produced the whipping tools. He then extended a whip to his compatriot and said with finality, "These should do."

The soldier lifted his foot off her back and dared her to run for her life. "RUN! RUN!" he roared. "Run as fast as you can! Today will be the last time you ever run!"

She fought hard to stand before springing away. She was soon out of my sight, with death pursuing her.

One soldier ran after her, leaving the other one to leisurely stroll behind.

I could tell that the first one had caught up to her by her ensuing cries and the sound of lashes against her frail bones.

I don't know what possessed me to follow them, but I did.

I walked to the front of the hut where she had crawled, looking both ways before proceeding. As I neared Grandma's place, her outcry ceased. The whipping stopped. There were no sounds coming from her.

The second I spotted the soldiers, I climbed one of the trees that once supported Grandma's hammocks. They were too engrossed in their mission to notice me. I held firmly to the tree branches and remained hidden but had a clear view. I could see Grandma's hut, the field behind her hut, and the water barrel to the front of the hut. I spotted all three of them by the water barrel.

This time she was fully naked, motionless, and face-down. Dirt and blood had caked on her body.

One soldier went to the water container and brought a bucket of water. One pried her mouth open so the other could pour water down her throat.

Her limbs twitched; but only slightly.

The Khmer Rouge acted as though it were their right to discipline and to kill.

They dragged her by the arms. Her head dangled, bouncing against her shoulders. The rest of her body was treated no differently than a log. Her stomach and knees scraped against the road as they hauled her westbound.

My eyes were wide open. I was in shock, and I forgot how long I had been hiding in the tree.

Grandma noticed me when she returned with the younger ones from the mess hall by the lake. She saw my tear-streaked face and the rigidity of my body as I climbed down from the tree.

I told Grandma and my parents what I had seen. They tsk-tsked and shook their heads and commented that my boldness could have gotten me killed.

"Don't ever do that again!" they admonished me. "Always pretend to be blind, deaf, and mute. Recklessness will get you killed."

That night my mind replayed Skinny Wife's torture.

The next morning I ran a fever and I was excused from my chores. No one stayed home to take care of me. It was an unbearable and depressing day. The fever climaxed into spinning walls and splitting headaches. I lay curled in a fetal position against the wall, rubbing my thumbs into my temples to ease the pain.

Father came to tell me that Skinny Wife didn't make it.

22. THE SUNDIAL (CIRCA JULY 1977)

To make up for the deficit in the labor force, children as young as eight were forced to work. I was a few months shy of making the cut.

Vunn, eleven years old, only returned home from the all-boys cooperative once every couple of months. He fared worse than we did when it came to hunger: his throat shrank from lack of solid food.

Each time Vunn returned home, he had to relearn the use of his jaw and throat. It was painful to watch him eat. One would think he was swallowing pebbles, the way he ate his meals. Tears gathered and fell in the corners of his eyes as he tried to force the food down, often getting it painfully lodged in his throat instead. He had to drink water often to ease the affliction.

Nuy was luckier than Vunn. She worked in the village, clearing leaves and branches from the muddy fields. She collected cow manure to fertilize crops, working alongside Mother Len's daughters and other children her age. During harvesting time they became human scarecrows, protecting crops from birds.

As the pressure to keep us alive mounted exponentially, Mother's resolve and her temper also grew daily. Now I alone inherited all the beatings, since Vunn and Nuy weren't home to share in the emotional stress created by the regime's violent throes.

In their absence, I lugged the water, gathered firewood, tended the garden, washed dishes and blankets, and took care of Black Ghost when Grandma couldn't help out.

Of all the chores, the one I despised most was acting as Mother's human alarm clock. As her health declined, she would come home frequently after a quick communal lunch to recharge with a power nap. To make sure she woke up on time, she would draw a big circle (about twenty inches in diameter) on the ground by the front of our hut with a long bamboo stick. She erected the stick in the center of the circle. It stood slightly shorter than me.

"See how the stick casts a shadow?" Mother then drew a radius with her finger from the base of the stick to the edge of the circle. "When the shadow reaches this line, wake me up; about thirty minutes from now. Don't let the shadow pass the mark or you'll be hit with this stick." She glared at me with severity.

One time before Mother took her nap, she ordered me to wash Black Ghost and White Ghost in the lake near Father Pea's home. While guiding my siblings to the water, Father Pea gestured for us to come closer as he sat dangling his feet from the patio. I ushered us closer. I was curious and filled with dread at the same time.

"Hello there! Have any of you seen my cat lately?" he queried.

We all gently shook our heads in denial. Black Ghost and White Ghost hardly talked to outsiders. One of us had to do the talking, or else he would misinterpret our silence.

"No, we haven't seen your cat lately," I blurted out.

"Have you eaten anything unusual lately?" he continued.

We whipped our heads, and again I said no.

"Be extra careful by the water! And yell for help if someone falls in," he advised.

This time I couldn't will myself to say "thank you" as we stepped away from his hut to the lake. A week ago Father Pea's orange cat had wandered into our garden, as it had done many times before, but this time was its last. Several times it had unearthed fish bones buried in the soil. We often chased the feline away with sticks and stones. They were effective at first, but gradually the cat became immune to our threats. Father baited it with a thumb-sized piece of fish. The creature was lured in and he seized its neck. It immediately sensed danger and began to yowl. He had to act fast before it attracted attention.

Father swiftly took the knife to the cat's throat, multiple times. This annoying feline didn't go down without raising a ruckus. The blood splattered all over him and the plants in our garden. Father's determination to feed us and to keep us alive drove him to kill his supervisor's pet.

Nuy, Mother and I were busy stoking the fire to boil water. We savored this bounty by adding more lemongrass, basil, lime, and fish sauce to mask the strange taste and its slimy texture. We offered a bowl of food to Mother, but she gently pushed it away, saying she was not hungry. She sat quietly watching us chew and bite into the cat's flesh and bones, sucking on the marrow as if it were sugar cane. She told us to eat slower, but to Father she said, "Our children only know of suffering, eating bugs, lizards and cats," with tears welling up in her eyes.

Even after death, the cat continued to nourish us as its bones fertilized the garden.

Our parents warned us never to admit anything when asked about the cat. If we were to reveal the truth, Father Pea was in a position to have all of us killed. He held the title of supervisor. He oversaw rice production and the rationing and distribution of communal food among the various makeshift kitchens in the village. Father Pea, the chief, and a few other supervisors met almost daily. One elbow rub with the head chief and one whisper into his ear, and Father Pea could avenge his cat's death.

Mother's distrust of our neighbors, Mother Len and her daughters, proved accurate because they snitched on us. They told Father Pea they had heard a cat's tortured cry at our place. They said it had suffered a slow death.

Father Pea knew.

"Well, hello there, Mother Yeng and children. Did my cat taste good? How come you didn't save any for me?"

Mother pretended not to grasp what he was saying, pulling her eyebrows together in a puzzled knot. We children kept a straight face.

"Stop pretending," Father Pea said. "Mother Len and her daughters told me you killed my cat. Just admit it!"

Mother denied it, telling her truthful version: "I didn't eat your cat!"

Father Pea looked furious; perhaps he was expecting us to confess and beg for mercy and forgiveness. He wasn't satisfied. He came to us children a few more times, searching for answers when our parents weren't around. We never betrayed our secret.

Father Pea's suspicion lacked evidence and he was deprived of satisfaction; however, discontent was slowly brewing within him and it would eventually come to a boiling point.

◆◆◆

Once, in the middle of the night, Mother pinched me. "Get up and go wash yourself! NOW! I don't care if it's midnight. Don't come back unless you're wet!"

I knew I couldn't reason with her. I forced myself up and walked down the steps, rubbing my eyes of sleep, while seething with anger and hatred.

Earlier in the day I had washed myself when I was lugging water. It must have been the lapse of time, the humidity, and the limitless chores which had created an odor offensive to Mother's nose.

As I stepped out into the night, I sniffed both armpits and thought they smelled fine.

I found Mother's action groundless, bordering on cruel and tyrannical.

I walked to the main road with dread penetrating my every step. How am I supposed to wash in the dark? Although I didn't have the pail with me, the mere thought of leeches swimming in it repulsed me. Did Mother forget the night when tons of slimy bloodsuckers punctured my body and feasted on my blood?

I hated her heart of stone. I hated her more than I hated the leeches.

I paced back and forth on the road. I didn't see sparks flickering nor flames leaping in anyone's hearth. The village remained eerily silent, like a graveyard. The trees and branches turned into moving shadows with their limbs and fingers reaching for me. If I listened hard enough, I could hear the shadows whispering in my ears, warning me to go back inside.

Tonight I felt alone. Father wasn't home. No one stood between Mother's madness and me.

I wished for my parents to trade places. When Father was home, I didn't have to do the chores so thoroughly. I didn't have to rise early. I didn't have to watch the sundial and be a human alarm clock. He would lug the water for me. He would never mete out the unthinkable punishment of sending me to the lake in the middle of the night.

Tonight, rage clouded my mind because I painted Mother as the devil and Father the saint, but I knew it was Mother who had been keeping us alive. When she was away at labor camp, we suffered in other ways. Father wasn't adept in the art of negotiation. Other than the fish he caught, he had never once procured additional rice and salt, as she did. With Father home, Uncle Rain and Grandma had no one to turn to for salt. Without salt, the edema in our bodies would distend us even more.

I thought of using Grandma's water, but it didn't feel right. Not too long ago, while she was gardening, a snake bit her toe. Her foot had turned purple to nearly black and her complexion had become sick from the poison. She lacked the physical and mental stamina for the simplest of tasks. Walking had become a chore and babysitting was almost unbearable.

Grandma had suffered enough. Right around the time of the snakebite, she was caught a second time with a bagful of corn near her place. They again tied her up, led her away, and poured angry fire ants all over her body. She had to endure their attacks for several hours, her legs and hands bound.

So tonight my conscience prevented me from going to Grandma's place.

I was worn down and had no energy to rage any longer. I begged for the first light to peak so I could go to the lake, but the night stretched, moonless and starless, and dawn seemed far away.

I decided that the best course of action was to wait until Mother surrendered to sleep, maybe another hour, before I could crawl back to bed. My legs were tired from pacing. I sat on the path in the front connecting to the main road, in an open spot devoid of scorpions and snakes. With my head between my legs and my arms hugging my knees together, I dozed off.

Nature delivered a light drizzle on my sleepy body. I had no idea how long I was out. I woke up confused by the gentle spray. By the time reality sank in as to why I was outside sitting on the road alone in blackness, the rain had subsided. The sprinkles didn't last: they were too brief to drench me from head to toe. I looked up and the sky was a black blanket encompassing the vast universe.

At that moment, nature beckoned, and my bladder responded. I was about to squat and pee, but mischievous thoughts sparked within me. I would finish what the rain had started.

I took off my shirt and pants, bundled them up, and tucked them between my legs as the dam burst. A tinge of satisfaction crept up my face. If Mother wanted me wet, she would get it. I felt thrilled and scared at the same time.

I put the clothes back on and fumbled my way back to bed. The second I lay down on my side with my back to Mother, she draped her hand on my body then patted me up and down lazily. I couldn't tell if it was the touch of a concerned mother who was glad her baby had returned home to roost or the touch of suspicion, seeking not so much the confirmation of obedience, but the punishment of disobedience.

Moments later, I heard Mother's heavy breathing; shortly after, her snoring.

Relief washed over me. I had survived the night without venturing out to the lake. Although I felt a slight guilt for this deception, I was too exhausted to be bothered by my conscience or by the dampness of my clothes or by my filth. I checked out for the night with a sense of victory.

◆◆◆

When I noticed I had missed the shadow on the sundial, I panicked. Despite the anxiety attack and the urge to run away, I forced myself to climb into the hut to wake Mother up.

"Wake up, Mother! Mother wake up!"

Mother fanned her hand at me as she mumbled incoherently. I withdrew my hands from her body, but remained by her side.

The stick shadow had passed the drawn line. She should have been up by now. I turned back to look at her face.

My eyes roamed from her face to the rest of her body, and the smallness of her frame alarmed me. I saw for the first time that she wasn't invincible. Death could come for her almost as easily as it could claim Black Ghost, her chronically-sick child.

I saw Mother's ribs protruding through her clothes and observed her sunken face and bloated stomach. She was as fragile as a hatched chick shivering in the cold. I could have mistaken her frame to be Nuy's, who was nine years old at the time. Mother was that tiny.

I envisioned black crows perching on our rooftop, cawing to mark our location for their master.

Mother's hair had thinned out to reveal the flesh of her scalp. Her face was pale and yellow, marred by hardship and malnutrition. Her hands and feet were bloated. Sadness enveloped me. I'd never seen her so vulnerable. The sorrow grabbed my emotions and refused to let them go. I had an urge to reach for her, to grab onto her and to hug her tightly before she withered away. I wanted to hug my mother, who had no time to hug me because she was too busy keeping all of us alive. I wanted to feel her warmth before time could undo her existence and take her away.

The child in me came out and I wanted so much to touch her, to feel her warmth. The adult in me, the one who had been battered and hardened by life, didn't know how to perform an act so natural between a mother and a child. I was overwhelmed with so much love and gratitude for my mother that I saw an invisible child detaching itself from me to plant a kiss on her gaunt cheek—then I shed tears.

I reluctantly shook Mother to disturb the serenity of her mind and body. This time failure was not an option. I would not be shooed away. I shook her violently. I felt horrible inside, as if I were some evil spirit preventing a sick person from resting.

After Mother finally sat up, it took her some time to absorb reality. As she came to full awareness, she realized her own tardiness. Steam shot from her eyes and nose.

"How could you be so careless? Didn't I tell you to wake me up?" Because of my negligence, she missed a vital transaction.

Mother was unforgiving. The bamboo stick smote my body and the welts formed instantaneously. I jumped up and down while she hit me with vengeance.

I was fuming with hate. I wanted her to die again. I felt betrayed by the child in me for wanting to hug her. I hated myself for wasting tears on her.

Mother's once-unshakable resolve was starting to crack. A will to survive dilated in one pupil while a slight temptation to surrender it all glazed over in the other. Sometimes the contusions on my body pooled tears in her eyes, and she would speak to me in a gentler tone filled with entreaty for the next few days—yet other times the open cuts failed to make a dent in her soul, and dark resolve shone through her eyes to stab me, hard and cold, in the heart.

I could not distinguish if she was my tormentor or savior. I felt her punishment and her deliverance all at once. Sometimes she talked about having all of us hang ourselves; yet other times, she worried parasites would kill us.

It felt like the Khmer Rouge had dropped me into a deep well, and while I was lost, stuck, and in shock, Mother would relentlessly dump water on me and expect me to rise with the water to climb out. But I was a child, and I was drowning.

I once broke the bamboo stick in two, believing it would be rendered useless and she wouldn't be able to hit me with it.

I couldn't have been more wrong.

Mother drew a smaller circle the next day, and when she finished ramming a short stick into the center of it, she told me that by the time she woke up, she'd better see a longer stick. Needless to say, I found a replacement stick.

No one was as excited as I was when the Angka conscripted children as young as eight to work. I queued up behind other children to distance myself from Mother.

A man about Father's age sat behind a small wooden table by the meeting circle and jotted down names and ages of children who were eight years and older. Those who failed to register (if they were found out) would not receive their allotted food.

As I stood in line, I felt hopeful. I could see clearly that I would be leaving with Nuy tomorrow morning to join her work group. I could see myself no longer being tormented by Mother's emotional stress. Elation danced within me.

"How old are you?" The man behind the table looked at me first before asking.

"Nine," I answered. I was seven and approaching eight, and I figured by adding more than one year to my actual age, I would be guaranteed passage to join the labor force.

The man sized me up and down. "You're not nine, not even eight. You look too small to work. Next year!"

My chest deflated. I might as well be buried alive. In desperation, I half-kneeled with my hands reaching for the man's arm in a plea.

"But I'm nine. I can do many things: gather wood, fetch water, garden. Please give me a chance. You'll see that I'm capable and hardworking."

The man was perplexed by my determination. He eyed me up and down again, knotting his brow. He probably thought I was crazy. No one in her right mind would want to collect cow manure. He shook his head and declared with finality: "Next year! Next in line!"

A girl about Nuy's age who was clad in crisp black clothes was next in line. Our eyes locked briefly as I sidestepped for her to pass through to the line. I sensed her unwillingness to work. Oh, how I wished to be in her shoes!

I walked home feeling defeated and depressed, thinking, *How am I supposed to survive Mother for one more year?*

23. THE GARDEN OF DEATH (CIRCA AUGUST 1977)

It was approaching dinnertime, and I carried the kettle to the communal kitchen. I was expecting six ladlefuls of watery rice porridge: that was the daily amount rationed to my family.

Instead of six, tonight it was five.

"There must be a mistake," I said to the two servers behind the counter.

I held up the line. People behind me grumbled and complained: something about their family members dying at home waiting for food. The two ladies behind the counter waved for me to move along.

Convinced I had been shortchanged, I stood there and refused to move. I stared at the servers. "Why am I getting only five? Only my brother is away; our family should be getting six."

One of the ladies leaned over the counter and whispered, as if to spare me the embarrassment. "Child, your mother isn't getting her food today."

Panic flooded my tiny body. I knew something bad had happened. Was she caught carrying rice or jewelry? Stealing corn? Or saying something offensive? To my knowledge, this was the first time one of us was purposely deprived of food. I became more worried as my reasoning and deduction led to one conclusion: Mother was in trouble.

On my way home I was too distracted to notice the bamboo groves, too distraught to steal a moment to eat. Somewhere in the back of my mind I wondered if somehow I was responsible for her punishment.

Something sinister had already been set in motion without our knowledge, an inferno needing nothing but a spark to ignite it. The spark came about when Vunn overheard Father Pea's tirade over Father's incompetence. This happened shortly after Vunn returned from his youth brigade. His two closest friends were Father Pea's sons, and my brother often overextended his stay at their house and would overhear things.

Vunn came to us with worries. He said Father Pea was mad at Father for not following orders, claiming Father would abandon his work midway to do something else. The supervisor construed Father's behavior as rude and reckless, beyond undermining his superior's authority, and grounds for punishment. According to Father, however, he was a mere Indian with too many chiefs to answer to. The head chief would often come to Father to tell him to do something else. If Father was busy digging trenches under Father Pea's orders, the chief would tear him away to move bales of hay. If Father was chopping logs by the mess hall, the chief would send him into the jungle to fetch more wood. Each time, the head chief reassured him that Father Pea had knowledge of his new job assignment: if not, he would be sure to communicate it later so Father wouldn't get into trouble. Unfortunately, the Indian worked hard, but his many chiefs lacked order and communication—or perhaps it was all a part of the head chief's design to wreak havoc in our lives.

"Father Pea mentioned sending him away to re-education camp," said my brother.

At the mention of the infamous word "re-education," the food turned bitter in my mouth. I sat there listening to Father defend himself to us. He told us not to worry; it was simply a misunderstanding. He seemed rather blasé about the whole thing, but Mother became perceptibly worried. Father thought she was overreacting. He told her the head chief's authority superseded Father Pea's supervisory level. There was no need to worry.

Mother couldn't sit tight. She wanted to clear things up and confront the situation rather than ignoring it, so she went to Father Pea to dispel any misunderstanding.

"Father Pea, my son heard you complain about Father Sann's performance," Mother began her explanation. "We understand you're his supervisor. But please know the chief also orders him around. If you were him, whose order would you tackle first? My son overheard you wanting to retool his father. I want you to know that all is just a big misunderstanding. Please don't scare us."

"Where's your son?" demanded Father Pea. "He sure has a big mouth! Perhaps he's the one needing the re-education!"

Mother was dumbfounded and shocked.

To diffuse the tension, she besought him with a gentler tone. "Father Sann, as you know, is one of the hardest workers, dependable and reliable. Because too many superiors order him around, it's hard for him to fulfill all the assignments to everyone's satisfaction. Perhaps it's best if you and the chief check with each other first before approaching him with tasks."

Father was caught in the middle, as helpless as a bird with clipped wings. He went to chop down trees as ordered by the chief and disregarded his supervisor's request to work in the village.

If the start of this incident hadn't already aggravated Father Pea, what happened next was sure to bring his blood to a boil. Father and another man went to haul logs back from the jungle via oxcart. Before they took the trunks back, they had to first set them on fire to kill the fire ants residing in them. Once ablaze, they had to put the fire out before hoisting them onto the oxcart. Unbeknownst to both men, an ember lay dormant. Somewhere along the way back, the gentle breeze stoked the fire to life and burned half of the wagon, rendering it unsalvageable. Because the other man was the driver, the blame fell solely on Father. He should have detected it early enough to prevent the flames from spreading out of control.

Father was defenseless.

The wagon belonged to none other than Father Pea, who had built it with his bare hands. The wagon incident must have boiled his blood. I overheard him confiding his frustration to his friends. "You know the saying 'to lose you is no loss and to keep you is no gain'? Well, here's a no-brainer. . . . Father Sann is slow and he can't seem to follow orders, as you all know. . .."

The group of men roared in laughter. Father Pea's was the loudest. This rambunctiousness abruptly halted as they saw me walking by.

At the time, we had no knowledge of the burned cart, only of Father's being ordered around by too many superiors. He was too ashamed to confide in Mother. Had she been informed of this unfortunate incident, she would have reacted differently by not reacting at all; so to punish her for being a thorn in their sides, they deprived her of food.

Since we were clueless about the burned wagon, what I heard put Mother over the edge. What made it worse was how I conveyed it: with gusto and conviction. I didn't know the names of the men; their faces eluded me completely as I told the story. In my head I could still hear the sinister laugh spewing out of Father Pea's mouth. By the time I was done telling, I had inadvertently mentioned Father Pea's name to Mother a dozen times. The other men I saw were left out of the story entirely. Now I had mistakenly created a sole antagonist and he was Father Pea, Father's supervisor, the man whose cat went missing.

My tattletale was the straw that broke the camel's back. Father might have been the log with no common sense and Vunn might have been the spark for mentioning the re-education camp, but I was the lighter fluid and the bellows.

I had created an inferno.

Mother was beyond outraged. She made me accompany her to Father Pea's place for the confrontation. She asked me to repeat in front of him what I had told her. Of course, he denied it. He claimed he would never say such hurtful remarks. He urged her not to believe a child's tale.

In the end we were assigned to a different communal kitchen and Father to a different supervisor. Our family was completely removed from Father Pea's group.

Subsequently, Father Pea ignored me and stopped telling me to scream for help if someone were to drown.

Overnight a wall had grown between Mother and the village. Father Pea was seething inside, and he managed to rally the people against her. The old-people exhibited a united front and they all ignored her. Through the grapevine, Mother was identified as an unreasonable and difficult individual.

Some of the old-people who had once come to her to broker their goods had turned against Mother. Some had secretly reported Mother to the chief, hoping to curry favor. Two good souls, Mother Lei and the lady with the sensitive bladder, warned Mother that the head chief was on to her and advised her to stop her underground market at once.

The head chief's visits became bolder with each passing day. He was no longer a shapeless shadow looming in our banana orchard, but a solid mass with stature and authority. He'd walk right up to our hut and gaze inside. We knew he was scheming, perhaps trying to catch us doing something incriminating, whether it was Mother with a bag of rice or Father with a basket of fish. We all sensed his ill intentions.

The sky hadn't yet brightened and the night hadn't yet departed. If Father had snuck out after midnight to set the net in the river, this would be the time he would go back to retrieve the fish and the net. Sometimes he'd stay there waiting for the fish to be caught. Sometimes he'd come home to rest in hopes of a more plentiful catch, but at the risk of having the unattended catch and gear stolen.

If he overslept and couldn't get up on his own, Mother would be his wake-up call—usually at dawn.

This morning Mother's internal alarm clock woke her up from a dreamless sleep. She heard Father's loud snoring. She was about to nudge him with her elbow when she detected the familiar dark form outside. The head chief's silhouette lurked by the water barrel and the hearthstone, less than five feet away. She shifted her body around in the manner of a sleeping child.

Mother eventually heard footsteps leaving our premises. She turned to make sure he was no longer there. She quickly broke into Father's snoring and told him about the chief. "Be extra careful today. The chief was just here snooping." Without saying much, Father quietly left to go to the river.

An hour had passed, and Father hadn't come back. The rising of the sun elevated our worry, as it had with his every trip. With every delay, we couldn't help feeling that his luck had run out.

The increasing brightness allowed us to search within our garden for plants to propagate. We'd unearth small shoots sprouting in a crowded space and transplant them somewhere else to grow and multiply. As we busied ourselves, we became consumed with anxiety. We would calm down only after Father's safe return.

As always, a pot of water was boiling over the fire in preparation for the catch. The vegetables had been washed and cut. A bucket of water had been positioned next to a tree stump being used as a cutting board. Hidden in the bucket was a knife to gut the fish.

An assembly line stood ready. We each had a part to play. I would usually remove the catch from the net, Nuy would clean the fish, and Mother would oversee the food cooking in the pot.

While waiting for Father, time evaporated like the water in the boiling pot. Mother poured an extra bowl of water to bring the level back up. She added more wood to the fire. We hunkered down by the flames and waited for Father to emerge with his bounty. It could be any moment now. Our ears were cocked to the road, filled with great anticipation; our mouths salivated.

As expected, we heard footsteps near the edge of our walkway which intersected the main road. Anticipating Father's arrival, we turned to look with expectant eyes, only to confront what we had feared most. The head chief must have sensed our sudden alarm. He walked straight up to us with speed and swagger. Sleep vanished from his eyes. Fear entered ours.

"Hmh, Mother Yeng, what's the pot for?" His inquiry sounded accusatory and threatening. "And where's Father Sann?"

Though we were caught by surprise, somehow instinct took over as we recovered from our initial shock. Now we behaved nonchalantly and put on indifferent and unreadable faces. I wore the face of a sleepy child forced to farm against her will.

"He's already left for camp," Mother explained.

"Really? And what's with the pot of boiling water then?" he continued asking with the same asperity. We understood his implication.

"It's for drinking and making soup," Mother pointed to the basket filled with heart-shaped leaves. They developed a slimy texture once cooked.

The water over the fire was boiling once again. It would be too obvious to let it keep bubbling. Right away Mother removed the pot and half emptied it into a smaller jug for drinking. She returned the pot back to the fire and emptied the leaves from the basket into it. A minute later she reduced the fire by pulling out a few burning sticks to snuff them in the sand.

The chief stood there watching us, as if he were mesmerized by the transformation of the vegetable soup, but we all knew his purpose: he was lingering for Father's return.

We silently prayed for Father not to come back—not just yet.

To make the chief feel uncomfortable, Mother told us that break time was over. "The soup is too hot," Mother directed. "Let's plant some more before we eat."

We obeyed and returned to the garden. Meanwhile, the chief followed us to the back yard and leaned against the hut to observe us.

"Mother Yeng, you have capable children," he broke into our silence.

She eagerly nodded before adding, "They work hard and sacrifice their sleep. This garden is really their doing."

Mother dropped her shovel and excused herself. She felt the unexpected urges of nature's messy call. On her way to the far end of the back yard, she broke big and small leaves in haste to punctuate its severity.

I sensed Mother's need to remove herself from having to carry on a conversation with the chief. She was discreetly trying to drive away the chief by making him feel uncomfortable. While she disappeared out of sight, Nuy and I continued digging and planting, but trepidation filled our every fiber and bones.

The chief turned to us and asked if we were tired and sleepy from having to wake up so early. We slowly turned to him with a what-do-you-think look, with the eyes of half-dead fish.

The chief sashayed from the wall to the trellises and roamed around the garden, leisurely inspecting the green chili peppers and the tiny tomatoes; then he stretched his body sideways to look out to the road. He bent his body back. From the corner of my eye, I could see him. He swung his head to observe our reactions. We continued our work as though we were untroubled by his presence. My eyes dared not follow the chief's toward the road because that would have been a dead giveaway.

Amid panicking, I managed to plant a small cassava sapling and rake the loose soil with my hands. I packed its roots in the moist earth, exposing the stalk and leaves to the air and sun. While my hands gently patted the soil, my eyes wandered over to Nuy, who was counting the pumpkin seeds to match the number of holes in the ground.

After the chief failed to gain our attention the first time, he overtly took a big step forward to find an unobstructed view of the road. The chief turned to look at us again, gauging our anxiety. My mind raced and concluded that today our luck would surely run out.

I continued to pray silently for Father's delay. I begged the gods, the spirits, and the power of the universe for an enormous miracle.

I wanted so much to run to the road to wait for Father and warn him, but I knew such an act would be self-incriminating. As I busied myself planting, I focused all my attention on the worms wiggling and burrowing in the soil. I admired the tiny plants, their roots, and their determination to grow. I marveled at the pumpkin seeds which Nuy was burying next to me. In a month their vines would sprawl, and in another two months the pumpkins would mature to the size of my head. My mouth watered just thinking of the orange flesh, and my nose could already sense its delicate bouquet.

I tried my hardest to remain distracted by the garden and to ignore the chief's presence, but most importantly, to refrain from looking out to the road.

The chief's milling around in our garden was approaching ridiculousness. He must have felt it, too, because he left soon after Mother returned from the bushes.

We exhaled a sigh of relief, but the familiar worry crept back in. "What's taking Father so long?" we wondered aloud.

About five minutes later Father appeared.

What delayed Father was his own doing. He had misplaced the fishing net. At first he jumped to the conclusion that it had been stolen again. His heart panged at the enormity of the loss: a loss so heavy, so irreplaceable, that it weighed him down to his knees. He should have waited by the net to prevent it from being stolen. He scolded and blamed himself for such carelessness as we later learned from him.

Father searched frantically for any net to replace the stolen one. He didn't care who it belonged to—if one was stolen from him, he felt he had the right to steal one back. It was a dog-eat-dog world: moral compass be damned.

He spent some time wading in the water but didn't come upon a net. The realization that he was searching in the wrong place sparked hope. This inadvertent mistake wasn't his first, and it wouldn't be his last.

When we saw Father rush down the walkway to our hut, we looked up to the sky with our palms together, saying "thank you."

24. THE BANE (CIRCA SEPTEMBER 1977)

It was late afternoon when we gathered under the tree at the meeting circle. This tree was lush and shady with easy to climb branches. A mandatory meeting was about to begin, but we were there early for another purpose. People were slowly arriving while I was in the tree picking its yellow fruit. Nuy was on the ground jumping up to grab and pull down the boughs so she, too, could help with harvesting. White Ghost and Black Ghost were busy retrieving half of the fruits that fell onto the ground from my poor aim. Our rowdy behavior alarmed a few people who were already there. They turned to each other first, as if holding a forum, before they yelled at us.

"The fruit's not edible! Stop picking them!" One man voiced the thoughts and consensus of many.

Mother nodded. "Then it should be strong enough to kill the worms in their bellies." She pointed at White Ghost and Black Ghost's ballooned stomachs.

The man said, "It might kill them first, before the worms do."

"I've no choice but to take such risk," she muttered.

After the meeting was adjourned, Mother bartered a clump of palm sugar to sweeten the bane. Nuy constantly stirred the pot and added wood to the fire. Already poison permeated the air and an unfamiliar toxicity assaulted the atmosphere, nauseating us with noxious fumes.

The contents in the pot began to thicken. The bubbles popped like mini volcanoes.

When the content cooled, Mother rolled small spoonfuls of it into balls the size of bird eggs.

Never once did I see her taste this concoction, as she normally would with any meal preparation.

To maximize the remedy's potency, Mother deprived us of dinner.

Nuy and I were given two balls each, while one and a half went to White Ghost and Black Ghost.

We obediently took the balls in our palms and popped them into our mouths. Instantaneously they offended our tongues. They were terribly bitter, and the palm sugar did little to disguise their awful taste. The concoction exploded with tingling irritation and the foul fruity-asphalt taste attacked our tongues. We chased the poison down with water, but our mouths were numbed with prickly sensations.

With all our might, we suppressed the urge to spit them back out. Mother admonished us to hold them in and reinforced the gravity of her seriousness with a piercing gaze.

White Ghost didn't fare well. Shortly after she swallowed, she retched. Mother cast a serious do-not-test-me look at her. White Ghost knew all too well Mother's impatience for insubordination.

She handed White Ghost another ball and a half, but she shook her head in a plea to forgo the disgusting compound. Mother's eyes searched for a hitting stick. White Ghost quickly relented by opening her palm to receive the bane. With bleary, wet eyes, she opened her mouth and redoubled her efforts in swallowing it yet again.

Within the hour, the poison seeped into our bloodstreams. My stomach started feeling strange, and my vision became drastically impaired. Everything turned blurry; nothing was solid nor still. The substance morphed and rendered familiar objects and faces into blotches and fireballs, all reeling in and out of focus, at times blinding us with blackness. The floor undulated beneath us, making us feel like we were drifting in water.

I lay next to my three moaning sisters, each of us a headless and limbless mass.

A raging headache surged inside my skull. The battle for dominance ensued as the pain in my head was mirrored by the torture churning inside my stomach.

I lost ownership of my body. The poison struck and annihilated the parasites. The worms turned stiff and hard. They felt like tiny nails being stapled to the insides of my intestines.

There were moments in which I didn't dismiss the possibility of Mother trying to kill us. After all, she had spoken so much about it that I thought she was executing it under the guise of killing the intestinal parasites. To make matters worse, Father wasn't home. My mind was easily led astray in his absence.

The pain dragged on and on and we tossed and turned, half in delirium and half in a comatose paralysis. My mind and body felt trapped in a kind of dazed purgatory, pushed and pulled, and thrust into the hallucinatory realm of pain and shadows. I was running from big snakelike monsters and from floating ghosts with white faces in black robes.

The worms churned and bellowed, expelling their toxins. They rumbled like angry thunderclaps. My insides felt stretched and coiled into a big knot, wrung by the force of thousands of tiny snakes. As the worms struggled against the poison, my body was forced to exhaust its last essence of life support. I grabbed my stomach and curled in a fetal position, begging for a miracle to end the suffering.

At this point I didn't care if I saw the next day or not: I just wanted it to be over.

Throughout the long night, I heard Mother's voice; garbled but near.

When morning finally dawned, Mother summoned us to rise and eat last night's dinner for breakfast.

My suspicious mind was soon put to rest and I was relieved to be alive. I swallowed the first bite of food and drank the first sip of water. This first dawn was a blur to me. I quickly ate and crawled back into my tiny space.

As the poison beckoned me back into a strange dimension, Mother forced the young ones to wake up. They moaned and groaned; then I passed out again.

Night came and we woke to Father and the smell of food. He had come back. We crawled to bed shortly after we finished our dinner. I was beginning to feel alive again. To gauge my wellness, I pinched my arm. I'd never thought of pain as an exquisite sensation until now.

On the second dawn, nature called the four of us into the far end of the back yard, all within the span of three hours. I was the third to discharge a mound of worms next to the other two. As I squatted, I already knew that over forty worms had come out of White Ghost and over thirty out of Black Ghost.

I discharged the parasites. After I finished, I came back to lie down.

I squeezed my stomach with both hands. It felt oddly empty: deflated, but in a foreign, yet familiar, way. I took many deep breaths and slowly fell back to sleep.

Father ventured to the far end of the bushes to count the worms. I had twenty-five, and Nuy had seventeen.

It was beyond my comprehension what prompted him to even bother counting the worms in our feces. His nearsightedness didn't help matters. To see clearly, he had to be a handbreadth away from the mounds. His action boggled our minds, but we chalked it all up to his eccentricity and his strange ways.

Only a few days ago, giant roundworms known as *Ascaris* had crawled out through my mouth and White Ghost's, as well.

My worms came out right after dinner, and White Ghost's in broad daylight. Two worms squirmed out and dangled from her mouth: it looked as if she were in mid-slurp of two long strands of noodles. She danced in fright with tears streaming as the worms swung from her mouth in midair. Her hand involuntarily yanked them out, half in fright and half in discomfort.

My throat almost joined her when I saw her plight. I had already experienced the gagging reflex a few nights ago. The worms had wiggled their way up my esophagus to my mouth. They were about one foot long. I quickly turned my face so I wouldn't have to see White Ghost's ordeal.

I was much in awe of Mother's insane methodology and her ability to heal us without killing us. How did wisdom or knowledge come to her with such ease? What possessed her to give us the poison which took us to the brink of death, only to yank us back to life? In a strange and bewildering way, I worshipped her, feared her, and loved her, all at the same time.

Not too long before we swallowed the poisonous fruit, Father woke abruptly from a vivid dream.

"*Sadok Sadom, Sadok Sadom.*" He kept on repeating the words when he shook Mother awake. "*Sadok Sadom, Sadok Sadom,*" he continued, chanting the words as she slowly opened her eyes. He told her of an old man with a long white beard in white clothes who held a cane.

The old man had come to Father a minute ago in his dream. "Child," he called Father. "Your children are in grave danger. They'll die soon if you don't do anything about the worms in their bodies. Please listen carefully. Find a Sadok Sadom tree and feed them the fruit. Please heed my advice. Remember the tree's name. . . *Sadok Sadom . . . Sadok Sadom . . . Sadok Sadom.*" The old man vanished into thin air as he shoved Father back into the realm of flesh and blood.

Mother ran down and began scribbling the word *"Sadok Sadom"* on the dirt with the tip of her finger. She knew the message was too precious to rely on the mind to recall. By writing it down repeatedly, the word engraved itself on her mind, her eyes, and her heart.

For the next several days, she made inquiries and chased the elusive words of the dream. Many told her that *Sdao* trees are everywhere, but the name *Sadok Sadom* was foreign to them.

"Never heard of it," they would say, or "Doesn't exist."

She followed every possible lead given by anyone who thought someone else was a bit more knowledgeable about plants, trees, and nature.

Finally, someone knew of its existence. He was a native man from a nearby village. He said there was such a tree in Phnum Sress, our village. How ironic that he led her to the tree I often perched on at the meeting circle. This fruit became as precious as gold after Mother used the bane to cure other dying children.

My cousins, Sida and Big Daughter, came to deliver bad news. They told us their parents were dying. Upon hearing this, the next day Father obtained permission from his new supervisor to visit them.

He was shocked to see his sister in such a skeletal form. Her head sank into her neck and her ears brushed against the protruding blades of her shoulders. She was nothing but skin and bones with a bloated stomach.

Uncle Rain appeared just as feeble and sick. Both of their bodies were swollen. Their listless expressions and grotesquely emaciated bodies stung Father's eyes into two misty pools.

The edema almost shared the smell and look of a rotting dead fish.

Uncle Rain tried to get up, but Father told him not to exert himself. Upon hearing her brother's voice, Aunt Khan opened her eyes to receive him. Father moved closer to his sister to peel away the layers of disease and starvation in search of the face he remembered. It had been more than six months since the siblings had seen one another in our village. Those six full moons eroded all that was recognizable of her.

Father continued to search, within that settling death, for the sister he had grown up with.

Finally there came a moment of recognition. At that angle he saw her once-youthful tenderness slowly ebbing away in the murkiness of her irises. In that flash of recollection, the fond memories of their childhood and adulthood flooded his senses. He was choked by an immense melancholy.

Their eyes remained fixed on one another as silence moved in to stop the beating of time. In this sacred stillness, both wondered how much of this reunion was real and how much was a figment of their imagination. The older sister extended her hand to her younger brother. He clasped her hand gently in his, like a clam protecting a precious pearl in the folds of its belly.

During their upbringing they had never once embraced nor even held hands. They only made contact when passing food at the dinner table, exchanging money, or sharing incense sticks when praying and bowing to the spirits of their ancestors. From their early childhood to their wedding days, to the birth of their children, and through many celebrations, their profound love and respect for each other had reawakened when their hands finally clasped under the terror of the Khmer Rouge. They felt the same blood pulsing through each other. The stillness had encapsulated their bond and placed it into the sacred well as a last memory.

Reality shortly broke their connection, telling them their synchronized heartbeats would soon stop. Instantly, the well of fond memories morphed into a well of deep sorrow, spilling silent tears down their faces.

Father eventually pulled himself together and uttered words of encouragement in his husky voice.

"Big Sis, you must fight hard to live," Father ordered her, pausing only to ease the pain in his voice. "Promise me that you won't give up! One day there'll be plenty of food to eat again. You must live for that day. You must live for Big Daughter and Sida. They need you. . .."

His sister's eyes welled up even more at the mention of her two remaining daughters. Through the windows of her eyes, Father saw defeat. "I'm not going to make it." She turned her eyes away from his. "It's already too late for me. My time is near, and he's not too far behind me, either." She was referring to Uncle Rain's weak health and mortality.

Father could sense her struggle to utter every word, her parting words. "Don't say that," Father told her tenderly as tears rolled down his face and caught in his throat. "There's always hope."

"My body's telling me otherwise," she said.

Father read his sister's thoughts, to which he quickly added: "We'll look after them." He was letting his sister know that Big Daughter and Sida could live with us when the time came.

She nodded knowingly and expectantly.

"Is there anything else I can do for you?" Father asked.

"Sugar," his sister blurted out. "I'd like to taste it one last time."

Father rushed back to the village. He reached out to the tall lanky man, who had helped build our hut, for palm sugar.

Upon receiving the sweet, he quickly stuffed it into his shirt and raced back to his sister.

My aunt bit into the sugar. She smiled at Father and thanked him profusely for granting her this last wish. She began to cry uncontrollably, saying how she'd wished Jon, Ti, Middle Daughter, and Tai could share this sweet with her. Father told her he would visit again with more treats. He commanded her again not to give up, but he could see the resignation in her once-bright eyes.

The day was almost over. Their last reunion ended all too soon as the sun slowly dipped below the horizon.

Father returned to us late that night and told us that his sister and brother-in-law wouldn't make it. He blew his nose in the dark. We were all saddened by the news as we struggled to fall asleep and lay in contemplative silence.

Aunt Khan soon became the sixth casualty. She departed this realm of suffering at age thirty-seven in December of 1977.

Out of nine people in their family, only three remained: Uncle Rain, Big Daughter, and Sida.

◆◆◆

Uncle Rain continued to hang on to life by a thin thread. His village of Tapan won third place for producing the most rice for China, our village of Phnum Sress received second place, and another village nearby won first place.

Meanwhile, the war slaves starved. Only five to seven cans of rice were allotted per hundred people per meal. I knew this because the rice porridge sloshing inside the kettle felt, looked, and tasted like water.

At meetings the children and adults were told how to respond when someone approached us with questions about our meals.

Two soldiers showed up in our hut after dinner.

"Did comrades enjoy dinner?"

"We did, thank you," we answered in unison.

"Did comrades have enough to eat?"

"Yes, we had plenty! Thank you."

"Would comrades like more rice?"

"No, thank you. We're full."

25. CAUGHT IN A WEB (CIRCA JANUARY 1978)

As an intermediary in the underground bartering system, Mother saw how riches were swapped between the new-people and the privileged old-people. Those who were once the bottom feeders rose to high ranks in this supposedly-classless society.

Sand and his wife, the woman with her chubby baby, were related to the head chief. Sand was the chief's oldest brother. With that kind of connection, it was no wonder they always had food to trade. Sand's wife, whose baby wore my sister's sweater, was living large and had the attitude of a prissy princess. Her collections of gold, jewelry, and precious stones grew in proportion to the dead around her.

The starving ones who had valuables would contact Mother to do the trade on their behalf.

She went to Sand's wife too often; but then again, she went to them all beyond her comfort level. Sometimes the counter offers were outrageously unreasonable.

"Five cans of rice for that bracelet," the wife haggled. The reason it didn't deserve ten cans was because she didn't love it as much.

Even when a ruby ring captured her heart, she'd still ask for a steep discount. Her eyes might widen at the sheer size and clarity of the stone, but she would still refuse to pay full price. The ring fit on her finger. Her mouth opened in astonishment as she outstretched her hand to marvel at the sparkling gem.

Sand's wife and Mother settled on eight cans, not ten—the full asking price—for the ring.

Mother delicately declined the five cans offered for the solid gold bracelet. She worried that the owner of the bracelet would strangle her, believing she had cheated them.

After she left the bracelet offer behind, she approached a few more people. The endless trekking, the daunting task of coming to agreement and arranging a transaction, and the constant anxiety of getting caught were part of her daily dose of stress.

As always, Mother was determined to find a buyer who would make the best offer. She knew their likes and dislikes: who fancied necklaces and adored bracelets and who liked everything but was three cans of rice short for the transaction.

She had to know everything, because it all meant survival.

She worked on multiple deals at once, before and after work, and during lunch and at dinner. She relayed counter offers between potential buyers and sellers.

Watches had become the hottest commodity in this egalitarian society. If any new-person still had one, he wouldn't dare walk around with it. Only those who reigned in this reverse class flaunted them shamelessly. They'd roll up their sleeves to showcase the watch on their wrist.

The fervor had even reached the chief's brother Sand. He, too, came to Mother.

If communism were a religion to the Khmer Rouge, wristwatches were their idols of worship.

Mother had been trying to fulfill Sand's request, with extreme urgency. A few full moons had lapsed, but the search was in vain.

An average timepiece with an automatic dial was worth five to ten times more than a solid gold bracelet, so it was in Mother's best interest (and ours) to satisfy Sand's desire. He had been pestering her for it since he had first approached her.

In desperation, she showed him two men's gold bracelets, hoping at least to divert his attention to something else as a way of buying time. He tried the bracelets on. He shook his head while observing his bedecked wrist. He looked to his wife and she, too, didn't fancy their styles, saying they were too gaudy or too feminine. He removed them and handed them back to Mother.

"If style is the issue, don't worry: I can find others that may suit you," she assured him.

"Sure, go ahead and show me more," replied Sand. "In the meantime, don't forget the watch."

She left Sand's place feeling optimistic, elated at the prospect that she might be able to profit from both a bracelet and a watch.

Mother came to Sand and his wife a few more times, bearing various pieces of jewelry. His wife was much easier to please than he was, although she drove a hard bargain. Sand was by far her toughest customer. She must have showed him well over a half dozen gold pieces.

Later she managed to gather three additional jewelry pieces at one time and was eager to show them to him first thing in the morning, anticipating the final payoff for her laborious search.

The following morning, she inserted the three bracelets into the folds of her waistband and headed in the direction of Grandma's place.

After she showed Sand the bracelets, instead of talking business, he went to summon the head chief, his brother.

"Mother Yeng, you're an opportunist who's gone too far!" yelled the chief. "Hoarding all the riches and refusing to relinquish them to collectivism is a serious crime, punishable by death."

Mother became deathly frightened. For the moment, her mind rejected this reality. It leaped and bounded into the safety of denial, suspended somewhere else and uncommitted to the present.

"Mother Yeng, have you heard a word I said?" the chief roared at her while she turned to the voice with a hollow look. Mother took in a deep breath. As she inhaled, her mind began to register the danger she was in.

"You're to be taken away, to be whacked and dumped," repeated the chief. She refused this ending. Her life hadn't come to its final chapter yet, even though it appeared to be written in stone. Her fate might have been sealed, but her mind escaped to the moon and stars.

"Mother Yeng, look at me! Your days are numbered. Mark my words."

Her mind had swung back to reality. Mother reluctantly accepted her fate. After all: though she had been warned before, she'd never planned on getting caught. She should have trusted her intuition and that uncomfortable feeling she felt around Sand. She had sensed his strong dislike of her; she should have heeded her conscience as well as the advice from trusted friends. Both Mother Lei and the lady with the sensitive bladder had warned her to keep her distance from Sand. These women had cautioned her about his deep-seated jealousy of her ability. Her god-like elusiveness as an intermediary taunted him. Because none of us had succumbed to death, we were living proof of her greatness; but Sand and the head chief were determined to take her down.

Our wholesomeness mocked Sand even though his own family was equally unscathed by death. In his eyes, we were inferior and should suffer the same loss as the others. We were neither old-people nor Khmer people. He grunted and hissed beneath his breath at our fortune.

Only now Sand had found a way to make us miserable. Mother knew she had fallen into his trap and knew without a doubt that he was determined to have her permanently removed.

"I don't possess any gold," Mother tried to reason. "Everyone knows I'm just a go-between. The most I profit is a can of rice, if that."

"No need to explain yourself," Sand yelled at her. "The evidence is in your hand." He looked to the chief, who nodded eagerly in approval.

It became clear to her these two brothers had banded together to destroy her.

She was convinced that once they terminated her, they would easily confiscate our prized garden. The chief and his brother had much to gain from our loss.

Mother thought they could have easily arranged an under-the-table deal with any new-people who would be more than willing to pay a hefty sum of gold to reap the fruits of our agricultural labor.

That morning Mother continued to plead for mercy with the head chief and Sand, appealing to their good nature, only to confirm they were full of malice. She even begged his wife, but she ignored Mother completely.

The chief sent someone to report her illegal conduct to the Khmer Rouge. By midmorning, news had spread about her imminent demise.

It reached me with a tap on my shoulder. I turned to see Mother Lei's concerned face.

That morning, while Mother was helplessly caught in a web of deceit, I was out and about exploring, oblivious to the gloom awaiting us. That day the bulk of the domestic responsibilities shifted back to my older sister. It was understood that on days her youth work group didn't have to work, Nuy was to resume her duties at home, relieving me of the burden.

That day I was one of the first children in line for lunch. According to the rule, children were to be served first and, supposedly, we were to have a thirty-minute head start before the adults came charging in from the fields. Even this early, I was maybe the fifth person in line. The children in front of me had been waiting all morning long: I could tell this from their restlessness. They were about my size, and I recognized most of them. After all, we swam in the same water and stood in the same line for food every day; but I didn't know them nor their parents by name—families seldom ate lunch together; only on special occasions could they afford such privilege.

Someone urgently tapped me on my shoulder. I turned around and saw Mother Lei's face, grave with apprehension. She pulled me out of line. Mother always spoke highly of her, praising her as one of the kindest and most sincere people in the world. "She's a pure Buddhist at heart," Mother would say.

We stepped away from the line. When we stopped, she turned me around to face her. "Geng, you need to tell your grandma that your mother's in serious trouble."

In that brief instant, I didn't grasp the enormity of her message. The word "serious" could mean many things. She must have read my blank stare because she rephrased it bluntly: "Your Mother's getting whacked and dumped." She dragged a forefinger across her throat, the universal sign for murder.

Although I was listening closely, nothing in the world could have prepared me for this development. I was beyond shocked. My jaw dropped as she pantomimed Mother's death. I was paralyzed by the news and was dazed in disbelief. Mother Lei shook me by the shoulders. "Go now!" She pointed eastward for me to run to Grandma's.

At first I ran toward the bend, half hidden behind the low brush, where my siblings and Grandma were expected to appear; but then I changed course and headed toward Mother's sewing station, hoping to find her there. About a half mile later I reached the sewing station, but she was nowhere to be seen. A sense of doom flooded my entire body and my heart pounded even faster as the pumping adrenaline gave me strength to race on to Grandma's.

I left the sewing station immediately and ran eastbound. Along the way, two soldiers leisurely patrolling the road hollered at me to slow down. I ignored them and ran with all the energy and speed my short legs could muster. Everything whisked by like a dream caught up in a nightmare. Midway through my journey, I began having abdominal cramps. I slowed down and grabbed my stomach in pain. I slogged painfully to Grandma's hut, and my mind unleashed horrible images of Mother's capture. I imagined her locked up like Uncle Jo, her hands and legs shackled as she sat in a jail. I pictured her being whipped into unconsciousness with blood seeping through her torn clothes like Skinny Wife. My mind was so overwhelmed by those images that I had to breathe deeper and walk slower to pull myself together so I could tolerate the pain.

A huge void grew in me at the thought of losing Mother forever. I turned my head to the left to look at the imposing mountain. My eyes became misty, and I fought hard to keep the tears from falling.

The blue sky and the slow-drifting clouds over the mountain contrasted with the stark emotions swelling within me. Here on the road I struck a deal with my soul and the invisible spirits of the universe. My heart murmured to the winds and begged them to save Mother. I went further, for good measure, making an offer of sacrifice as I told the gods and the spirits to take me instead and to spare her. I told them with remorse how I didn't mean it when I wished Mother dead. I was simply angry with her and couldn't think straight. I begged for their forgiveness: I sincerely loved her, and I felt that love intensely and deeply. I would gladly die for her. Whatever bravery and restraint I had in the past were now dissolved into tears. I just wanted Mother back. I wanted her to return safely to us.

For the next few hours I searched and sought people for information. I was dazed and afraid and had forgotten all about lunch. Around late afternoon, we all converged at home, anxiously waiting for news of her whereabouts. Only when dinner was ready and Nuy handed me the kettle to fetch our meal did I finally feel hungry.

It didn't come as a surprise this time when Mother didn't receive her ration. Food was the last thing on my mind. All I saw, repeatedly, was her beheading. I hauled five ladlefuls instead of six, that night. Upon arriving home, I was shocked and surprised to see her. For that moment, I truly believed the gods had heard my plea and honored my offering.

I handed the kettle to Nuy, who was busy preparing dinner by the front of the hut. I was so thankful to have her as my elder sister. Gray smoke from the hearth swirled upward into the night. She was boiling a pot of sour vegetable soup using watermelon rind and lily stalks. I should have helped her prepare dinner, but instead I charged right up to the corner of the hut and sat across from Mother and Father. Black Ghost was sitting on Mother's lap and White Ghost was sitting near them both.

I caught Mother's last phrase as I was sitting down.

"Mother Lei and others said that they will come for me tomorrow." She stared blankly into a corner, then shrugged with an absent-minded frown. Her blank gaze shifted downward to her hands where they were gently rubbing Black Ghost's shoulder blades. She continued, "They said that I was lucky to come back tonight."

I interrupted her. "Mother, where were you? I was looking everywhere for you! Did they take you away and chain you up like Uncle Jo?"

She shook her head and again formed an empty frown. "I was mostly with the chief and Sand, defending myself." They had dispatched an informant to summon the Khmer Rouge, but no one knew why the soldiers had failed to show up to escort her away. After waiting indefinitely, the chief had sent her back to work. "By then the news of my imminent demise had reached everyone. A few cried, just thinking of the small children I'd leave behind."

Mother talked as if she were disconnected and removed from the story: as if, when tomorrow came, death would claim some other unfortunate soul. She was still in shock, I could tell, and she refused to accept that tonight would be her last night.

Part of me believed she would be killed tomorrow and the other part hoped for a miracle to spare her life. Again, I silently and fervently prayed for deliverance and offered myself up to take her place.

I sat there listening, numb and exhausted but wide awake.

"Mother, what if you're really gone tomorrow?" I asked her flat out. "What'll we do then?" The dazed look on her face vanished. She seemed strangely unperturbed and untroubled, but she was shortly absent again. We sat there, waiting for her to come back to us.

I searched the faces around me, trying to understand how they were taking it all in. I wondered if everyone felt the same overwhelming sense of loss. The sun had already sunk and darkness had crept in when the sorrow within me turned my family's faces into the faces of mourners. Father's face appeared sad, but in a resigned and stoic way. Perhaps he was mentally preparing himself for the solo journey of keeping five children alive and wondering if he could do it alone.

Nuy was solemn as she walked up and down the stairs bearing food to our eating corner. The fact that she didn't ask me to help her with food preparation spoke clearly of our dire circumstances. White Ghost's face was noticeably sunken; she sat quietly listening and not making a peep. Black Ghost slouched on Mother's lap as if she, too, sensed an undertone of melancholy.

My eyes wandered back to Mother. The silent ticking of time pulled down yet another curtain of darkness, preparing for the moon and the stars to appear. As the night turned black, my heart became weighed down by unbearable grief and my eyes were transformed into two overflowing ponds. I turned slightly aside to wipe away the tears.

We sat quietly. Although we were within arm's reach of one another, our thoughts were so distant that we didn't see the food Nuy served.

Mother's blank gaze disappeared, and she finally returned to us. She took a long deep breath followed by a long exhale, a sign of defeat.

"I'm not afraid of dying. I welcome an end to this misery."

I managed to nod, realizing I was also accepting her death. With this acceptance came the images of Mother's final seconds on earth. Two men brandishing rifles would lead her somewhere remote. They would kick her legs to force her down on her knees. She would stare unflinchingly at the pre-dug hole as she extended her neck for a quick death. With a spade in hand, a soldier would jump up to strike her with all his might.

It was a somber night. Even the cicadas and crickets sang the tune of our hearts' heaviness. We grieved and lamented in our own silent ways. Deep down we were hoping it would prove an empty threat. It felt like we were in a nightmare trapped inside a dream, and we couldn't escape the void to find the light.

Mother wore a mask of absence and indifference, as if she had already been separated from us. She caressed Black Ghost's gaunt cheek in an unusual way. Her hands gently touched the sunken part of her face, as if gauging how much time would pass before Black Ghost would join her in the afterlife. White Ghost walked over to her to be loved for the last time, too. Mother looped her hand around her waist before she pecked her cheek and ruffled her stubby head.

Mother's tenderness toward my younger sisters caused more tears to pool in my eyes. I felt too old to be hugged and caressed by her, yet my body yearned for her touch, at least this once. I couldn't recall the last time she'd shared the same warmth with me. The countless months of hardship had created an ocean of distance between us. It'd be too awkward to hug her now. I sat across from her with tear-stained cheeks, wondering if she could feel my sadness and if she knew that I loved her unconditionally.

That night, with each bite of food, I was reminded that this would probably be our last meal with Mother. The soup was tasteless and it was difficult to swallow, even though I hadn't eaten all day.

This was how our hearts bid goodbye: solemnly and awkwardly, with the uncertainty and fear of the dark surrounding us.

26. A NEW MASTER (CIRCA JANUARY 1978)

In the morning we woke up to discover that both Mother and Father were already gone. Shortly after, Nuy left for her youth brigade. My two younger sisters left by themselves to go to Grandma's.

I was home alone and uncertain if I should continue my chores because I was in a state of abject terror.

Shortly after everyone left, the familiar sound of gunfire riddled the village once more: a sound which took me back to the forced evacuation. This time it wasn't the sound of rifles emptying shells into the air, but rather the sound of men firing into each other's flesh, the sound of men battling to the death. The wind ushered voices of panic, uncertainty, ambush, and of change to our village. I thought that if I were to step out onto the road, I would be caught in the crossfire of bullets ricocheting nearby.

Despite the danger, I rushed over to Grandma's place. The road was empty, but the gunfire sounded so close. I looked around first before stepping out, and I did not see a single Khmer Rouge; it was as if they had all abandoned their posts to engage in the crisis at hand.

When Mother returned home, we learned there was a new Khmer Rouge group in town, a change in management. A new faction called Beyorp had destroyed the old faction, Nerady.

Everything felt surreal: the arrival of the new faction couldn't be a coincidence. The higher powers had granted me my wish! My heartfelt prayer had entreated the universe and spirits to rescue Mother, and I was certain it had happened.

A few days later, the new faction was everywhere. The new soldiers were clad in black just like their predecessors, but unlike the previous faction, this group didn't wear red sashes on their upper arms. Although it was a minute change in appearance, the subtleties meant the world to us, especially to Mother.

Mother shaved her head this time as a gesture of humility and a new beginning. The Khmer Rouge were busy killing each other and were not at the chief's disposal, to deal with her swiftly.

Suddenly the names Nerady and Beyorp assaulted my ears. This new faction came to "clean house," and we, the war slaves, rejoiced.

Beyorp rallied all the village leaders to sit around a mound of jewels. They were praised for a job well done and were told to pick out a piece of jewelry as their reward. Many leaders, including our head chief, saw this was a trick and thus behaved humbly and did not touch anything. They removed and executed the few who selected an item from the bounty.

They told us that the new faction pursued the corrupt and the power-mongers. We even attended a meeting to hear its pledge to protect and serve the people. The Beyorp soldiers were our liberators and our suffering was unnecessary. They apologized to all of us and promised a perfect utopia from now on.

With the new faction in place, the chief and his brother Sand stopped their accusations and left Mother alone.

At first we wanted to believe that Beyorp was a kind and benevolent faction: how could the group not be better than Nerady? Our assumption caused our behavior to become brazen. I had the audacity to venture into the cornfield behind our hut and bring back a basketful of corn to cook, in broad daylight. Grandma also became brave. Despite her previous capture for stealing corn and her torture with fire ants, she harvested from a nearby cornfield under the moon and walked out with a bucketful.

Uncle Tek stole and killed a pig. We ate in abundance to make up for our prior deprivation.

The same happened to Uncle Rain, who still lived a couple of villages away. He, too, stole and slaughtered a pig. He and his two daughters ate for the six family members who'd died from starvation.

We were beginning to feel normal again and our spirits recharged.

But our new benevolent rulers quickly made it clear that they disliked our thievery. Stealing did not belong in a perfect utopia. Even though they spared Mother her life, our tormentors in the village of Phnum Sress were essentially the same, and eventually our chief and his brother reverted to their old ways, heartless and psychotic. Greed and corruption thrived once again. The chief turned his eyes back to our garden.

The only one who changed was Mother. Her underground operation came to a screeching halt and she became the cornered creature that couldn't bite back.

The vigilance of the new faction deterred Father from going to the water for fish.

The garden was our only subsidy. Compared to others, we still had a lot; however, our situation became so dire that our escape plan became more urgent—but Mother reconsidered. She refused to run away. She knew that once captured, our deaths would be absolute. The Khmer Rouge didn't allow redemption and forgiveness. Worse yet, the chief and his brother would ensure we would never return alive. If we were to be successful in our escape, the chief and his brother would be relentless in tracking us down. No one knew if the situation on the other side was better than here. Escaping west to Thailand was an impossible feat due to the long distance. District Three, which lay south of District Five, was our only viable option: we had no choice but to risk it all. Mother was scared, indeed, after her close call with execution.

A plan had already been set in motion. Uncle Jo, Uncle Rain, and Father had been in contact, leaving Mother out completely because they didn't want to be dissuaded by her.

The three men worked out the logistics. They agreed on a time, a date, and a designated place—two rendezvous points, in fact. It was a thunderous, rainy day when Uncle Rain came to our hut for the last time. Ironically, it always seemed to be rainy and stormy when he visited us.

Father and Uncle Rain stood and talked under the edge of the roof with their voices muffled by the angry sky. Their bodies were drenched as they conversed. Shortly after Uncle Rain left, Mother returned.

Mother roared at Father. She was loud, even louder than the thunder. I was thankful that the sound of the heavy rainfall and roaring sky drowned out our disagreements. "You go ahead without me. I'm not leaving this place!"

"Don't be like this. We have to escape, or at least die trying." Father attempted to reason with her.

"My mind's already made up. Ask the children to pick sides: stay with me or go with you. Let them decide."

My family was splintered in the same way the lightning had recently struck a tree in our back yard and ripped it into two pieces.

I sat in a corner, resting my face on my knees and contemplating the choice I would soon have to make. I already knew the answer.

I always knew the answer. Their tension and disagreement over running away was old news. Uncle Rain's visit was mostly about escaping, but the moon and stars had failed to align themselves for us to commit the deed. Often, half of us were away at labor camp, thus we were never whole enough to disappear together. The other factor was the floodwaters. All of us would have to be excellent swimmers and in great health to survive the five- to ten-mile stretch of water.

This time around, there was a strong sense of finality of our departure and separation. Even if the moon and stars were a on collision course, there was no turning back.

Melancholy settled in me, for I knew Black Ghost and White Ghost would remain with Mother because of their ages and their inability to swim. I was ashamed of how readily I chose to side with Father. Mother's heart of stone and her innate ability to keep us alive lost to Father's blindness. My conscience refused to die. Father would need me to navigate a way through the unknown. I was willing to go with him to the end.

We never conversed among ourselves as to whose side we would choose: we were afraid that once we said it, our bond would be forever broken. Luckily it remained intact; for in the end we didn't have to choose sides.

Mother had an unusual dream. She dreamed of her wedding day, where everyone was smiling and laughing. She took this to be a good omen that the spirits were telling her to go with us. She began our escape preparations in earnest.

It was early April of 1978, exactly three years after the forced evacuation, when my parents reconciled a few nights before we vanished from the village. Their coming together as husband and wife was so rare that they were able to exactly date the time of our escape—because nine months later, another baby came into our desolate world.

27. FUGITIVES (CIRCA APRIL 1978)

"*Wake up*... wake up... time to go."

It was around one in the morning when our parents pulled us from our sleep. In the dark, we silently grappled with our pre-assigned bundles we were taking with us. Weary and afraid, we headed east first to make sure Grandma's place was empty, and then we walked south, with the huge lake to our left.

We couldn't bring much of the essentials with us. The much-needed mosquito net remained inside the hut. We used blankets, baskets, and pots to form some semblance of human shapes sleeping inside the net. This was our effort to conceal the absence of our bodies. The night breeze gently swayed the mesh, giving the illusion of someone stirring from within. If one were to stand by the stairs, one would not notice the vacancy inside until sunrise.

I carried a pack of our three best blankets. Vunn carried a pot, and in it were a few bowls and utensils, cooked yams and cassavas, and a jar of honey which Father obtained by smoking a huge beehive in the bamboo forest at the same spot where he and Uncle Rain had previously extracted a honeycomb.

Father also melted and reshaped most of the jewelry with the use of a hammer and a tiny cast iron pan over a scorching fire in the back yard. We were on the lookout while he heated the gold and hammered it into an oblong shape bigger than his thumb.

We all knew where the gold was hidden. His strides were awkward. He often paused to grasp the seat of his trousers to shove the gold back inside. Each time he sneezed, it launched like a torpedo out of his rear end. He wore a perpetually constipated expression. All of this would seem comical in another time and another place, but tonight it was about pure survival. We were all at risk. Mother and White Ghost each carried a bundle proportional to their sizes. The vinyl floor mat was atop Nuy's head and Black Ghost was in Father's embrace as we set out.

Our steps were extra quiet as we threaded our way out of District Five. We knew our own carelessness could invite death. Rodents scampered and snakes slithered quietly into the reeds. The moon was majestic. Its imposing roundness hovered almost directly above our heads. The invisible wispy clouds intermittently disrupted the luminescence. Should we detect any moving silhouette, we were to drop to the ground.

We forded a river. Its water reached my neck. At times I found it easier to float than to wade. I kept the blankets dry by raising them above my head. Because of her light body, Black Ghost now clung to Mother, leaving White Ghost's heavier weight to Father. White Ghost perched on Father's shoulders as we journeyed through the moving waters.

We crossed beyond the familiar boundaries into fields that seemed to stretch endlessly into the edge of the void. White Ghost was now walking on her own. Black Ghost was bouncing in Father's arms. We climbed up and down the dikes dividing the rice fields into gigantic squares.

The connected fields hindered our speed. We were five to seven miles from District Three. We had to circumvent the lake and backwater, climbing up and down the connected rice paddies and embankments: it took much longer than it should have. As we ventured farther, the dikes rose higher. Our hands reached and pulled for one another when we clambered up, and we held on tightly for support when we dropped down the dikes. We felt much safer when we had disappeared in the field but felt exposed and vulnerable when we reappeared on the causeway. These fields were mostly barren with brown dirt. Farming tools were left scattered in the field from the previous day's work. Seven bodies tirelessly hurdled through the fields, which looked like one endless giant checkerboard, racing against time.

Uncle Rain, Uncle Jo, and Father, however, were familiar with the layout of the fields. They had worked hard, dredging the soil during the canal building to redirect the flow of water. They cultivated the land while soldiers were roaming around holding guns and cracking whips. Their collective knowledge of the landscape would have given us comfort had the three men been together. Unfortunately, the escape plan included parting and regrouping at two future rendezvous points. We were to meet up with Aunt Sing, Grandma, Uncle Jo, and his son Rern at a specified location, and then Uncle Rain and his two daughters would arrive at another site.

We relied solely on Father to navigate our path. After climbing in and out of many fields and taking shortcuts by going diagonally through deep trenches, we became somewhat disoriented. Father had difficulty leading us out of the maze, with his impaired vision. It was hard to find any bearing at night because the fields fell off into the fringes of blackness.

Hopelessness and frustration were reflected in Father's stride. We followed closely, though we tried not to pressure him. We kept quiet while our hearts raced in panic. We backtracked and climbed the same dikes repeatedly because Father had lost his way.

Our eyes darted in all directions, searching, probing, and analyzing our surroundings for both danger and safety. We looked over our shoulders in panic, thinking the Khmer Rouge were chasing us.

Eventually we emerged from the endless rice fields to a vast clearing of hedges, low brush, and reeds. In the open, we spotted a handful of horses eating grass. They snorted and neighed to warn each other of intruders.

The dry riverbanks of the low country provided little coverage for us to remain hidden.

Occasionally the clouds dimmed the moonlight. Our pace quickened as our trepidation soared. Each passing second put us closer to exposure and a few feet nearer to danger. Fate took control, now. My heart pounded in my throat. The night air fell upon us, warm and muggy, as we traversed the earth with the foreboding feeling that we might never reach safety.

The seconds turned to hours and the distance grew to three or four miles from the start of our journey before we reached the designated point marked by a wall of mangroves, palms, and a few other scattered trees.

No one was there. Uncle Jo's group hadn't yet arrived. It could mean two things: they had been captured, or they were running late. We knew it would take Grandma longer to get here. Her health had been declining since the snake bite, and every so often she needed to sit or rest. She was always at the edge of exhaustion.

During the wait, we heard the loud neighing and urgent galloping of horses. Our anxiety elevated tenfold, and instantly we sought cover in the shadows of the mangrove bushes and crouched behind trees. Before the spirited steeds came into clear view, my self-induced paranoia leapt to the worst conclusions: I was convinced the Khmer Rouge were on horseback, aiming their guns at us.

Relief swept our moonlit faces like a balmy breeze when we saw two wild four-legged beauties arrive, playful and alone.

Now at ease, we gazed around and found a dry bowl of rice positioned on a banana leaf in front of a small cluster of palm trees. Judging from the brown banana leaf used as a placemat for the bowl, the rice was perhaps two weeks old. A half-burned incense stick had been erected in the middle of the rice. It appeared to be a sacred offering by someone in mourning, and despite the smallness of the offering, I could feel the tremendous weight of its sacrifice. What a waste of food, I thought. Why would someone be willing to feed the dead while the living starved? We didn't take the bowl of rice for fear of upsetting the spirits. Tonight, of all nights, we needed their blessings and protection.

Vunn walked out from behind the tree with two chunks of burned, crisped rice in his hands: another offering to the spirits, it seemed, but less extravagant because they came from the bottom of the pot. He kept the bigger chunk for himself while offering the smaller piece to us. It was roughly the size of my palm. Nuy and I both rushed to it, but I snatched it a millisecond faster.

Tiny black ants could be seen crawling in and out of the crust. We smacked them violently to shake them off. I broke the rice crust in two and gave a piece to Nuy. We ignored the few stubborn ants and began chewing. It was like munching on cardboard.

Both Black Ghost and White Ghost were fatigued, and they collapsed over the bundles. My parents blended in with the shadows next to the mangroves. They were whispering to each other. In the open field the two horses snorted loudly before galloping away to play elsewhere.

We soon noticed a tiny silhouette among three bigger shapes heading our way. Right away we knew it to be our long-awaited family. Amid our excitement and relief in our reunion, we had to press onward into the unknown; for fugitives must remain on the move or risk being captured. Mother had to disrupt Black Ghost and White Ghost's temporary rest.

We threaded through the fields in silence for another hour or two. The dimmed landscape slowly changed from wild reeds and grass to wild water spinach, twisting and clambering to the height of my waist.

It was now past four o'clock in the morning, and we decided to rest for a couple of hours to regain our strength.

Mother quickly unfurled the blanket and vinyl mat so we could lie down.

I lay on a blanket with Nuy. The water spinach caressed our bodies and they limited our peripheral vision to only the moon. I was too tired to even feel afraid.

Dawn broke through the sky as soon as I shut my eyes. Suddenly, Father crawled over to us on his stomach. Our legs were brushing and rustling against the water spinach.

"Shhh! Don't move!" Father whispered the urgency of a serious threat with a finger on his mouth. "There are people out there! Maybe Khmer Rouge! Lie low!"

At the mention of Khmer Rouge, paralysis swept through me and I stopped breathing. In the stillness, our ears detected a group of men bantering with each other as their feet tramped through the field. My anxiety ramped up as their treads grew louder. Their laughter had quickly ceased, but not their movements, as they thrashed their paths with sticks and machetes to ward off snakes.

As luck would have it, they soon veered away and no longer headed in our direction.

Our breathing became normal again as their voices drifted farther away. Slowly, one by one, our heads popped up to see the receding figures shrinking away in the distance. We remained uncertain if they were commoners or Khmer Rouge.

Fright stirred us into restlessness and no one could fall back to sleep. We were feeling more hungry than fatigued. The little food we had packed in the pot and the water in the canteen were soon depleted. Mother contemplated an alternative to end our hunger and thirst. She instructed Uncle Jo and Vunn to fetch firewood. Meanwhile, a few of us girls busily broke the most delicate part of the water spinach. We quickly placed a pot over the small fire, started by a tiny lighter. We seasoned it with a dab of honey. It was mostly water and empty calories.

◆◆◆

After our short meal, we remained hidden in the water spinach. The sun was levitating slowly in the eastern sky. We cautiously crossed to the edge of the field where shrubs and trees concealed our presence. To my surprise, I saw a paved road.

The adults observed the road carefully to see if it was secure to traverse. We had made it safely to District Three. We did not rejoice because we still worried about being captured or forced to turn back to District Five by roaming Khmer Rouge soldiers.

We remained hidden from the empty road behind trees and bushes, biding our time. Soon the road began flowing with wayfarers and oxcarts. Vagrant travelers like us and natives came out of nowhere and headed in various directions. We found comfort in the flow of masses trickling into street traffic. With that sense of safety and fitting in, we emerged from the bushes to continue our journey. Shortly, we regrouped with Uncle Rain, Big Daughter, and Sida, and soon we arrived in Dalam. Residents there didn't welcome the throngs of homeless flocking to their district. They saw us homeless folks as a dead weight, ones who would eat their food and starve their already-deprived children. "Go back," they said. "There's not enough food here, either. We have suffered enough! You coming here is like a nail in our coffin."

Going back wasn't an option, so we pressed onward. We knocked on the doors of strangers for food, only to be shooed away.

Eventually we encountered a kind old man and his old wife, who didn't have the heart to say no to us hungry children. They fed us their porridge and watched us lick their bowls and spoons. They told us that many people in District

Three had suffered casualties the last few years. Life hadn't been kind to them either. If we had shown up earlier, they wouldn't have been as generous and giving.

The adults demonstrated to us how to thank the old couple for their generosity. We took turns approaching them, pressing our palms together, and bowing our heads slightly, saying, "Thank you for your kindness."

At one rest stop, we came upon another spiritual offering. Someone had discreetly placed a bowl of rice atop a tree. Big Daughter found it and she was thrilled. The rice was dry and hard, but she was a smart girl. She took out a familiar jar, the same one we had given her family a while back to hide salt in the fish sauce. This time the jar stored water. She took a swig before pouring it over the stale rice. She then handed me the jar so I could take a drink. The water reeked of stinky fish sauce, but I was too thirsty to decline. Big Daughter swirled the bowl in a circular motion to soak the rice in the water. About five minutes later, she and Sida ate the rice faster than I was able to count my fingers and toes.

By the time we arrived at another village, it was already past noon. We sought the village chief to ask for food. "We have leftover rice." The chief pointed his finger to a big pot on the table next to him. "Let me find someone to make porridge out of it so you won't choke on it. I've seen too many people die from eating solids after starving for too long."

A lady came to scrape the rice from the bigger pot into a smaller one. She set the smaller pot over the burning fire and poured a small bucket of water into it. Already I could tell that the porridge would be dense and hearty. She then returned to the big pot to scrape the crust off the bottom. Chunk after chunk of golden rice crusts came loose. To see such bounty was unreal. It was as if we had landed in another world. Our eyes bulged out of their sockets and we salivated like a pack of mongrels. The lady turned to the chief. Her eyes silently sought his guidance; for she found it difficult to refuse us.

"They can have it after they eat their porridge," said the chief, addressing her concern.

That lunch was the best meal we'd had in months. The rice crust was a slice of paradise—crunchy, fresh and tasty.

This chief insisted that we rest for the night. We happily obliged.

He guided us to an empty hut nearby. That evening we joined the mess hall for dinner. We each ate a bowlful of rice. It was more than we could have dreamed. We were accustomed to sharing less than a bowl of cooked rice in a gallon of water among seven mouths.

By the time dinner was over, we children begged our parents to remain in this village without even knowing its name. The adults, too, wanted to settle here. They saw possibility and potential in this town.

Unanimously, the adults approached the kind chief. To our surprise, he welcomed all of us to be a part of his collective unit; however, by noon the next day we were on the road again.

The reason had to do with Mother's dream. The dream was essentially the same, except this time she was not smiling on her wedding day. She interpreted this unhappiness as a bad omen.

The adults were at war with one another. My two uncles were the most furious with Mother. They wanted to stay. Father was neutral, which further enraged them because they took it as a sign of indecision, a weakness in a man who deferred to his wife.

Everyone was in discord and the chief angrily dismissed us with a look of disgust. "Beggars can't be choosers!" The chief, sounding much like he was insulted, began to yell. "I don't have time for ungrateful people! Good luck to you all! Now, get out of my face!" He chased us away with a wave of his hand.

Mixed emotions swept through us as we walked away. This might have been the best place for us, but somehow we had turned it down. The loads we carried felt unusually heavy as we became vagrants once again. The regrets of not staying in this village grew as we encountered difficulty in finding refuge elsewhere. We were still homeless three days after we left the kind chief.

Many of us harbored resentments toward Mother. Uncle Rain and Uncle Jo, especially, were in the forefront of the cold war against her.

Along the way, we witnessed a man die from eating too much. One minute he and his daughter ate with us in a mess hall; then the next he collapsed as he stood up to walk. His daughter, who was about my age, threw her body over his and wailed. A few locals rushed over to console her.

One man was quick to ask the right questions, for the look of the dead man said it all. "He hadn't eaten solid food in a while, right? And he ate just a moment ago?" The girl nodded yes to both questions.

"Are you alone?"

The girl nodded again.

"Don't worry. . . we'll take care of you."

"At least he died full," another voice echoed. "He was luckier than most."

As the days wore on, faces of strangers or other vagrants who were equally lost and desperate for food and shelter became familiar. Although we were all displaced, we considered ourselves more fortunate than the Vietnamese family of five we encountered. This family wasn't fluent in the Khmer tongue. They found it difficult to approach strangers for food and shelter because many villagers would throw them out like stray dogs. How they'd survived this long was beyond our comprehension, and we never knew how many of their family had already perished.

The Vietnamese family approached Father for help. They followed along with our group for several days. Every time we stopped somewhere to beg for food, I would see Father include them in our group's total headcount. Instead of fourteen, he would say nineteen. It was hard not to see it as his chance at penance—a chance to redeem his soul and our souls for not preventing our Chinese-Vietnamese neighbors,

Didi and Wonhing, from being massacred. This guilty conscience was alive and breathing in the deepest recesses of all our minds.

This time I saw Father's resolve to save the Vietnamese family, but he couldn't help them after we arrived in Ou Tom, or Big River. It wasn't for lack of effort on his part: he approached the new chief on their behalf, seeking the same treatment for them as had been granted to us.

Chief Sern looked at Father in astonishment. He was bewildered and moved at the same time. "You mean to tell me you're trying to save others when you and your family are drowning? Don't get yourself entangled like dead shrimp! Consider yourself lucky that I'm willing to risk my life for your family. You have no right to jeopardize mine!"

Father thanked the new chief for his benevolence, although he couldn't help feeling scalded by his words.

Map 4: Big River

28. THE BIG RIVER VILLAGE (APRIL 1978 TO DECEMBER 1978)

Life regained a sense of peace and normalcy in Big River less than two weeks after we left District Five. Our acceptance in the village had transformed Mother into a warmer, happier person. There was no need for her to play various roles to ensure our survival. She gladly worked in the fields. The chief assigned her to work in the communal kitchen later, which freed her to care for Grandma and the young ones.

During our stay in Big River, my family of seven lived with residents in a sturdy house raised on wood masts and concrete columns next to a rapid river. We didn't know our hosts: fear taught us to keep to ourselves. Be deaf, dumb, and mute was the steady mantra. Anxiety stifled our curiosity and turned us into mules. Throughout our stay, new faces sporadically entered the house and disappeared a few days later. These residents were in and out of labor camps and thus in and out of our temporary home.

Houses stood on both banks of the river next to trees of unknown ages. Their branches reached out for each other as if protecting and preserving the tranquility within. I marveled at our luck daily and took to heart that there could be no better paradise than this. I didn't have to work in the garden anymore and I relished my newfound freedom.

To access the communal kitchen and to visit Grandma, we would walk upstream and cross a huge concrete bridge.

Grandma and Aunt Sing had taken refuge with another family near a lake where we often swam with other children. Uncle Jo and his son resided elsewhere, but they often visited Grandma's. As before, all the grandchildren were self-sufficient, and we congregated at her new place. When told it was time for lunch or dinner, we would find our own way to the mess hall.

Lately Grandma couldn't get out of bed to trek the short distance for meals, so one of us would take her share back.

On days I didn't frolic in the calm water, I'd bathe in the rushing river behind our place. I had to hold tightly onto a branch or risk being pulled away by the current.

Nuy and Vunn were mostly away working in their youth groups. Mother, Father, Uncle Rain, and Uncle Jo worked their hardest to ingratiate themselves with the chief, sincerely acknowledging him for risking his life to save us.

Amid the District Five Khmer Rouge hunting us down and the District Three Khmer Rouge investigating our past, we moved twice before settling in on a ground-level concrete storage shed. This shed was located diagonally across from the communal kitchen. Its structure was tinier than the hut we had in District Five. It was small, but at least our family enjoyed privacy.

I was no longer burdened with the responsibility of collecting dead branches. When we needed wood to boil water, I would discreetly smuggle it from the stockpile outside the mess hall. The communal kitchen was a big box-shaped building, spacious but enclosed. Wooden benches and chairs were lined up next to a cooking area. The building was accessible by two entries: one from the southwest side and the other from the northeast. The north entry was also the kitchen area.

Next to the kitchen and against the wall, a tiny long-tailed brown monkey resided in chains. People came and went and the monkey behaved like a puppy, jumping up and down and swinging around for attention.

The monkey bit me as I opened the door to make sure no one was near before stealing the firewood. Mother walked me to the chief to show him the bite. Before the chief sent us to a doctor who lived one house down from him, he jokingly said, with a smirk and a wink: "That monkey is smart. He didn't want you stealing his wood."

Right away I felt guilty and averted my eyes to the ground.

Mother jumped in to scold me, knowingly rescuing me from my shame and the momentary awkwardness. "Didn't I tell you to replace what you took?"

Looking at my feet, I nodded, although I knew she had never uttered those words. In fact, she was the one who had directed me to the stockpile in the first place.

Mother continued, "Tomorrow you'll report to the chief so he can put you to work."

I remained silent, afraid of having to work.

Before she pulled me away by my good arm to lead me to the doctor, Mother emphasized once more, to the chief: "She'll be here tomorrow to help with the firewood."

Less than a minute later, we arrived at the front door of an old man's place. With his rotten, stained teeth, he looked older than Grandma. He was chewing a betel nut, and many of his front teeth were missing. My bite wound, which was covered with bright, thick congealed blood, alarmed him. He came closer to inspect it. This was my first time seeing a doctor during the reign of the Khmer Rouge. As I stood in front of him, I wondered why this doctor could practice when many doctors were executed; but before I walked away that day, I knew the answer.

The old man spat out the contents in his mouth. He reached into a small pouch around his waist, pulled out a tuft of shredded leaves, and put it into his mouth. It smelled like spoiled plants—tobacco, perhaps. He pointed to the big water barrel and instructed me to rinse my wound. I scooped up the water with the coconut shell, poured it over my arm, and walked back to him. He reached for my wounded arm and chanted an incantation with his eyes shut, as if to channel all his energy to evoke the cure.

I looked at Mother to solicit her take on this, but she was unreadable. The doctor finished chanting and opened his eyes, zooming in on the wound. I thought he was done and tried to pull my arm away, but he steadfastly held on. Then, with no warning at all, he cleared his throat and spat everything in his mouth onto my wound. I winced in disgust and wanted to pull my arm away and run from him; but to do so would be construed as impolite, which would make Mother look bad, so I endured.

I turned to look at Mother again, but this time she quickly turned her face away. On our way home, she told me I could rinse it off if I wanted to. With or without her permission, I intended to wash away the slime.

The next day Mother accompanied me to the chief's place. The monkey bite hurt and the pain smarted throughout my arm. The chief was too busy to ask how I was feeling. There were people standing around waiting for him to assign work. Mother took off immediately. Upon seeing me, the chief gestured to a girl who was around my age and told her to go with me to collect firewood. He handed her a machete.

The girl and I walked off together, speaking casually. I told her about the monkey bite. She told me her general background, mentioning that she was from Phnom Penh and was the youngest in her family. She had suffered severe casualties. Her immediate family had been reduced from seven members to only four.

We crisscrossed a wet marshland to reach a cluster of trees and mangroves. We found a dry tree branch about the thickness of my wrist. It was too big to break with our hands, so I pulled down the branch and held it tightly. Opposite from me stood the girl whose left hand gripped the branch. She held the machete with her right hand. She had one foot of space to bring the blade down on the branch. She brought her arm back, took a deep breath, and swung the machete down with her eyes closed, planting the blade accidentally into my pinky finger.

It cut diagonally, deep into the bone, more than halfway into my finger. I let out a bloodcurdling howl.

She looked horrified at the mishap.

Blood spurted from the wound. Instinctively I clamped down, applying a ring of pressure at the base of the finger to minimize the loss of blood. I was seething with anger as I ran back. She came after me, apologizing, but I was too angry to even look at her. Blood continued to ooze out, dotting the wet marshland. Dizziness and colorful specks plagued my vision. I was disoriented and had to focus to find the chief's place. I somehow knew that if I were to lose more blood, I would faint. I raised my pinky finger high above me, applied extra pressure at its base, and increased my strides. The girl tried to keep up with me, but I continued to ignore her.

I returned to the chief with bloodstains all over my clothes. He was aghast at my injuries, both the swollen monkey bite and now the half-broken finger.

The girl came up behind me and said, with her eyes downcast: "It was my fault because I don't know how to use the machete. I accidentally chopped her finger." I didn't know how to respond to this and wasn't even sure if I was more upset at my injury or at the fact that she didn't know how to handle a blade. Where had she been the last few years?

In bloody frustration, I screamed at her; but my attempt at anger instantly withered into sobs and my throat squealed several octaves higher, "Why didn't you tell me earlier that you don't know how to chop? If you had given me the machete, I promise you, you wouldn't have lost your finger!" I immediately wiped away my tears and was embarrassed at displaying such vulnerability.

The chief looked at me, then at her. He told the girl to go home, and she ran away as fast as she could.

He led me to the doctor again. I winced, knowing where we were headed. En route, he kindly said to me: "You can take as much firewood as you want from the kitchen and you don't have to go to the marsh anymore." I nodded in response. I was tempted to ask his permission to return home, too, but that would seem ungrateful now; so I decided to go through the motions and see the doctor once more.

The doctor performed the same rituals. He chanted again before spitting tobacco on my finger. At least this time he didn't clear his throat and empty all the contents in his mouth. Another surprise occurred: he wrapped a piece of white gauze on my pinky.

"I don't give this to everyone, you know," the witch doctor said as he winked at me.

The gauze struck me as profoundly odd: out of place and time. It reminded me too much of the past. I recalled seeing it packed into Mother's abdomen to soak up the pus and infection from the botched tubal ligation procedure.

"Keep it dry at all times and don't remove the fabric for five days," the doctor instructed me. "If you follow my instructions, your finger should heal nicely. If not, it'll become infected and possibly fall off."

On my way home, my mind wrestled with the doctor's advice: to rinse or not to rinse. In the end I opted to wait out the five days not because I was afraid of losing my pinky finger, but because I treasured the gauze. It took a couple of months for my finger to heal, but the scar remained.

My paradise was Uncle Rain's hell.

After three long years, fate had finally caught up to Uncle Rain and brought him face to face with the hitherto nameless and faceless phantom that had haunted him since the start of the forced evacuation in April of 1975.

Uncle Rain had a short period of relative bliss in Big River until he encountered a familiar face. The minute he saw the man out in the field, what little hope he had managed to preserve abandoned him. This chance encounter happened when the two toiled in the same field. Time stood still. Their gazes locked. One worried; the other oozed venom and bile. One felt trapped; the other considered it to be his lucky day. One had promoted democracy; the other had sided with communism.

Uncle Rain had always known communism to be destructive for the country and believed it would adversely affect all our lives, but he had no idea of the magnitude and the harm it would unleash. He hadn't foreseen how it would eventually kill his wife and children and plunge the country into a dark age.

In the years prior to the forced evacuation, Uncle Rain and his nemesis rallied public support for their political beliefs. They each stood on opposite ends in this political tug-of-war. Although there were many people standing with them, rallying, debating, and opposing each other's ideologies, these two were waging a personal war, a silent war that was deadly and cutthroat. After a victor was declared, there was no handshake, no conceding of the throne to sleep well and to be free of worry, and no packing up the office to do consulting work. It was about how to make it out alive and remain hidden, keeping the family safe from persecution.

One man remembered bitterly: his heart was full of contempt. The other forgot. The man who had forgotten had seven beautiful children and a loving wife to go home to. He left the government post two years before the Khmer Rouge had laid claim to the land. The other man remembered, because his hatred for Uncle Rain was intense. It was as though his life's purpose was to eliminate Uncle Rain. The day the Khmer Rouge won the civil war, this man became powerful and had the ability to remove anyone with a simple flick of his finger.

Now they met again. Uncle Rain didn't know that this man had been demoted. His once-omnipotent status was now reduced to a mere supervisory level. He would eventually be demoted further, to a rank slightly above that of a common laborer.

So for now, the man turned and walked away from Uncle Rain, impatient to file a case with his superior to expose a counter-revolutionary working in the fields. That night Uncle Rain imparted his newfound knowledge to his two surviving daughters. "Should you never see me again, you're to go live with Aunt Yeng and Uncle Sann. Always obey them and respect them like they're your parents." Big Daughter and Sida solemnly acknowledged his directives, accepting his imminent death with uncommon mettle.

As expected, Uncle Rain's past came into question. They interrogated Father, Mother, and Uncle Jo, numerous times. They dredged up our past, from what we did for a living, to whether we had sympathized with the Khmer Rouge. My parents downplayed their roles as capitalists, telling them how they could barely scrape by as a haircutter and a photographer supporting five children. When asked the reason why our family later moved closer to Thailand, my parents responded that they wanted to be closer to their parents, who weren't in good health.

When the investigators asked how long Uncle Rain had worked for the Lon Nol regime, my parents said, "Two years, from 1971 to early 1973." They knew honesty now would serve us all well. They emphasized to the interrogators that he was discontent with the government, which had been full of corruption, nepotism, and incompetence. By saying Uncle Rain was dissatisfied with Lon Nol's Social Republican Party, my parents scored him points with the current master. "He went to work on the farm from early 1973 to 1975."

While my parents were attesting to Uncle Rain's innocence and his devotion to the utopia, orders came for him to leave Big River at dusk to transport supplies back from a nearby village. Receiving an order to work at dusk was never a good thing. Uncle Rain braced for his own demise and imparted pearls of wisdom to his daughters, instructing them to get along with us and to do more than what would be asked of them.

Big Daughter, thirteen, and Sida, seven, were devastated by his parting words. They accepted the finality when he wiped away his tears. The tears of one last goodbye. He walked away from them in a trance, leaving his heart behind. He seemed to accept that he would never come back to them again.

It came as a huge shock when they sent him on a mission to transport the supplies back; however, the belief that they could come for him at any given moment never left him. Each time they sent him on a mission at dusk, he presumed it would be his last. This overwhelming fear threatened him for a few more months until he learned that his nemesis no longer held power. There was unrest within the ranks of the Khmer Rouge.

Mother was speechless about her pregnancy.

She didn't find out until the middle of her second trimester. Everyone, including men and children, felt the fatigue, headaches, and cramps normally associated with symptoms of early pregnancy. Mother hadn't been menstruating regularly, and when she did, only a few drops stained her undergarments. To miss four or five months of bleeding was common for women who were malnourished and under immense stress.

Mother asked the midwife for a strong herbal concoction to abort the baby, but the midwife told her it was too late in the pregnancy, as she estimated the fetus to be at least five months along.

She looked at her stomach and rubbed it with bewildered surprise and a resigned look. "Do you seriously think my stomach is large enough for five months? Just look at it." She pointed to her belly. "It's at most one or two months. I've given birth to five children and endured two miscarriages. I'm not new to this baby business."

"You already have five children; another one isn't going to make a difference." The midwife eyed Black Ghost and White Ghost and me, adding, "Abortion is too risky. You might lose your life and leave them motherless."

◆ ◆ ◆

Mother had been making friends with the natives in Big River. She wanted to send a message to her siblings in District Five to let them know of our safety and whereabouts.

Around September of 1978, when high tides flooded the prairies which separated Districts Three and Five, Uncle Tek, Aunt Hang, and three other people stole a canoe to find us. This occurred after Mother had successfully bribed an herbalist with a gold necklace to deliver a message to Uncle Tek. She found this healer approachable, for he was in the business of saving lives rather than destroying them.

The herb doctor worked for the Angka; he was free to roam from village to village and district to district looking for medicinal plants. Mother figured that at most she stood to lose the gold chain. Her instinct paid off when he personally whispered the message into Uncle Tek's ear.

The discovery of Mother's unwanted pregnancy was soon eclipsed by our happy reunion with Uncle Tek and Aunt Hang; however, this bliss was short-lived when Grandma's health took a turn for the worse.

With the reunion, Uncle Tek and Aunt Hang delivered news of those who lived and died in Phnum Sress: news which included more deaths than survivors. They estimated the population had been reduced in number from roughly one thousand people to no more than four hundred. Mother Len lost a daughter—one of the two daughters who had snitched on us about the missing cat. We also learned that the head chief had given our garden to someone we knew for a whopping twenty-five leungs (over thirty ounces) of gold.

There were days when the communal kitchens didn't open. When life became that much more unbearable, the villagers looked to us for inspiration. They marveled at our family's successful escape: a family of five small children that had vanished in the middle of the night without a trace.

Soon people in Phnum Sress were no longer just talking and reveling in our success. As each day passed and we were still at large, their hope and courage grew from the size of a pebble to the size of a boulder. When they couldn't endure their suffering any longer, they risked it all, like we did. Several families abandoned their huts in the middle of the night. Unfortunately, many people didn't escape as we had. The Khmer Rouge captured and killed many. Mother Len's family met such a fate, and they were old-people. If the old-people couldn't bear to live in District Five any longer, there was little hope left for new-people to survive.

The Khmer Rouge from District Five trailed after fugitives. They approached all the village chiefs in District Three and demanded they turn over any escapees they harbored. Fear made even the most kind-hearted people betray their humanity. The fugitives who weren't killed on the spot were thrown back into the lion's den. The Khmer Rouge forced them to chisel and excavate stones and pebbles in the mountains to create roads and tunnels. They deprived the slaves of food and water. All died a gruesome death in the end. Those who jumped off the trucks to run away ended up with bullet-riddled bodies. The soldiers were vigilant in capturing fugitives. They swept through District Three weekly. We were fortunate because Mother's dream had led us to Big River and Chief Sern.

Our escape made the Khmer Rouge and the head chief even more determined to find us, to make an example of us and to deter others from running away; but we were at large and as elusive as shadows in the sun. We were hiding in plain sight.

Both Mother and I had seen Khmer Rouge detectives pounding on the door of the communal kitchen in Big River and overheard their conversation with Chief Sern. He shook his head and denied that he harbored refugees. He protected our lives at the risk of losing his own.

29. DEATH, BIRTH, AND A NEW DAWN
(JANUARY 1979)

War broke out around us, again. This time it was between the Vietnamese and the Khmer Rouge. Bombs rained down on us without warning. The Vietnamese were taking over Cambodia and killing off the Khmer Rouge.

Big River was rapidly thrust into life-preservation mode. Collectivism ceased to function because people felt the need to be with their loved ones. In the mayhem, the good chief did his best to distribute food on a first-come, first-served basis. Vunn and Father grabbed buckets from our home to rush over to the granary for the rice distribution. They ran back home to empty the buckets so they could return for more rice. By the time they returned to the granary, there was nothing left.

The chief lost control of the crowd. The civility of standing in line abruptly ended amid bombs raining down and volleys of gunfire erupting from different directions. People stampeded over one another to grab palm sugar, salt, and dried fish. Vunn managed to seize a live rooster. Uncle Jo captured a piglet.

In the ensuing chaos I had to fight a mob of people for firewood from the communal kitchen while Nuy shored up our water supply. Our neighbors rushed out of their houses, hauling baskets and disappearing into the woods. The few families that remained were busy digging trenches nearby. From the front of our shed we could see one family shoveling the dirt as if digging a well for water.

If Mother hadn't been pregnant or if Grandma wasn't lying on her deathbed, we would have been digging trenches or running into the forest for protection, too. For now, the little concrete shed was our bomb shelter.

Another bomb dropped nearby, and my heart jumped into my throat.

Uncle Rain and my two cousins moved in with us during our time of need. All ten of us (and soon to be eleven) were cramped inside the confined space for at least a week. At night, before weariness won us over, we speculated about the distance of the nearest mortar attack. It started out ten miles away, then decreased to five, then three, then finally one. Most of us managed to sleep through the bombardment, but Mother was wide awake. It was impossible for her to sleep when she knew that her own mother was gasping her last breaths.

Grandma's breathing slowed. We all sensed her end was near, but her determination secured her a few more precious hours. We took turns spooning drops of salty water into her mouth to ease the pain in her throat. My aunts dabbed her face with a clean cloth. We comforted her in our own ways, telling her how much she had meant to us, not to worry and to go in peace. We each said our goodbyes: all except Mother, who was now in labor.

Only our family shuffled about openly; everyone else had fled or remained hidden. To travel from the shed to Grandma's place, we passed a huge body of water with lilies floating on its surface. Another mortar exploded, and its sonic waves shot through the air, causing abrupt and violent ripples in the water. I looked up to see the sky filled with dark smoke and red streaks, as if ribbons were on fire and drifting back down to earth.

I was scared for my life each time I ran back and forth to give Mother an update on Grandma's state, or to whisper in Grandma's ear that the baby hadn't yet arrived.

Nearby, mortar shells thudded. The vibrations coursed through the ground, and back and forth I ran. Each stride and each boom conjured an image of my small body blowing up into bits.

Despite her fierce determination, Grandma exhaled her last breath on January 8 of 1979. Her head collapsed slightly sideways with her mouth opened. Her eyes were tightly shut, but I could see tears of goodbye were pooled and unfallen in the corners of her eyes. Grandma missed her newborn grandchild by one day.

Mother tossed and turned. The concrete floor was hard on her back and the straw mat was of no help. She cried in her sleep as the newborn cried in her arms. The half-mile trek to see her mother's body seemed, for the moment, an eternity away.

Immediately after the newborn entered our war-torn world, Nuy and I washed the blood-soaked towels and sarong and delivered the news to our aunts and uncles. We told them the baby girl's name was *Sy* in Chinese, or Small.

The baby was so tiny that one push was all it took for her to arrive. She was nicknamed *Glath-Glo* (or "Half-Kilo" in Khmer). She was tiny and fragile and didn't look to be more than five pounds.

Mother truly believed Half-Kilo was the reincarnation of Grandma's old soul. Her instant bonding with the newborn helped her mourn the loss of her mother.

Three days after Grandma passed away, people came out of hiding to return to their homes. The gunfire and mortar explosions had ceased. People's voices grew louder as some rejoiced that the Vietnamese had defeated the Khmer Rouge. We were too absorbed in our loss to partake in the jubilation. While people roamed the country to look for relatives, we were busy constructing a coffin and laying Grandma to rest.

We gathered by the base of a hillock next to a winding road. I mourned and ached, unable to accept that she died at the cusp of our family reunion.

It was in Big River that Uncle Rain, Big Daughter, and Sida bid us goodbye. They left to find their other relatives. I was anxious when they left. The turmoil and frenzy of people carrying possessions and hauling the old and the weak on makeshift stretchers or in hammocks with sturdy poles left me with emotional angst. I felt trapped in a perpetual motion of separation and death, wandering aimlessly without hope of survival and feeling as if the world were detached from me; as though I didn't belong to it. I fought hard to keep my eyes dry when Uncle Rain and my cousins took to the road and disappeared at the bend beyond the bridge.

Uncle Jo then left with his son Rern, and soon after Aunt Sing, Aunt Hang, and Uncle Tek departed as well. Although I knew in my heart that we would be reunited, my world had been blown apart. The absence left me addled. With every parting there was always the lingering doubt that I might not see them again.

Two days later, we took an oxcart and headed to Mongol Borei where Mother's elder sister resided with her husband. It was a focal place for all my maternal relatives to converge and regroup. Mother instructed Father to commission the oxcart and a driver to transport our belongings and ourselves. Father and Vunn had to walk, but my thirteen-year-old brother walked with a shamed face. He still felt embarrassed by his foolish conduct a few days ago.

Vunn had gone swimming by the edge of the village in a deep ravine flanked by enormous trees. The trees bore fruit which looked like snow peas with rows of black seeds. Once matured, the pod opened and the seeds fell into the water. His curiosity got the better of him. For some reason he inserted one of the seeds into his ear to see if he could flush it out with water. He must have wedged it in there tightly because it refused to dislodge, and he panicked.

He ran to Father for help. He complained of the discomfort and the growing pain. I made a snide remark to voice my anger at his stupidity: "Just leave it inside and let a tree grow out of his head! He brought it on himself!"

Father smacked him on the back of his head. "See? Even your sister is mocking you. You're the oldest; you should know better than to be so stupid!"

Vunn was tongue-tied and his eyes avoided ours.

Once the baby was born, Nuy and I were kept busy. Mother constantly called on us to do chores: boil water, wash clothes, change diapers, hold the baby, or cook meals. Half-Kilo and Mother weren't the only ones who demanded our time. Black Ghost's chronic cough and her frailty consumed most of our days, too.

Black Ghost's posture assumed a hunched-over look. She was the picture of an "in-between" person, always looking like a ninety-year-old woman fighting for life. She had trouble breathing and she coughed acutely, with clenched fists. After she had exhausted every air bubble in her tiny lungs, she reverted to her hunched and sullen posture. Her rectal prolapse was as pronounced as ever.

Around that time, someone told Mother with certainty that Black Ghost had tuberculosis, which we had long suspected. Food alone couldn't save her. She required proper medicine; but where would we go for the cure? Mother brewed strengthening broths to prolong Black Ghost's life. It was all she could do.

During our daily turmoil, I found Vunn to be a nuisance. Now that he was no longer away at the labor camp, I felt suffocated having him around all the time. He was never called on to help with our messy and disgusting chores: all he had to do was gather firewood and fetch water. The previous four years had changed me forever. I had entered the countryside with my youth and innocence and left the war with only emptiness inside. Vunn entered with his slingshot and his clay balls and left with a seed in his ear.

Cambodia was teeming with barefooted vagrants covered in gray rags. Each person carried his total material worth on his person and orphans were scattered and lost. Everyone was in search of his or her bygone life. Our wagon squeaked as we lumbered out of Big River. We flowed into foot traffic filled with distraught war slaves, here and there encountering Vietnamese soldiers and their armored tanks.

Pots and pans clanged together in torn wicker baskets held aloft by two people connected by a long pole.

A mother carried her entire world in two baskets: a child swinging and bouncing in one and her personal belongings in another.

A lone child about my age was resting under a tree when our wagon passed her. She was not lost, but she had lost everything.

A man with missing legs trudged onward, without crutches, willing his way ahead with his hands and arms.

A teenage girl and an old woman were nodding off in a horse-drawn wagon as they headed in the opposite direction from us.

My mind took in these vignettes of people reeling in the aftermath of the Khmer Rouge, trying desperately to regain some semblance of normalcy. It was like piecing together a broken vase when half of it was shattered and destroyed forever. We could never bring our lives back to the way they were; all we could do was pick up the few remaining pieces and attempt to live in a world of abject ruin. We were less than a third-world nation: we were a forlorn fourth-world nation, drowning in crisis and catastrophe.

As our wagon rolled down the paved roads and dirt paths, many of the weary travelers and passersby turned to stare at us. A few bore their eyes enviably on our oxcart, coveting such luxury as a wagon; but many were sizing up our family members. To see our family so large in number was to take stock of their losses. Our togetherness stirred in them memories that were once wholesome and happy, of a past where they, too, had had a mother, father, siblings, and children. I could almost read their thoughts and feel their anguish.

The wagon slowed to a stop in front of a huge two-storied red brick building. Nearly twenty people rushed out to greet us. Many were faces I once knew but had forgotten. Several I remembered. Strange how some people could leave an indelible mark while others remained as elusive as a cloud in the sky.

I remembered Mama's elder sister Lan and her husband, but not their adopted son, who was Vunn's age. We reacquainted ourselves with Uncle Yi and his adoptive family: our great-aunt and great-uncle and their children.

It was here that we immediately reverted to our Chinese language. It felt odd to now say "Mama and Papa." When we inadvertently called out "*Mae* (Mother) or *Pok* (Father)," the adults would knuckle our heads; this was their way to restore our Chinese culture. In no time at all, we abandoned the Khmer Rouge's lingo.

The red brick building stood in the middle of a flat farmland flanked by sugarcane fields which looked like rows of miniature bamboo trees. It felt surreal—had I died and gone to the land of candy? Although all the larger stalks had been harvested long before our arrival, I was more than content with what was left for me to forage. I developed an addiction to the sugarcane. I couldn't function until I got my fix several times a day. Throughout the day, I would sneak over with a knife and remain there chewing and sucking on the sweet nectar and spitting out the fiber after it lost its sweetness.

♦ ♦ ♦

With reunion came division. We set our sights on Thailand and rolled the invisible dice of life and death.

We immediately prepared to head west, storing up food and rest. Part of the preparation included finding a blacksmith who could melt and mold gold into a certain size and shape, as dictated by Papa. Drawing from his last experience, he specified the girth of each piece to be a little larger, rounder, and an ounce heavier. If it was too big and heavy, gravity would slide it out of its cavernous hiding place. If too small and narrow, a sneeze or a cough would launch it like a rocket. He knew the right shape and size to maximize its snug fit and minimize its discomfort in the rear.

It was Papa who suffered discomfort during our escape from District Five to District Three back in April of 1978; but it was Mama who had thought of the idea. Now our other relatives would march into Thailand with gold hidden in their hindquarters as well.

It was also at this red brick house that Mama nurtured her weak body back to life. The last four years were about saving us. Now that we were nearly out of danger, she had time to rejuvenate her mind and body by soaking in the sun, eating nutritious food, and exercising.

Part of her zeal included sweating away the edema and ridding herself of jaundice. She volunteered to do most of the cooking and washing. Mama strategically moved the cooking area into the sun. It was hot and humid, and the temperature soared above one hundred degrees as she fanned the fire into a raging inferno. She layered her body with clothes, blankets, and towels from head to toe. This was our Mama pointing a dagger at her heart—in effect to harden her resolve and improve her own well-being.

She roasted a huge batch of green beans and stirred it with all the energy she could muster. Her clothes quickly became drenched in sweat while dizzy spells and black spots assailed her vision. We rushed to steady her and told her to take a break. She waved us off, drank some water, and pressed on.

The next day she cooked extra rice and left it to dry in the sun. She threw herself into jumping jacks if there was nothing else to do. The following day she roasted the dry rice and jumped more in the heat and humidity.

Mama's brothers, who were adept at butchering pigs, were called upon once more to display their skills. It was evening when they yoked and dragged a brown cow into the house. They led it to an enclosed space surrounding the staircase and brought in with them whatever tools they had at their disposal: a sledgehammer, a hoe, and a machete; then they shut the door to prevent the cow's escape.

Upon hearing the cow's frantic moo, we children ran out of our rooms to the landing by the staircase and craned our necks to see the beast below. The space was dimly lit with oil lamps. From the top we saw the cow attempting to back away, to no avail.

The men below glanced up at us and yelled for us to go back inside and not come out. We ran back to our rooms and braced ourselves for what we knew would come next. The five of us older children shared a room. My parents and the newborn were in the next room. The creature's cries of torment pierced our ears as we lay in our own corners on the floor. It was hard to sleep knowing a life was about to be extinguished in the most inhumane way imaginable. Next door, Half-Kilo was crying but Mama was unable to calm her.

Right before the men swung their first blow, someone commanded a concerted effort to aim at the throat and head. The slaughter then began, and the ensuing madness. The sounds of struggle between prey and predator—between life and death—bounced violently from the dimly-lit room below straight through to our ears and to our hearts.

The swishing and bludgeoning sounds, the loud mooing and scampering, and the shouting and crying of human voices transported me back to another event. My mind kept flashing back to our Vietnamese neighbors waving their farewells to us. I envisioned their bodies mutilated and their lives extinguished in the same manner as the cow below.

After endless onslaughts (and perhaps as many as two to three hours later) the cow stumbled and crashed into the wall, rattling the house and keeping everyone on edge. It mooed and moaned in pain, as if begging for release.

Half-Kilo was still sobbing.

"I didn't know that killing a cow would be this difficult," uttered one uncle as he panted.

"We could've killed twenty pigs by now!" hollered another.

The men reached deep down into their reserves for one last round and the final finish. The charging, ramming, crashing, and crying slowly ceased as the cow painfully surrendered to the mercy of death. I tossed and turned. My mind returned to the little hut and I saw the mournful faces of our Vietnamese friends waving their goodbyes. Naked, they were bludgeoned to death and their bodies were tossed on top of other bodies. The Khmer Rouge and informants collapsed in exhaustion.

The cow was silenced.

My uncles were spent. They called it a night.

When we woke up late in the morning, Mama had already cooked a huge pot of beef stew and enough rice to feed an army. For the next few days, Mama and the others were busy marinating and preserving the rest of the thinly-sliced beef in the sun. The dried beef and the roasted rice and beans would last us through our escape.

30. OUT OF THE FRYING PAN AND INTO THE FIRE (APRIL 1979)

Shortly after the Vietnamese declared victory in Cambodia, most of my paternal relatives converged in downtown Svay Sisophon, which neighbored the rural town of Poipet, our hometown before the Khmer Rouge forced everyone out. When the regime ended, we had no home to return to. We had all become squatters, and none of us dared lay claim to any buildings or land. Everywhere was a temporary shelter, everyone was homeless, and thousands of children had either been abandoned or orphaned. Like so many people, we no longer viewed Cambodia as livable. Thailand seemed to hold all the promise.

In Svay Sisophon, we took refuge in a small apartment on a busy corner with Papa's sister Wui's family of six, along with strangers. Our temporary living quarters were a single-story unit with common walls. Behind it were taller buildings showing the same wear and tear from weather and the neglect and destruction caused by the Khmer Rouge. A vast lake shimmered directly in front of our unit. There was no furniture in the apartment: just one empty room, and we all crammed to sleep on the floor. There were at least twenty people in the same space, temporarily bound together by circumstances.

It was here in Svay Sisophon that we counted our family's losses. Tears filled our reunion.

"How and when did my father and brother die?" Papa asked his sister-in-law Dai.

The sister-in-law answered, "Your father first, then your brother, all within the same year. No one had enough to eat. You know . . . same story: overworked, no food, and no medicine." She paused, then dabbed her eyes with her neck scarf. "The same happened to my two children." Her family had been reduced from nine members to five.

Papa cleared his throat, trying to still his rising pain, but it was useless. Tears pooled in his eyes. Tears were in all our eyes.

Aunt Wui asked Uncle Rain about Aunt Khan: "How did my sister die? Did she die before the children, or after? Did she suffer much?" Uncle Rain couldn't answer right away. Each time he attempted to speak, he found himself choked with tears. Papa had to take over the story of their deaths.

Aunt Wui's daughter Lin fell from a flimsy plywood bridge while en route to join her youth brigade. She didn't know how to swim, and she might have drowned had someone not rescued her; however, she never fully recovered from the accident and her life withered away from malnutrition and other maladies.

We children listened as the adults exchanged stories. We shared our sorrow and suffering with each other. Unfortunately, when the stories were finished, we didn't feel any relief. No one who had survived this atrocity would ever fully recover from the trauma.

I lost Grandpa and Grandma, three aunts (Uncle Rain's wife, Uncle Jo's wife, and Skinny Wife), one uncle (Papa's brother Gunn), and nine first cousins (five of Uncle Rain's children, Uncle Jo's son Kearn, Aunt Wui's daughter Lin, and two of Uncle Gunn's children). That was fifteen people out of my family of forty-six: a thirty-two percent casualty rate. Nearly a third of us who marched into the countryside during the forced evacuation didn't make it out alive.

I remembered with fondness a time when we used paper money to purchase noodles and ice cream in Cambodia. Life was easy and simple before the Khmer Rouge destroyed my country. A song rose in my memory, and its familiar melody thrummed inside my head. We all sang it together many moons ago, until its words were forbidden under the Khmer Rouge and its tune was silenced.

We sang this song without fully grasping its meaning as the Khmer Rouge marched us away from our homes in April of 1975. Now, after having lived through and survived four years of communism cruelty, this song felt like it had never reached its crescendo. It failed to encapsulate our suffering and misery. It was as if it were written with black ink on white paper, devoid of red—the color of blood—and the true meaning of evil. This song tells only half the truth.

We have a road,
But no one walks on it.
We don't buy with money,
But we trade with leaves.
We have a house,
But no one lives in it.
In haste we live in chicken coops,
And get shit on.

The other half of the people drowned in blood. The Khmer Rouge pursued a classless and stateless society by eradicating everyone and everything standing in its way. We lived in perpetual fear and under the constant threat of execution, disease, and starvation. The Khmer Rouge's obsession with achieving a free society with no division or alienation failed. Not only did communism fail to produce equality; it exacerbated inequality and ramped up corruption. It killed one-third of its population.

Unfortunately, the casualty rate continued to climb.

◆◆◆

Uncle Jo and his son Rern were the first to leave the red brick house and attempt the escape to Thailand, but they failed. The Vietnamese soldiers captured them and threw them into a makeshift jail in Svay Sisophon.

Every day Mama visited her brother and nephew with food while we children frolicked in the lake and searched the bottom for clams. After we retrieved a pocketful, we would sprinkle them with salt and leave them in the sun to sizzle on a metal plate. After an hour the clams would split open, their tasty insides cooked. It was my favorite part of the day.

Many people flocked to this city, so finding firewood was a daunting task. I was always paired up with a cousin or my brother. Everywhere we went, our eyes searched for dry limbs on trees. Big Daughter, Sida, and I came upon a huge junk heap piled high with car parts. We ventured in and found other children already there, playing.

The cars were missing tires and cushions. The windows were all smashed. I wondered if Papa had come here a few days ago to scavenge the tires to make our sandals. We had needed protection for our feet in the jungle. Papa measured and cut the tires to make thong sandals.

Big Daughter came upon a car that we could play in. She crawled through a front window and took to the wheel. She insisted on Sida and me joining, in the back. We both climbed through the broken windows and together we sat uncomfortably in the skeletal, stripped body of a taxi. We drove that ravaged taxi down memory lane. I had often ridden in one of these with Mama and Papa to visit relatives and friends.

"Where'd you young ladies like to go?" Big Daughter turned around to ask us as she pretended to turn the wheel.

"To eat ice cream in Thailand," I told the taxi driver.

"Don't forget, we want to live in Thailand too. We're not coming back!" Sida chimed in.

"No problem. That'll cost you one hundred cans of rice."

We found the whole pretense amusing and laughed at our own silliness.

We exited the taxi when the heat became unbearable and climbed down the deep ravine next to the junkyard for a quick, soothing dip; then back up to the cars before setting out on our mission to gather firewood.

◆ ◆ ◆

Out of necessity, my family stayed in this town longer than we wanted to.

We moved to a two-story building across the street when our relatives left for Thailand, but we often shared our unit with strangers when they asked if they could stay for a few days. One such squatter stayed with us for nearly a week as she combed through the city for her missing relatives. She later left our place, having reconnected with her surviving family members, but she never left my mind.

One morning while she was staying with us, she left her neck scarf on the wall partition that separated the kitchen from the big room. One end of the scarf was bulky and heavy. Right away, I knew it contained her valuables. I led Mama to the article and she unwrapped it to discover many colorful gold bracelets, rings, and necklaces. "What a careless person," she said as she took the treasure upstairs.

About thirty minutes later, the lady raced inside and ran to the wall where she had hung her world. Her eyes narrowed, reflecting the madness and panic swimming inside her head when she didn't see it.

I calmly told her, "My mother has it. She's upstairs. I'll go get her for you."

When Mama came down, she lectured the lady. "How could you forget something this valuable? Of all the places, you left it in the kitchen. People come and go all the time around here, in case you haven't noticed. You're lucky that we found it first. Had it been someone else, you wouldn't have been as fortunate." As Mama handed the scarf back to the woman, she added: "Everything should be there, but double-check to make sure."

The lady put out both hands in supplication to receive her scarf and jewelry. She thanked us effusively, saying: "You and your family are good people. I'll pray to Buddha to look after you all." She only remained a few more nights, for she soon found her relatives.

Like the jewelry lady, other people came and went while we remained.

We had long since consumed the dried beef, rice and beans which were to sustain us in our escape. It was never easy keeping eight stomachs full under any circumstances. We had to replenish our bags of perishables many more times before we found our guide.

Uncle Jo and his son immediately found a guide to lead them to Thailand the day after they left the jail. Coincidentally, Uncle Rain ended up commissioning the same guide. He was to depart in the morning, and Uncle Jo was leaving in the afternoon of the same day.

Uncle Rain, Big Daughter, and Sida came to our place to borrow a gallon-sized plastic container from Aunt Wui. She handed the container to Uncle Rain, saying: "If possible, I'd like to have it back after you're done with it. It'll be difficult to find a replacement. We need it for our escape too."

Uncle Rain took the container and said: "Once I'm safe, I'll have the guide return it to you. Thank you for letting me borrow it."

I told Big Daughter and Sida that we would see each other in Thailand someday. With that, my uncle and cousins left, carrying the container with their bundles. They headed for the border with their traveling group and their guide.

Roughly three days later, a shirtless man came to deliver the container, around noon. I was on my way out to swim in the lake across from our building when I ran into him by the front door.

He softly asked, "Do you know Mr. Rain?"

I nodded. "Yes, he's my uncle."

The man handed me the container and said: "This is from Mr. Rain. Give it to your parents and tell them that he has safely made it to Thailand." By the time I placed the container in a corner where my aunt kept her belongings, the man was already halfway out the door.

As the afternoon sun dipped into the horizon, everyone heard of Uncle Rain's escape. We surmised that Uncle Jo and his son had safely crossed into Thailand, too, with the same guide who led them.

The real news came two days later. The few survivors from Uncle Rain's group didn't truly escape. The guide had conned them all by abandoning them in the jungle to die. It was highly unlikely that anyone made it to Thailand. More than likely, we were told, they all perished in the jungle.

We were all stunned by the enormity of this unexpected loss. I couldn't believe I had just lost three more cousins and two more uncles. Shock and anger stifled my ability to mourn. My eyes burned with rage. All I could do to relieve the pain in my chest was to put a curse on the con man. I condemned him and his next ten generations to die of thirst and hunger; that each would experience the cumulative agony and death of his victims and that they would suffer as long as the moon and the sun hovered in the sky.

It was unbearably painful to know how much agony my uncles and cousins had endured, to come so close to salvation only to die at the hands of greedy men.

After the shocking news, our hope of leaving the heinous wreckage of Cambodia for peace and prosperity in Thailand vanished. There was serious discussion of us going back to the red brick house, surrendering to a bleak and dismal life.

Hope slowly revived when we learned that Uncle Jo and his son were still alive. The Vietnamese soldiers had rescued them from dying in the jungle. They were once again incarcerated for attempting to escape from the country the Vietnamese came to liberate. They had no word of the fate of Uncle Rain and his daughters. We assumed they had all died.

It was early May of 1979 when both father and son were released again. Uncle Jo's desire for freedom was so unquenchable that when he and his son were set free again, they immediately attempted their third escape.

Shortly thereafter, my family entered the jungle.

When Uncle Rain and my two cousins, seven and thirteen, attempted to escape to Thailand, they joined a group of forty-seven people and left on the morning of April 15 of 1979, exactly four years since the Khmer Rouge invaded Cambodia and forced everyone out to the countryside in April of 1975.

After following the guide for hours, passing over hilltops and boulders and curving around bends in the wilderness, the guide stopped. He then pointed straight down to his feet. "I'm currently standing in Cambodia." His same finger slightly rose and pointed to the front of his feet. "The land before me belongs to Thailand. Just cross over the mountains and you'll see Thai civilization. It's about one or two miles away. My job is done here."

Someone in the group climbed the tallest tree, and sure enough, a great view of the ridge splayed majestically before his eyes. Lured by wishful thinking that freedom was finally coming to fruition, he yelped to everyone below: "I see the mountains! I see the mountains!" Everyone jumped with jubilation. They were no longer tired, having been rejuvenated by the prospect of freedom.

All transactions were settled on the spot. People paid their dues in gold. Before the guide took off, he convincingly stated: "You're practically there. If you want, I can help you take whatever you don't need back to your relatives to let them know you're safe and sound."

People ate, drank, and washed their faces with resources they would have otherwise conserved. A haze of happiness danced and swirled around the group. They were busy consuming their provisions to lighten the load and wash the grime away from their hands with precious water. The frenzy fed on itself. Everyone agreed that things borrowed must be returned. Some even sent food back because, after all, abundance was now within reach.

Uncle Rain handed the empty water container to the guide.

The "one or two" miles described by the guide turned out to be endless. Finally over the mountains, they saw no sign of civilization and scarcely any living creatures: only a universe of dirt, brush, and trees merging into a lush jungle which seemed to expand into infinity, testing their will to continue the journey.

It was only then that they realized that they had been duped.

By then everyone in the group was experiencing dizzy spells, hunger, and thirst. Regrets for consuming and wasting precious resources clutched their insides and took permanent residency in their hearts.

Gullibility wasn't something anybody could afford to risk; yet here they were all left with their folly. How could one have foreseen deception when one had been mentally confined in perdition for so long? All they could do was blindly hope and trust.

Half of the people immediately turned back. It was through them that we learned of the others' fate.

Uncle Rain was determined to leave this forsaken land. Remaining in Cambodia was as suffocating to him as placing a plastic bag over his face. He was already dying a slow death, often submerging himself in grief, recalling the deaths of his wife and children. A thousand painful memories coursed through him each day. The only way for him to find any remnant of peace and happiness was to search for it elsewhere, in Thailand or in another country.

Cambodia had once been a gentle land and a mighty empire, but it had since lost its essence to the dominant powers of France, China, the Soviet Union, Thailand, Vietnam, and America. Each of these countries took part in Cambodia's suffering. They were the culprits that muddled his bright world, killing his wife and children. The cut was deep, deeper than any man should have to endure.

Uncle Rain's desire to escape this ill-fated country obscured his ability to see beyond the boundaries of death and safety. His knowledge of politics was prolific, and his hate was strong and intense, boiling in the plasma of his blood. The hate was pulsing and alive, compelling him to charge forward with his two remaining daughters.

Unfortunately, April was the hottest and driest time of the year, the cruelest month to be lost in the jungle. The sunbaked ground burned the feet. The refugees moved sluggishly forward like earthworms wiggling and inching along on hot gravel. Except for scattered birds fluttering their wings from tree to tree and a rodent or lizard quickly scampering away, all was quiet.

By mid-afternoon, Big Daughter was struggling. She wasn't feeling well. Something she ate or drank earlier was waging a battle in her. They had to stop many times for her to step into the bushes. The discharge slowly drained the life force from her and caused her strides to slow and become feeble. Her mouth was parched. Soon she hacked a dry cough, so forceful that she retched. White froth foamed in the corners of her mouth, her lips cracked and bled, and her stride wobbled.

Uncle Rain carried her bundle and supported her body while Sida trailed closely behind as they navigated the labyrinth of the wilderness. No one seemed to have any water left and, if they did, they were discreet; for sharing meant putting their own lives at risk.

Out of desperation, Uncle Rain took a small bowl with him behind a tree. He returned with urine in it, offering it to both children. Big Daughter, her stomach already upset, shook her head; but Sida took a sip. Others in their group also resorted to this method to alleviate their parched throats.

Delirium came early for Big Daughter as they trudged along slowly but relentlessly, winding their way against time. The sun was their compass: west was where all hopes lay. They followed the afternoon sun until they couldn't take another step. Everyone lay down to recharge their bodies and to calm the alarming palpitations in their chests. Soon sleep came to banish everyone's despair and exhaustion. Uncle Rain dozed off next to his two daughters alongside the twenty other people in their group.

Their only hope of salvation was to be captured by warring factions. They were so desperate they might have welcomed the Khmer Rouge with open arms.

An hour or two later Uncle Rain woke up in a strange daze. His mind was slow to register that he was lost in the jungle. Even when he saw Sida lying next to him, his frayed sensibilities were slow to waken. He saw bodies lying nearby under the shade of bushes and trees. His mind returned to focus, and finally he recalled being lost.

Panic rose in him. Where was Big Daughter?

He held his breath as he scanned the jungle for her. "Big Daughter! Big Daughter, where are you?" His panic woke everybody. Soon everyone joined him in calling her name. They spread about the perimeter to find her. The jungle was the master of deception. A wrong turn could lead to permanent separation from the group. Thickets and trees weren't to be trusted as bearings, for they looked the same everywhere. The group's voices became the collective bearing point; they expanded, hoping to find her—all in vain.

The group had decided to forge on and encouraged Uncle Rain to join them. They told him Big Daughter had most likely become delirious in her search for water. Her vomiting and diarrhea must have caused her to succumb to dehydration and pass out.

All Uncle Rain could do was shake his head like a maniac, refusing to abandon Big Daughter, refusing to lose her in such an absurd manner, refusing to lose her forever. He told them all to go on without him. Time was slipping away. Self-preservation and instinct took over. His group reluctantly marched away from the spot where they were sure to die, should they linger.

With everyone gone, Uncle Rain told Sida to stay put while he continued searching and screaming for Big Daughter in the unforgiving and infinite expanse of the jungle. He couldn't venture far. He often returned to check on Sida, but she was too tired and had fallen asleep. He screamed until he lost his voice. By midnight, he was in despair. He huddled to sleep with his seven-year-old daughter, his mind teetering on the edge of insanity.

When he woke up the next morning, Sida, too, was gone!

Immediately he hollered her name as he slung the bundle over his shoulders. He walked in circles, crisscrossing and at times cutting through thickets, trees, and bamboo, shouting the names of his remaining precious children. "Big Daughter, Sida! Sida, Big Daughter! Big Daughter, Sida!" His world was quickly slipping away.

Eventually he stumbled upon Sida hiding behind a tree. Sudden relief overtook him.

He slowly approached her. She was hugging a tree and her eyes were closed.

"Daughter, daughter . . . what are you doing?" he gently whispered, afraid of startling her.

"Nothing Pa. Nothing. I'm just playing hide-and-seek with my friends."

Sida's response was too much for him. He raced to her and hugged her tenderly. Tears of pity and tenderness blinded his vision. He carried her in his arms. He pecked her cheeks and promised himself he wouldn't lose her again; for she was his only solace now—his entirety.

Sida meekly pleaded in his arms as though he were her deliverance, "Pa, water. Pa, water. Pa, water. . . I'm cold."

He knew his primary objective now was to save Sida; and with that he carried her farther from where they were, away from Big Daughter. He murmured to the morning sky, "Please forgive me, Big Daughter. Please forgive me, my good daughter. We must go. We have to leave you behind." Each step he took felt like the piercing of an arrow as he moved onward and away. His eyes were two gushing streams. He was losing the battle not just to the elements, but to time. Shortly thereafter, Sida let go of her grip on his arms and passed out.

He often had to stop and take short rests, for Sida grew heavier with each second. After he had caught his breath, he would pick up her limp body again and march a few hundred feet, then stop again. Time was running out within the barren jungle. There were no grubs to feast on, the lizards were too quick to catch, and there was no water. He looked up at the sky and knew that rain wasn't coming anytime soon.

He mustered his remaining strength to carry Sida westbound, praying that he wasn't going in circles. Slowly Sida came back to him. Groggily she muttered, "Water . . . water . . . water. . . .." These were her last words as she slowly drifted out of consciousness.

It was high noon, the sun was directly in the center of the sky, and Uncle Rain had lost his bearings. Where was east? Where was west? He stumbled upon some recognizable bodies from his traveling group. He would soon be one of them, if there was no water.

Subsequently he heard the rushing sound and saw a blue body of water on the horizon, shimmering in the glaring heat, not too far and within reach. Its glassy surface beckoned him. He thought this would be where he would find Big Daughter. He hurried through the mist with the speed of a father carrying his dying child to a doctor. He was determined to reach it, to cup the water in his palms and feed it to Sida, where she would drink hungrily and thirstily.

He felt a cool breeze brushing his cheeks. His body was cooling down; he must be near the water. He followed the mist and lost track of how long he had been searching for its source. He pursued the mist, always hopeful. How happy he would be to see Big Daughter waiting for him by the water! It was only a few steps away, he told himself.

He never reached the water.

Something snapped his mind back to Sida, who was no longer breathing in his arms and who had turned stiff. He laid her down and patted her face. "Sida, Sida, wake up, wake up!" On his knees, he wept over her.

Within twenty-four hours he had lost his entire world. It was in this desolate wilderness that he contemplated ending his life. He wanted to hang himself—it would be so easy to end it here—but according to Buddhism, suicide was condemned as an act of cowardice, the most unforgivable of all sins. If he were to kill himself, he might not be able to see his family in the afterlife. He was afraid his reincarnation would be a repetition of this one, where he would be endlessly confronted with a similar predicament, losing his family over and over in a vicious cycle. He dared not drape a strip of fabric over a tree branch to end it there: he must let this miserable destiny come full circle and die at fate's mercy. His thoughts eventually wandered to a loophole in Buddhism: that if he were to die in the same manner as his children, it wouldn't be suicide. Death had suddenly become a thing of beauty, like drugs to an addict or flowers to bees.

All this time Uncle Rain had been trying to outrun death, but now their roles were reversed. He had turned into a predator, and death was now his prey. His sole purpose was to rejoin his wife and his seven children. He yearned to be with them again, to be free of sorrow. He imagined a family reunion with smiling faces and heartfelt embraces. He was on a mission to seize the devil by its horns.

First Uncle Rain had to find a suitable place to bury Sida. He ruled out the ground, lest wild animals devour her. Eventually he placed her on a sturdy bush of thick undergrowth. He pecked her cheeks and forehead and whispered softly, "Pa's not far behind, my child. I'll see all of you soon." He then pulled out two shirts from the bundle he carried. Tears streamed down his face as he covered her from head to toe. He even tucked the fabric under the weight of her slim body. His sensibilities left him. At this moment, he wondered how there could be tears in his eyes when he was as parched as a cowhide.

Now he prowled the jungle with nothing left to lose. He had lost all but the will to meet death head-on.

The end was within reach and he could feel it—he could sense its presence, but waiting for it would take too long. He became impatient. To speed up his appointment with death, he must empty his own reserves; yet death proved itself to be slow and elusive. The harder he pushed himself, the more lucid his mind became. His head was too clear and too bright to enter eternity.

Determined, Uncle Rain pushed on, trying to dim his mind of thoughts and his vision of light. He continued to crawl on his stomach. He welcomed the dryness in his throat and the fatigue in his limbs. Eventually, he succumbed to unconsciousness.

He came to in the void; and with consciousness came misery. Death had failed to show for his appointment. Once again Uncle Rain crawled, hoping to enter eternal rest to find his family waiting on the other side.

Blackness came upon him and he remained unconscious throughout the next day. But unwelcomingly, fate and destiny intervened: around noon, something unusual happened—it rained.

Uncle Rain remained unconscious as his life returned against his will. The downpour pelted his body, but he didn't flinch. It was nighttime when he awoke to find himself lying on the moist earth. When he opened his eyes, three other people from his group were sitting across from him: two males and one female.

To the side of his body was a bowl filled with rainwater they had collected and saved for him. At this point, any attempt to refuse the water would be no different than hanging himself. With much effort, he managed to reach for the bowl and awkwardly bring it to his lips.

The first sip was a waste: the water gushed out of his nostrils and pain splintered through his head. Not a single drop of that water quenched the desert of his mouth and throat.

A young man in his late teens told Uncle Rain to dip only his tongue into the water to allow the wetness to absorb into his body. He did as instructed, dipping only his tongue into the bowl. Even that was excruciating, as the wetness turned razor-sharp. It sliced through his esophagus and then through every inch of his intestines, tearing through the nerves of his body. Water had become a foreign object in his flesh. He didn't think he would make it.

He had lost the ability to moan since he lost Sida. The three saviors shook their heads at his suffering. Ultimately, the teen's advice proved effective. The pain slowly dissipated as the dryness in his throat reverted to flesh and blood. Slowly, his voice returned.

The rain restored his life, but it failed to bring him happiness. To Uncle Rain, this divine intervention was nothing more than another act of cruelty.

Later that night, his saviors gave him plain rice soup. He immediately felt energized, and instantly death backed away.

They continued their journey. Time was once again slipping away, to their detriment. Uncle Rain tried to get up, but he had lost sensation in his limbs. Like crutches, the two men assisted in propping him up, but he struggled as a quadriplegic would. He waved for the three to continue without him, but they simply refused. The two men supported him until he was able to walk again.

By the time Uncle Rain could stand on his own, they had arrived at the edge of what was dubbed the "danger zone," with bamboo spears placed in pits throughout the jungle. They were deceptively covered with leaves and brambles. A careless move or a misplaced step could cause a person to fall in on the sharp spears. Contraptions with spear-like heads were suspended above their heads and they were also mounted to tree trunks. A misplaced arm would release hidden arrows.

Mines were rigged to trees and bushes with thin, transparent fishing line. If a foot caught hold on a snare, a chain reaction would lead to detonation. Even exercising extreme caution didn't guarantee safety if fate refused to be on one's side.

The four navigated through the death traps and stepped over dead bodies. They were cautious, but no matter how careful they all were, danger was always only a hand or a foot away. Despite his extreme caution, the old man in the lead pressed his knee down on a line. He froze and his face paled.

They all cried, "Hold still!"

They traced the line to assess the danger.

Fortunately, the tip of the grenade was rusted from prolonged exposure to the elements. The man slowly pulled back his knee, leaving the dud hanging in its original position.

The group of four arrived in Thailand on April 18 of 1979. Later they came upon three other people from their group, but no others. Three months later, on July 18 of 1979, Uncle Rain was flown to America to live in Fullerton, California. He experienced severe depression and post-traumatic stress disorder and although he was in a bright place, his mind whirled in the past and remained there. He was a man holding the ghosts of his children and wife in his heart, and his memories of their love and suffering followed his every step.

Uncle Rain had a severe case of Posttraumatic Stress Disorder (PTSD). The therapist encouraged him to write down his story to comfort his soul. He did as advised and completed his journal three months after his arrival in the states. He put the journal away to forget it, but it became a demon in his closet, and he never had the courage to relive those painful memories. For many years to come, Uncle Rain had purposefully lost himself to work and insomnia.

He later moved to Fresno, California, to live a life of solitude. The intensity of his agony had slowly ebbed away with time and distance, but like flotsam and jetsam sinking to the ocean floor, memories of the experience were often dragged in with the tides.

He pulled the monster from the closet years later. At my request, he read his journal to me for the first time since he had written it in 1979. For one entire day we cried together over a horrific past that felt as raw as though it were only yesterday when we left Cambodia.

31. ENTER THE JUNGLE (MAY 1979)

It was evening when my family finally met our guide and his son. There were a dozen other families in our traveling group, totaling approximately sixty people. Our family was the largest in number and the smallest in age. The guide was a bit older than Papa. He had a teenage boy assisting him. The guide promptly led us on a narrow footpath into the fringe of the dense forest. The shadows deepened rapidly as the sun's afterglow surrendered to the enveloping darkness, but our eyes quickly adjusted, and we were able to see the narrow path as we shuffled forward in single file. Our family was in the middle. The old guide was leading the way while his son brought up the rear.

We walked in silence with both dread and anticipation accompanying our every step. By this time tomorrow, assuming we were still alive, we would be free.

As we braved the unknown once more, I prayed silently for safety and protection. I made numerous promises to the gods and the spirits that I would become a better person and the world would receive the countless good deeds I would perform. I even apologized to the spirits for the error of my ways, for having neglected them when we were safe, only to petition them again when we faced danger. I admitted to the powerful beings how I had taken advantage of their benevolence countless times, and I pleaded with them, candidly, to forgive me for my shortcomings and to look favorably upon us one more time.

The silence continued as we walked. Occasionally a baby wailed, or a man cleared the phlegm in his throat. Someone sneezed. There were two babies in our group: our five-month-old Half-Kilo and a young couple's one-year-old.

I didn't sleep well on our last few nights. I was haunted by the absence of my cousins and Uncle Rain. I pictured our own demise the way my cousins and uncle might have met theirs.

A few days before our departure, Mama shaved all of our heads with a brand new razor. After she finished with Black Ghost, she turned the blade on her own hair. Except for Half-Kilo and Papa, the rest of us had shiny, shorn heads. This happened every time my hair grew a couple of inches long, but this time my hair was barely one inch when she shaved it off again.

With bald heads, we knelt with incense sticks and bowed before our food offering to our ancestors and Buddha. We asked for protection, for no harm or misfortune to befall us, and for a safe journey to Thailand.

In Buddhism there were various meanings and interpretations to baldness, including peace, devotion, and humility. Mama had purposely timed our baldness to invoke humanity and compassion from any subversive criminals or bandits in the hostile jungle. This was her reasoning as we prepared to leave Cambodia to seek a better life in Thailand.

While we were packing, I asked Mama if we should have more water in case we ran out. "With what, Geng? Do you want to carry it in a bowl? Go ahead, if it makes you feel better!" Mama had a point. My heart sank as I was plunged into yet another involuntary memory. I saw Uncle Rain, Big Daughter, and Sida walk away with the container they had borrowed; then the con man handing me the same container. I imagined Uncle Rain and my cousins had been swallowed by the jungle and died of dehydration.

Mama read my sullen face and she was quick to comfort me. "We have one water bottle, one canteen, one kettle, and the baby's bottle. If it helps, I'll leave you in charge of the canteen."

I eagerly nodded and promised to be its safekeeper.

I was nine years old when we entered the jungle, running for our lives again. Wild vegetation and brush pricked our arms, sliced our feet, and poked our eyes. Every step was heavy with trepidation. Night quickly plunged the jungle into pitch blackness. Whatever shred of hope we harbored for freedom and opportunity seemed to have evaporated. The night felt thick with foreboding.

The guide and his son lit torches. The flames danced and flared, leaping and flitting as if they were two giant fireflies. The guide often turned to check on his son. They signaled to each other by moving their torches in a circular motion, sideways, or up and down.

After one hour of walking, the guide sent a signal to his son. "Okay, we'll stop here and break for five minutes." The line came to a stop on the narrow path. We set our belongings down to stretch our aching backs and tired legs. The old man walked around us. We saw the two flames moving toward each other. Our next break would not be for another two hours. "Stifle your coughing, sneezing, and crying," the guide cautioned as he returned to the front of the pack. "Follow me closely and do not sidestep. Danger lies ahead."

During the break, Papa handed each of us a pair of sandals made from car tires. We struggled to insert the thong between our toes while at the same time passing the kettle around to quench our thirst. I took only a small sip because I had guzzled a quart right before we met up with the group.

This was my own effort to reduce our water consumption on the journey. I had overdone it, because I could feel water sloshing in my stomach, resulting in a bellyache.

When the kettle was passed to Mama, she topped off the baby's bottle, added more sugar, and shook it. Half-Kilo was tiny and bony, partly due to Mama's own malnourishment and inability to produce enough breast milk to satisfy her appetite. She wailed of hunger almost constantly, and since there was no baby formula to supplement the milk, water and sugar would have to do. Under normal circumstances Half-Kilo would be spoon-fed rice soup. The infant quieted down to drink and soon fell asleep again.

After we transferred the sandals from Papa's baskets to our feet, he took the vinyl floor mat from me and the bundle from White Ghost. My load had been reduced to a three-pound bag of freshly roasted mung beans that I slung over my shoulder along with the water canteen Mama had entrusted me with. We were to drink out of the kettle first, to minimize spillage through the spout and lid. Mama quickly transferred her bundle to me to free up her other arm for cradling the baby.

We quickly discovered the sandals were more of a nuisance than a blessing. Given that we had gone barefoot for many years, they hardly qualified for the "essential" category; but the sandals made it on the journey the same way the damn cameras did during the forced evacuation in 1975 because Papa was adamant about bringing them. Because he was Papa.

In less than five minutes of walking in them, we abandoned them. The sandals and their wire "threads" made it feel as though there were hot nails beneath our feet. The collective weight of all the sandals almost equaled the weight of one tire.

Here, in the hours of uncertainty, Mama questioned her own fate again in marrying Papa. "You used wires in the shoes? What were you thinking? Never mind that they weighed a ton! I told you to throw them out. Why don't you ever listen to me?"

"Shhh." The guide turned around with his torchlight. We hushed immediately. We followed the torchlight and kept our concerns and worries to ourselves.

The path eventually narrowed and transitioned to a carpet of small saplings, leaves, and brambles underneath our feet. We kept our eyes on the burning torch ahead as we wound our way around trees and impenetrable groves. At times the guide slowed so his son could catch up when people in the back fell behind. This was when we stole moments to relieve ourselves at the spot where we stood or reach into our bags for food and water. It usually took only a moment for the second torchlight to catch up.

More signals were passed between the two torches that moved in a circle, sideways, or in an up and down motion; then off we meandered and wove into the deepest vortex of the unknown jungle.

Two hours later we exited the darkness and emerged into the pale moonlight, a starry night above us. We were now snaking through an open field of undergrowth and smaller trees and elephant reeds. The clear view of the heavens above did little to calm our anxiety. We couldn't ignore the overwhelming feeling of danger lurking in the shadows surrounding us. The guide's quickened strides, his total focus on navigating his way, and his silent gesture with a finger over his mouth meant one thing: hostile territory. Not one person, neither young nor old, complained of weariness. We knew that tonight our resolve was being tested. We remained in absolute silence and concentration. Thankfully, the babies were asleep in the comfort of their mothers' arms.

We marched on in a dreamlike stupor. We obediently followed the guide and his torch into another thick forest, twisting around big trunks and seemingly impenetrable shrubs. He led us with the urgent and careful quietude of a deer. It felt as though we had repeated the same trek all night long, circling, backtracking, and rewinding. *Did Sida and Big Daughter feel the same? Was this the despair they felt when they were lost and dying of thirst?* It was difficult to be free of suspicions. I wondered if their bodies shriveled nearby and whether my feet touched the ground they'd walked on.

It was impossible to calm my nerves, especially when we detected heavy warfare raging nearby in the heart of the jungle. Based on the sound and trajectory, we were heading straight toward the fight. Suddenly the line paused, and the torches froze in the guides' hands as flames leaped upwards in blackness. We halted our movement and stilled our breaths.

It was remarkable how Black Ghost and White Ghost didn't get startled at the sounds of battle. Perhaps previous exposure to the ugly sound of mortars and artillery had made it natural to them, but Half-Kilo was beginning to fuss. Mama tried to breastfeed her, but she let out a frightful cry and refused to suckle.

Mama quickly pulled the baby bottle from her pocket and fed her the sugared water. Somewhere behind us, another baby began to cry. Someone in the group muttered softly, "Maybe the babies know something we don't." With that comment, the air instantly hung heavier and tenser than the second before. The guide waved a new signal with his torch to his son, telling him to change course to a longer but safer route. The shooting shifted farther to the right of us as we put a greater distance between us and the conflict. It was hard to know the exact time. Judging from how tired I felt, it must have been past midnight.

The detour eliminated any chance for a short rest. Despite sensing that the night was full of peril, my eyes betrayed me and felt heavy. When Black Ghost couldn't keep up any longer, Papa had to empty one basket and divvy up the belongings among us older kids so Black Ghost could sit in it. I tried my best to silence my yawning. Mama resorted to pinching and tugging at us to chase the sleep away. It barely helped sharpen my senses. My entire body was numb with fatigue. I was like a walking zombie. I would have been pleased to be left behind, if given the choice. I couldn't care less about tomorrow when I was too tired to continue living today. Mama was behind us, making sure that all her ducklings were in line.

Out of nowhere, guns exchanged fire directly in front of us with ferocity and blinding brightness. This paralyzed us. We were caught in the crossfire. The blasts split the air and deafened my eardrums. I was no longer a walking zombie, but a frightened animal. The brightness lit by the submachine guns revealed a dozen men fighting nearby. The men shouted in Khmer, "Over there! Over there!" They then stormed away to pursue their enemies. There were more men crouching and chasing after them. We felt the heat emanating from the barrage of gunfire and we quickly took cover nearby among the vegetation. The battle continued between the two unknown factions. The jungle was pitch black except when the volley of gunfire lit up the night. Bullets whizzed loudly, both near and far.

This is it. Our end is here. My body braced itself for bullets.

I was next to Nuy and White Ghost, and a thick wall of reeds pierced our backs and sliced our arms. We heard Half-Kilo somewhere to our left. She was crying at the top of her lungs. We were separated from Vunn, Papa, and Black Ghost. We could only hope they were unharmed. In front of us, the guide and his son struggled to put out their torches. We lay frozen for maybe half an hour, too tense to feel pain and discomfort.

The factions barked commands to each other as they continued firing and running. There was no doubt we had compromised our position. The two babies screeched hysterically, to the point of hyperventilation. I pictured Mama stuffing the sugared bottle into Half-Kilo's mouth, but it was no consolation. The sound of gunfire combined with the baby bullhorns was deafening.

I tensed up tenfold after realizing that both sides could exploit us to advance their positions.

The battle eventually moved away from us. These unknown factions chased each other as soldiers yelled and fired randomly in the dark. Injured men screamed in pain and dead men collapsed silently like trees in the forest.

Their distance meant our safety. The scared voices of wounded men sounded more distant and remote. The gunfire eventually petered out, but the two babies were far beyond comfort. We remained immobile for another fifteen minutes to ensure our security before crawling back out to continue our journey. The infants eventually calmed down.

By now I was wide awake, and I prayed for dawn; but the night dragged on, slower than ever. Time always crawled when I consciously willed it to speed up. Two hours later we exited the jungle onto flat, open moorland. The moon had shifted its position and dipped lower in the dark sky. We didn't cut through the open field due to safety concerns. Remaining out of sight and taking a longer detour decreased the chance of detection, the guide said. It felt like four in the morning.

Just when I dreaded entering another jungle, the guide unstrapped the basket on his back and told us to rest until sunrise. Here we restored ourselves with roasted green beans and roasted rice and water. The old guide moved from group to group. He whispered the dangers of the next phase, telling us how critical it was to listen to him. We were instructed not to deviate from the path—to walk slowly and cautiously to avoid tripping over explosive ordnances. He warned us of bandits: should we encounter them, we were to obey their every word. He especially told the women to cooperate and not to resist any unwelcome advances.

We had less than two hours to close our eyes and rest, but how could one sleep, knowing this? My head was still ringing from gunfire. As I lay there, my eyes caught sight of the most bizarre-looking caterpillars. They were fat and long, the size of my big toe. They glowed and had red and pink fur.

A pair of them wiggled their way into the jungle. Such crawlers would disgust me, but they were so extraordinary that I was hypnotized by their beauty. Eventually their bodies disappeared out of sight and, before I knew it, I was pulled from sleep. We were to set off once again.

We entered the danger zone. To the left and right of the unmarked path were huge rectangular pits along the jungle landscape. In these pits bamboo spears lay inverted with their sharp tips pointing upward: we came across two bodies decomposing in one of them. The pits and the bodies didn't unnerve me as much as the rafts suspended above our heads. They were latched onto trees in a conspicuous manner, ready to spring at us should we step on a snare or a trap.

We walked cautiously until we finally met a group of Thai soldiers who were easily distinguished by the language they spoke (which I immediately recognized from my childhood, having lived so close to Thailand before the forced evacuation.) I was relieved to have at last reached Thailand, our destination and our salvation.

With the tips of their guns they divided our group into men, women, and children. A group of five soldiers led the women away, and another group of five led the men away. A few of them remained to guard the children while others searched through our belongings. They found gold buried in shoulder poles. They unraveled the bundles and took whatever pleased them. They reached into pots and pans for treasures buried in rice.

A soldier reached into my bag of roasted mung beans and fished out a silver Seiko watch. That was all they managed to steal from us. The gold was well hidden in both of my parents' hindquarters.

Mama was returning to us from behind the wall of trees and thick bushes—I could tell this by the sound of my baby sister's high-pitched wail. While the soldier was busy patting her down, Mama stealthily pinched Half-Kilo's thigh. The two women with babies strapped to them were the first to be released, followed by the elder women. The rest of the females remained behind. I spotted their nakedness through holes in the trees and undergrowth. Shortly after, Papa and all the men came back. We were instructed to retrieve our belongings. We quickly packed and retied everything as best as we could. When we appeared ready, two soldiers led us and another couple and their baby to the edge of the forest. We were the first two families to exit the jungle in our traveling group.

They indicated we were to proceed onward, into an awaiting crowd. We did as told and walked out into the morning light and into civilization, where Thai citizens immediately handed us water in clear plastic bags. That was when I realized that my canteen was almost empty.

One man jotted down our names and instructed his helpers to give us a few pounds of rice and a blue tarp tent. We were immediately ushered to the left to stake out a spot so we could set up our shelter. We were in a shantytown filled with tents and clotheslines, living among other Cambodian refugees who, like us, had successfully escaped hell. We had arrived in the Nong Chan refugee camp in Thailand. Within days we were once again reunited with relatives: Mama's siblings (Uncle Jo, Uncle Tek, Uncle Yi, and Aunt Gai) and Papa's sister and sister-in-law. I found more contentment and peace here than I had known since the forced evacuation.

32. DANGREK MOUNTAINS (JUNE 1979)

My parents had converted some gold into Thai money and we were able to purchase wares from street vendors who were Thai citizens. I put on a new t-shirt and shorts and even had a new pair of yellow flip-flops for my calloused feet. I savored durian ice cream, drank coffee, and enjoyed a bowl of noodles, and I even swam in a small river with other children. I was in paradise.

What was familiar to me was foreign to my younger siblings. White Ghost and Black Ghost yelped "hot" when touching a chunk of ice. They didn't know how to walk in flip-flops. They stared at a bar of soap, asking if it was edible. Papa gave all of us medicinal lollipops for our intestinal worms. We were told to eat them for many weeks straight before the efficacy would kick in. However, we were never given the opportunity to know if they worked—and Papa didn't have an opportunity to buy corrective eyewear for his poor vision—because the buses were waiting for us.

Buoyed by hope and its promising tomorrow, my relatives lined up to climb onto the buses.

We were next.

We hauled our belongings half a mile to a fleet of buses. As we approached, two soldiers ushered us to a coach that was already half full as more people waited to board. The Thai military guarded us with rifles. In front of our coach were other buses already packed with people; they were being driven away toward the late afternoon sun.

Behind our vehicle several more empty buses lined up, all waiting for their turn to pull forward. To the right were thousands of soldiers standing sentry over the masses, brandishing rifles and facing the crowds, keeping them at bay. Some of the Thai people shouted in their native tongue and many tried to force their way through the guards to give us food and water sealed in small plastic bags tied with rubber bands. Some succeeded in passing the provisions, but many failed because the wall of soldiers pushed them back, intending to keep these two worlds apart. In the frenzy, it was impossible to differentiate cries of joy from those of sorrow. Ignorant of the Thai people's warning cries, we continued to smile, not knowing what they were attempting to convey to us.

We had no idea why they offered us food, but we fought for it nonetheless. We thought they were just good Samaritans showing compassion for those less fortunate. It was especially difficult for my enormous family to compete with others for the handouts, since we were encumbered by small children. We couldn't rival the bigger and stronger people for the scattered donations.

Papa was busy shoulder-poling two baskets full of pots and pans, tarps, a vinyl mat, blankets, roasted beans, and raw rice. Mama had Half-Kilo hammocked to her body and dragged Black Ghost by the hand. The rest of us carried belongings while we struggled to obtain additional charitable items. I carried the same canteen filled with water and an empty ice cooler box which could hold about two gallons of liquid. We bought the cooler to store ice to suck on in the sweltering heat, but now it became the container for the pouches of water which our tiny hands gratefully reached out to accept.

In those few minutes of standing in line, our family collectively obtained two four-pound bags of rice, several packages of instant noodles, one bag of salt, one bag of sugar, and five bags of water. In the chaos, we pushed and shoved each other over the donations the way children scrambled after candies falling out of a piñata. Those who were bigger and faster had the advantage. We were the children whose little hands were empty because the bigger people snatched the goods first, but what little we procured was enough to make us excited and content.

When we were no more than ten feet from stepping onto the bus, someone yelled from the crowds in one of the Chinese dialects, which my parents understood.

"Wipe the smiles off your face! You've all been duped! You're to be dumped and thrown away!"

After hearing this, the expression on my parents' faces changed drastically, as if they were staring at the faces of apparitions.

Mama shouted the news in Khmer to warn everyone. Our smiles vanished instantly. The same person continued, "No one will survive this ordeal; it only leads to purgatory." Now I was shocked and rendered speechless.

What had felt like a parade procession just a minute ago had turned into an inexplicable nightmare. The news traveled fast. Instantly there was mayhem and panic, both inside and outside the bus. People were begging and crying for mercy and compassion. Some brought their palms together to pray to Buddha for protection, while others pleaded for clemency from the soldiers. A few attempted to crawl out through the windows, but they didn't get far because soldiers rammed them back in with rifles.

It was our turn to climb aboard. Seeing our reluctance to proceed, two soldiers immediately pushed us and forced us inside.

We got onto the bus in haste. Once inside, we scurried about as if a grenade were going off. We grabbed any available seats. I sat on an aisle seat in the center of the bus on the right side next to a man and his daughter, who was about

White Ghost's age. The rest of my family was scattered throughout the bus.

A few Thai citizens broke through the line and came running to us. In these few precious seconds, they tossed rice, water, candy, noodles, sugar, and other essentials through the windows. Some had tears rolling down their faces. Now that we understood where we were headed, we fought like cats and dogs for those handouts.

The man who sat next to me monopolized the entire window and wouldn't let me squeeze in with him for the freebies. He even kicked me back with his leg and used his rear end to block me from reaching the window. Through sheer determination I managed to get close enough for a handful of mint candies. I reached through the window again, and just when I thought I was about to get a bag of rice, he snatched it from me. His savage and greedy behavior ignited within me an intense rage. This meant war in a dog-eat-dog world: one where you die, and I live. I wouldn't go down without a fight.

I was shaking inside, but I wasn't deterred. In a split second I stole a bag of rice and a bag of water from their pile. I felt completely justified: the items would have been mine had he only shared the window with me. I tried to snatch more, but the father instructed his daughter to keep watch.

She eyed me like I was a snake.

There was another split second where I managed to get another bag of water from their loot. This happened as the father handed more items to his daughter and she was momentarily distracted.

When the bus revved its engine, the donors backed away from its fumes and dust. Just like that, the much-desired, charmed paradise receded into the background.

On the bus, we exploded in hysteria. The babies and children cried from discomfort and hunger. The bus sped along, keeping pace with the other buses, police cars, and military convoys. Two police cars with sirens and lights swirling followed us closely. Behind the police were more buses and military convoys filled with soldiers. Worry over the unknown chased away my appetite.

Since the bus continued without stopping, Papa had to empty a bag of water into the icebox to use the bag to catch Black Ghost's urine and diarrhea. There was no toilet inside the bus. Even when the bus stopped for fueling, we weren't allowed to step outside. This was obvious when soldiers leaped out of the convoy to surround the bus, aiming rifles directly at us. We later learned of buses flipping over or crashing when the passengers attempted to sabotage or hijack the moving vehicles to avoid being dumped and thrown away.

We weren't accustomed to the smell of burning fumes and vehicle motion. As the bus bounced up and down and swayed and wound its way into the night, my nauseated stomach churned wildly. To ease my misery, I popped a mint candy into my mouth; but the relief lasted only as long as the candy did.

The suffocating fumes and sounds of regurgitation from people throughout the bus caused me to vomit. I had the foresight to empty water into the icebox to prepare a bag. We were trapped inside this rolling purgatory for over thirteen hours. The subhuman atmosphere inside the buses reeked with the stench of fish, urine, and sweat mixed with feces, vomit, and fright.

They were taking us back to Cambodia. The ride should have been short—two to three hours at most—but the Thai government maintained a ruse to give us a false sense of security that they were taking us somewhere far and safe. When the bus first left, it drove toward the setting sun, heading west and away from the mountains, away from the place where everyone feared being "dumped and thrown" away. Someone on the bus attempted to calm us, telling us we were not going back to Cambodia, which lay to the east of Thailand. Because the ride was long, we were more convinced of the ruse. After the sun disappeared, the bus made many more turns and drove us to our doom.

I dozed off. As I slept off and on, my mind bounced with the motion of the bus, back and forth down memory lane. While the bus rolled into the night, my mind recalled images of the past. In those fleeting moments, tears streamed down my face. The phrase "to be dumped and thrown away" could only mean one thing. Though my spirit had thus far withstood this latest blow, it now cracked. We had come so far. I cried because I was afraid. I cried because I didn't want to die. I cried because that was all I could do.

The babies must have sensed the distress, too. They wailed ceaselessly as the bus rocked us uncomfortably towards an unknown fate.

The night eventually faded to gray. Soon gray turned to morning with a tinge of orange. The bus lumbered onward in an upward incline and the sun rose with glorious rays. The sky was an intense blue and nearly cloudless. The view outside was serene and lush with greenery. I felt detached from this image of nature's glory and beauty. All that was good and beautiful belonged to fortunate people. Not even that which was discarded came to us unfortunates, not even the air we breathed nor the water we drank.

It was now five in the morning, thirteen hours after our departure, when the bus slowed to a full stop on a dusty mesa surrounded with trees. The second the door to our bus opened, the military soldiers stormed in to surround us. Two of them forced us out, brandishing the universal language of weaponry. The soldiers harassed and harried us. We were all used to walking barefoot and as such, we had mindlessly kicked off our new flip-flops while on the bus. I managed to collect my sandals from under the seat and gathered all the essentials I stowed, but the rest of my family left them behind, along with some of the essentials. We simply didn't have time to gather all our belongings.

Once outside, the soldiers yelled and waved their guns at us, making us march and join the rest of the refugees, who were standing on the precipice.

The bus drove away as soon as the last person stepped off.

Our family stood behind thousands of people. It was hard for me to see beyond the wall of bodies. I was curious and managed to squeeze my way to the front. What I saw shook me to the core. It was a steep cliff. I spotted people far below and wondered how they got there. Even farther down, trees stood as small as blades of grass.

They had dumped us at the top of the Dangrek Mountains. The mountain ridges splayed east and west. We were standing on the northern peak, looking down and southward at vast wilderness in Cambodia. Straight below lay a steep and abrupt slope littered with unmarked land mines.

This area had long been a disputed domain between Thailand and Cambodia. Hundreds of years ago, it belonged to the kingdom of the Khmer people. Since then, the soil of Cambodia shrank as its neighboring countries waged wars to stake claims and expand their territories.

We refugees appealed, with our palms together, for the soldiers' mercy. We cried out our reluctance to go down the cliff. The soldiers, looking stern and serious, weren't moved by our pleas.

My family stood near the inland mesa, away from the cliff but with our backs to the ledge and our faces to the Thai soldiers. On cue, the soldiers fired rounds into the empty sky and screamed in Thai for us to jump; but the sea of people, terribly frightened, took only two steps backwards toward the edge, then inched forward again. The people behind us shouted at us to move forward, away from the cliff, so they wouldn't fall off.

Mama told us to move with the crowds. "Don't put your pole and baskets down," she told Papa as she sternly looked at our faces. "Always stand and move with the people. Do not draw attention to yourself."

Gunfire blasted into the sky every five to ten minutes, and like bamboo trees, we swayed back and forth. The people who stood closest to the ledge were precariously hanging on for dear life every time we fell back a few steps. They cried to us in the front, "Don't come back too far; we'll fall off! We'll die if we go down! There are land mines below." We continued swaying two steps backward and two steps forward for at least an hour. With no warning at all, a soldier walked over and reached into Papa's left breast pocket.

Papa was instinctively taken aback. He reacted by fending off the hand that had stolen from him. The soldier immediately pointed the tip of his gun barrel at Papa, who quickly surrendered with his hands in the air, crying out, "Please don't shoot."

The soldier then proceeded to fish out the lump of Thai money from Papa's pocket. He snapped off the rubber band and unfurled the roll of money. Leafing through the wad of cash, he found a few white pills sealed inside a tiny plastic bag.

Papa brought his palms together, "Please give back the medicine. Take only the money."

The soldier was irritated at first; but after seeing the fright on our faces, his demeanor became subdued. I didn't know if our shorn heads solicited his compassion the way Mama had intended by shaving our heads, but he did stuff the medicine back into Papa's pocket.

He even spoke to us in broken Khmer: "Go, go, go . . . down, down, down . . . water." He pantomimed the cliff and the digging in the ground to get to the water.

We didn't quite know what he was trying to say to us. We were all puzzled, but he was determined to communicate his message. He squatted and pretended to dig into the earth. With his hands, he cupped the invisible water from the ground and splashed it into his mouth. From this we concluded the soldier was trying to tell us that water could be easily found in the ground. Sensing he had succeeded in getting his message through to us, he returned to his position to guard against us once more.

It was now eight in the morning. Our desperation rose faster than the sweltering heat and humidity. We couldn't leave the premises to relieve ourselves. We relied on family members to shield us from others with a towel or a blanket at the nearest tree trunk. The air was heavy and rancid, mingled with the smell of sweat and urine.

People eventually grew weary from standing, so they would momentarily sit down to rest. Despair was gnawing on the faces of even the bravest and strongest. Papa tried to squat, but Mama gently kicked his foot and motioned with her chin for him to get up.

A lady who was a bit older than Mama sat with her two teenage daughters. They were no more than six feet in front of us. The mother sat on the dirt. A few minutes later she appeared to be lost in a trance. Her eyes pierced through the ground in front of her while she whipped her head and said, "Don't go down. Don't go down. Please have mercy. Please don't force us down."

It was around noon, over six hours since we had arrived. There wasn't a breeze in the air. The trees were still. The air felt heavy and dust caked our skin.

I needed a distraction to take my mind off this new hell. I looked around and found scattered sticks and stones at my disposal. I dug two parallel rows of holes. There were twelve holes and each of them contained four pebbles. I improvised a game of mancala, but I needed a partner. Nuy and Vunn declined, too distraught to play. I looked at White Ghost with pleading eyes and saw she was eager to learn. I was thrilled that someone was willing to play. I let her go first, but she took too long to make her moves. My eyes absorbed my surroundings while I patiently waited for her to empty the stones from one batch and drop them one by one into the others.

The birds glided in the air with their wings spread in the distant blue sky. The sun peeked through the trees. The rifles stalked all of us as soldiers pointed them randomly at the distraught refugees. The soldier who stood closest to us aimed his rifle at me, then shifted to my parents, before reverting to me. Although I noticed it, I ignored it. All morning long those guns had been busy pointing at all of us.

Another gun was aimed at me, then my family, before finally landing on the lady with the two daughters.

White Ghost was in the middle of dropping in the pebbles when suddenly, and seemingly in unison, a barrage of bullets was fired at us.

Everything happened so fast. The birds fluttered away, the sunlight shattered, and a burst of heat blasted our faces and bodies. Plumes of smoke lingered in the air. Everyone shrieked. A veritable stampede ensued.

They shot the lady in the face! Specks of her blood and brain pelted my cheek and shirt. We shrieked when we saw her faceless body collapse. A fragment of her skull landed at the base of a nearby tree. My stubbly hair contained chunks of her flesh!

The two daughters screamed in horror, their faces contorted by rage. They hyperventilated as they held their mother's headless body. They couldn't catch their breaths as they continued their bloodcurdling howls while hugging her body and rocking it back and forth. Both daughters were trapped in indescribable agony, frozen in one hellish instant of time.

The suddenness of it disoriented and stupefied everyone. Instinctively we grabbed our essentials before stampeding over one another to jump down the cliff. It felt as if we had been swallowed into an apocalyptic world where cruelty and pain had no boundaries.

Farther away, another man was shot in the thigh. His family scrambled, he hopped, and together they took a leap of faith and plummeted down the cliff.

In those few seconds, we blindly pushed and shoved each other down the sandstone escarpment. Papa tossed the pole and baskets down so he could grab on to Black Ghost. Mama leaped down with Half-Kilo in one arm and a small bundle in the other. Vunn and Nuy jumped down, holding on to a few possessions.

Our bodies tumbled down, as though some mischievous child had kicked rocks over the cliff and took pleasure in watching them skip and roll down the hill. We grabbed tree roots, each other, and rocks and boulders to decelerate the fall, mindful not to let go nor to lose sight of our belongings.

As much as I could, I lowered myself down on my rear end and slid before coming to a stop where the slope flattened out, still clinging onto the icebox for dear life. The cliff was steep; it felt like a three-hundred-foot fall. Our tumble caused people below to shove farther out. People were screaming in frantic and some ran through the barren field, aiming for safety in the woods but forgetting there were land mines. These unfortunate people unwittingly triggered the mines and eviscerated themselves.

The explosions coupled with the whizzing sounds of the gunfire created a cacophony of death and devastation. The massacre continued, and in it I envisioned my body and my family pulverized by flames. My mind returned to the difficult years under the Khmer Rouge, the battle for my life, how I had survived. It all seemed to be ending.

This mass of humanity numbering in the thousands rolled down the steep precipice, chancing the land mines rather than getting shot up above. Mounds of wounded people sprawled at unnatural angles, unable to continue the insane descent due to broken and mangled limbs. Family members separated. Babies and small children wailed, and old people moaned, but I was enraged to tears. Hate burned within me. I hated the Thais, now: not only did they lack compassion, but they were eager to mete out vicious cruelty.

Why were we condemned?

What had we done to deserve such a harsh sentence?

Why did we have to crawl through so many obstacles, only to meet our ends?

I felt betrayed by humanity, by the spirits, and by the powerful forces of the universe. The entire time we had dreamed of Thailand as being our saving grace. We believed it was a pilgrimage we must make if we were to survive; but we couldn't have been more wrong. The Thais were no better than the Khmer Rouge.

Map 5: Dangrek Mountains

33. DOWN THE MOUNTAINS FROM WHENCE WE CAME (JUNE 1979)

It was only after the present receded into the past that we learned the statistics of those fateful days. Back then, we didn't know there were well over one hundred buses working around the clock. We didn't know the buses ran non-stop for four or five days. With roughly sixty people jammed into each bus, the estimated number of refugees was a staggering forty-five thousand men, women, and children. It was estimated as much as ten percent of the refugees perished in this atrocity.

At this point, we were no different than the emaciated Jewish victims who had suffered in Nazi concentration camps—except that our supposed liberating army of Thai soldiers dumped us into a sea of land mines and flying bullets. The genocide continued, and the world had yet to hold the Thai government accountable.

Though our arms and legs were bruised, no bones were broken. Behind us jutted the brown precipice from which we had dropped. Below us spread an array of discarded souls, lost and bewildered. In the distance a faint line could be seen of people leaving the desolate mountains.

Those who had arrived first were tossed into the farthest fringe. They were to pave the path for us, with their lives. Fate had wedged them into a dangerous predicament. They had been stuck here a few days longer than we had. Their sustenance had long been depleted and some resorted to drinking urine to survive.

To dawdle the hours away would mean certain death. They had no choice but to chance fate and hope that their next stride wouldn't be their last. These men, women, and children were the trailblazers. They charted and cleared the path for us to follow. This path would eventually be our lifeline out of perdition (a vast area filled with unmarked land mines intended to divide and isolate Thailand from Cambodia completely) and we would later step over their decaying carcasses. We became forever indebted to them.

In the meantime, there was nowhere to go. We waited patiently for our turn to descend the mountain and navigate around the mines. We were at a standstill there for three days and two nights.

After the big fall, it took time to regain control over our nerves. Once we were settled, the first thing that came to mind was water. We looked inside the icebox and found that four bags remained intact in an inch of water. That was all we had for eight dehydrated people.

Mama pulled out the baby bottle to refill it. We untied one pouch and emptied half a bag of water into the bottle. The rest of the pouches were transferred into the canteen.

A new rule was made: no one was to drink water without permission. Papa slung the canteen around his neck.

We then salvaged the last drops of water from the icebox and placed them in a bowl. It was barely half full when we each took a small sip before passing it to the next person, treating it as our most prized possession.

We looked around to see if others were equally distraught from not having enough water, only to realize that we were the most ill-prepared. In the flurry of flying bullets, we had leaped down, leaving behind some of our vital provisions. Others fared better than my family, mainly because they were all older and stronger.

I looked upward at the lurching cliff: so imposing and so out of reach. I wished somehow I could climb back up to retrieve the rest of our belongings—but then more shots were fired and more people jumped down.

I gazed up to the sky and pictured a set of wings growing from my back. With wings, I could fly away. A silly and stupid thought, I scolded myself. I looked down at the bloodstain on my shirt and shuddered again at the image of the hole in the lady's head. When I looked up again, I saw worry cascading down my parents' faces like hot wax dripping from candles. They fought back the tears, but it was useless. A sinking feeling assailed me again.

Amid the ground rumbling under our feet and gunshots ringing from above to deter people from climbing back up, we implored, "Papa, we're thirsty."

With shaky hands Papa unscrewed the canteen and gave each of us a half capful. The cap was no more than two inches in diameter and one inch deep: it was barely a gulp. After savoring the water and licking our lips, we reverted to our positions, sitting and squatting under the scorching sun. We were feeble and hungry. Aside from not having enough water to drink (let alone cook with), there wasn't even firewood to roast more raw rice. Mama opened a package of instant noodles, broke it into pieces, and doled them out as equally as she could, and we were each limited to a mouthful of roasted rice.

Suddenly another explosion erupted, smoke spiraled upward, and the smell of sulfur mixed with charred human flesh assaulted our noses.

It was now five in the evening. Again, we begged; "Papa, our throats hurt."

The canteen was three-quarters full. Papa poured half a capful and told us to share it. He dipped his tongue into the water to demonstrate. The cap was passed from one person to the next. When it was my turn, I stuck my tongue in. It felt so refreshing. It took all my willpower not to drink it all and face the consequences later. White Ghost's hand was immediately in my face, impatient for her turn.

Tears pooled in our eyes. What was the point of having gold when no one was willing to trade for it? The ground was dry on an incline. Despite the Thai soldier's pantomiming the digging for water, we knew with great certainty that there was none underneath.

Half-Kilo was always hungry. Mama stuffed her nipple into the baby's mouth, but after suckling it for a few minutes, the baby wailed out of frustration from the lack of milk. Mama defaulted to feeding her the sugared water. Even the baby couldn't drink till she was full because the bottle would have to last her until raindrops graced us from the sky or water seeped upward from the ground. Both scenarios were highly unlikely to happen any time soon.

The merciless sun faded gradually into cool dusk. Our tired minds surveyed the desolation of our world. We knew we had to spend the night exactly where we had been all day. When it was dinnertime, we shared another packet of instant noodles and we each ate a teaspoon of sugar and drank a half capful of water.

The stars and moon twinkled above. The galaxies and constellations looked oddly serene. My stomach roiled, twisted, and turned. My lips cracked. My throat hurt and my heart beat irregularly.

"Papa, I'm thirsty. Can I have another sip?" Black Ghost begged.

He unscrewed the cap and slowly poured the water. "Here, pass it around."

It was barely one ounce of water for eight people: a few drops per tongue.

That night we slept in our sitting positions. Some of us hunched over our belongings for support. I managed to curl into a fetal position even as I was plagued by despair, spent by agony, and clutched by hunger; yet this was just the first night.

Land mines detonated around us.

Above us, the soldiers continued killing those who attempted to climb back up.

Each explosion yielded more death and destruction, followed by cries. People roared into the night like a pack of wolves howling to the moon. It was impossible to sleep. My stomach was aching from lack of food and water. I felt detached and numb. My empathy for others finally abandoned me altogether. I was grateful that it wasn't my family stepping on those mines.

I decided to stop praying and making deals and promises with invisible spirits who consigned me to a fate in which I felt perpetually suffocated. It seemed as if I had been living underwater and holding my breath for as long as I could remember. Why should we have to go to such lengths just to survive? The injustice was mindboggling.

Although forty-five thousand people were stuck in this hellish purgatory together, we had never felt more alone. Our burdens were our own.

The line finally reached us on the morning of the third day, after we drank the water that Uncle Jo had brought back to us, after his desperate journey through the minefields.

We merged in with the crowded front line, but the queue was still slow to move. The sun rose quickly to the center of the sky and the lack of food in our stomachs made us languid. Even though I simply stood still in one place, black spots invaded my vision, making me lose my balance. We chewed on roasted mung beans and raw rice for energy, but they also caused terrible stomachaches and diarrhea.

The people below were moving at the pace of an aged turtle. We, in turn, moved at their pace. Each step was precise and methodical. We lifted one foot at a time to place it immediately after the person in front of us raised his foot. Our eyes were focused and locked on the person in front of us. Our minds had to remain acute because there wasn't any room for second-guessing.

Explosions occurred randomly everywhere, always followed by screams and cries.

There were many times when we didn't progress at all and stood as still as trees on a windless day.

Mines riddled the ground. Time and elements conspired to wash away and erode the topsoil to expose some of the metal caps in the dirt; however, not all mines graced us with such an appearance. We couldn't sit or walk freely. Our survival depended solely on those who had already trekked the path and gifted us their footprints. We endured this slow march just as much as we endured starvation and fear, an added layer to our already-shattered souls.

The line ahead eventually curved around a wall of shrubs before venturing and disappearing into the fringe of the forest. Unfortunately, the mines didn't end there.

One time, the line stopped completely, and our feet froze in their places. Word traveled to us from those in the front that we wouldn't be moving for a long time due to an impassable juncture where grenades were wired to trees and brush and mines lay dormant in the ground, both visible and invisible to the eye. Wires were crisscrossed, linking the grenades and mines together to achieve one purpose—total annihilation to trespassers. A few hours later we heard that the Vietnamese soldiers had arrived at the scene to neutralize and dispose of the explosive ordnances. We had waited several hours in the same spot by the time the line moved again.

The Vietnamese forces now ran Cambodia, and although it didn't come as a surprise, we were nevertheless in tears; for they had once again come to us as liberators. Not only did they free us from the Khmer Rouge, but they also saved us from the Thai government's affliction and apathy. There were many explosions inadvertently detonated as they tried to defuse the bombs. The Vietnamese soldiers suffered casualties.

The smell of putrid decay assailed our senses long before we came to the scene, forcing us to pinch our noses. Over two dozen bodies lay scattered to the left of a small patch of shrubs. Some had missing limbs, and some had intestines spilling out of their stomachs. Flies buzzed around, feasting on rotten flesh with maggots wiggling inside. These bodies had been here at least five days because clear liquid oozed out of their skins like viscous sap dripping from a tree.

We gagged. Papa reached inside his pocket for a tiny tin of Tiger Balm. We rubbed the menthol ointment under our nostrils to help alleviate the foul smell. It worked briefly, but the stench returned. The smell of human decomposition thickened with the rising temperature, and it lingered at the tip of my nose. When I breathed it in I felt disoriented, but I had to remain focused. I couldn't wait to put a great distance between myself and this scene. It was difficult to shield our eyes from such gore, especially when we had to walk through the field of carcasses.

Shortly after we crossed through the carnage, a lady with two daughters about my age sped up from behind us.

They were moving quickly, asking people to excuse their rudeness as they wiggled through the line. Suddenly they cut past Nuy and White Ghost. One moment Mama was focused on placing her next foot, and the next second someone tapped on the shoulder. "Excuse us, we need to pass through."

Mama turned around in alarm. She did a double take at seeing the lady and the girls. "Excuse me, who the hell are you? Why are you between my family?"

The lady pressed her palms together. "Please let us through. Our family is ahead of us. We need to catch up to them."

"Look, lady, everyone's looking for someone! We're walking in each other's footsteps here. If you haven't noticed, mines are everywhere. Didn't you just step over dead bodies?" Mama's voice rose two octaves higher and her eyes burned with contempt. "You can get us all killed!"

"Please, I beg you. They're at the front. We got separated during the big fall."

Mama fiercely whipped her head. "I can't. Not if it endangers my family."

"Have mercy, please. Others were kind enough to let us through." She sounded extremely irritated with Mama.

Tension mounted. The people closest to us watched with a nervous intensity. No one shifted. A silent warning of imminent danger went off inside our heads. It was as if we were swimming in a sea of gasoline with two crazy people standing on the shallow shore ready to strike a match to burn us all in flames. The smell from the dead carcasses still lingered in our noses. If they were to throw punches at each other, their feet could easily stray off the path and trigger a detonation.

"You're the one with no heart, risking the lives of others for your own selfishness," Mama rebuked while pointing her fingers to the people in front and back of us. "Why should your family be more important than ours? Step back and let my family pass or we'll be standing here all day!"

The lady shook and glared at Mama. Poison and hatred shot out of her eyes.

Mama countered her stare with the same venomous look. She was formidable and unflinching.

The atmosphere became charged. A stalemate ensued.

Begrudgingly they stood their grounds like tigers fighting for territory. Each was ready to pounce at her opponent's slightest move. Those nearby remained paralyzed, beyond distress. This could take a considerable amount of time, and time was our worst enemy while our feet were treading through minefields.

It was a hot day, and their hostility sucked all the oxygen out of the air. The sun scorched my head. I dreaded this encounter because I knew Mama wouldn't back down, having stone-hearted her will. I understood her resolve the way I knew the back of my hand. She would stand there until tomorrow. There was only one winner, and the lady had better be a gracious loser or else the two hotheads would kill us all in one fell swoop. I shuddered at imagining that ending: the image of our bodies lying at this exact spot, with strangers stepping over us.

About ten excruciating minutes later, the woman relented, knowing Mama would not give her an inch. She motioned to her children to fall back and indicated the rest of us should go in front. The line was once again moving. We had a good thirty to forty steps of catching up to do. The lady and her children trailed us demurely for the rest of the day.

Papa balanced a pole on his shoulders. One basket contained pots, pans, and our meager sustenance; the other contained Black Ghost. She was caged like a diseased animal, wide-eyed with apprehension. It was strenuous for Papa to carry such a load. His shoulders were tender and tight with pain. Uncle Tek was considerate to offer his help, but he was in poor health and in no shape to carry the loads. Papa had to endure this suffering alone. Two of Mama's three brothers were with us only briefly. Unfortunately, Uncle Jo was obligated to stay with his in-laws' group and Uncle Yi with his adoptive parents. Aunt Gai remained with her in-laws. Only Uncle Tek stayed with us.

Papa was certifiably blind without the benefit of corrective eyewear; his movements were slow. He channeled all his energy in placing his foot correctly in someone else's wake. In this threatening jungle, however, danger lurked and detonation was only a footstep away.

To alleviate the pain from sawing deep cuts into his already-tender right shoulder, he rotated the pole with a slight twirl so the two baskets spun to opposite ends. The child in the front ended up in the back and the pole ended up on his left shoulder. Occasionally, when it became too much to endure, he would reluctantly set the yoke down.

Papa set the baskets down with his knees slightly bent.

It was a millisecond, but in that split second our world sped up and slowed down at the same time.

"Bomb!" we yelled while pointing to the basket with Black Ghost in it.

Papa's legs shot straight up in panic, taking with him pots and pans and the child in the basket.

Black Ghost cried in panic and instantly struggled to get out of the basket in midair. We all hollered at her to stay put.

Black Ghost's weight alone should have triggered the blast. We should have been blown away, but we weren't. Mama pressed her palms together and raised them as high as she could with the baby slung in her arms, frantically saying, "Thank you, our protectors. Thank you for saving us." Her voice was shaky but laced with intense gratitude. The baby stirred and cried from our uproar.

Black Ghost exhaled a sound of relief and reverted to her sickly state once more.

◆◆◆

I took it upon myself to attend to Papa's bad vision after the bomb scare. After all, I was the one who had broken his eyeglasses so long ago during the forced evacuation. I could still feel the cracking of his eyewear under my foot with as much clarity as I could imagine the inferno emanating from the bomb, had it not been a dud.

To be his eyes, I stayed close to him, navigating the path and instructing him to step over tree roots, stones, and holes in the ground. One time he asked if a gnarled tree branch was a dead snake.

Again, our walk barely progressed. We camped the night no more than a quarter of a mile from where Papa had set Black Ghost on the mine. We were essentially immobile. We urinated and defecated around the spot where we laid our mats to eat our meager meal. These were the exact spots camped in by those in the front from prior nights. That night we each had a mouthful of roasted mung beans and water for dinner.

We were tired and dirty. The hard ground, rigged with explosives, no longer seemed threatening to my weary body.

The explosions felt almost rhythmic, although not quite a lulling lullaby.

Sleep pulled me deep into a fantasy filled with steamy bowls of beef noodles and cones of cold ice cream.

Before I took a bite of either, Papa's voice called out, "Hey, you!" The noodles and ice cream vanished before I could taste them. I opened my eyes to see the object of Papa's concerns.

A man wandered aimlessly toward us, calling for his mother and waving a flashlight. From the rasp in his voice, we guessed he was an older man. He appeared lost and helpless. The flashlight beam became brighter and brighter as he came closer. Instinctively, Papa reached for the big shoulder-pole.

I propped myself up on my elbows, trying to make sense of the situation. Papa yelled again, "Hey, you there!"

The flashlight searched out Papa's voice and immediately found his face. He raised an elbow to block the harsh light. "Stay away! Don't come any closer!" Papa proceeded to swing the pole at him, to chase the man away.

"I'm looking for my mother. She's old and sick!" The man responded. "We've been separated for many days now. I need to find her. Please help."

Mama's voice blared over the man's plea. "I don't care who you're looking for! A man of your age isn't the same as a child looking for his mommy. You're a grown man. You should know better—wandering around like this can get us all killed!"

"I warn you, don't come any closer!" Papa's pole made a swooshing sound. The man sensed the threat and retreated a few steps.

The flashlight quickly bounced off Papa's face in search of a new direction. It swayed back and forth and sideways like a giant firefly. We were relieved the minute he distanced himself from us.

Anxiety and anger mushroomed wherever the man was headed. People screeched at him not to come near them. They called him terrible names and told him to go kill himself. Shortly thereafter, the man turned off the flashlight to be swallowed by the surrounding darkness, so he could be invisible and free of people's verbal assaults and physical threats.

I lay back down to sleep, thankful that the danger had passed while coming to the realization that the old man had just become a walking time bomb.

The stars suspended themselves above my eyes. They winked at me from a distance. I wished I could reach out to them. *Is that where America or France is? What do they eat and drink? What's it like to be born as one of them?*

A boom echoed in the distance and the ground shook, jolting me out of my reverie.

A few minutes later, another bomb went off nearby and people cried out in horror. The heat and smell of burnt flesh and sulfur wafted our way. Someone nearby said that it might have been the old man who was looking for his mom.

◆ ◆ ◆

The ground beneath our feet eventually transitioned from dry loose dirt to leaves. Footprints became more obscure and our steps more daunting. It was more frightening than walking through a jungle full of venomous snakes. At least we could chase snakes away with sticks.

Mines covered in leaves were more a game of chance, a sort of Russian roulette with thousands of people pulling the trigger. To maximize our chances of survival, we further reduced our pace. Any deviation increased the risk of annihilation. Each second spared was a second added to our lifespan.

Vunn took the lead, carrying our rolled-up blue tarp tent. I followed him, but stayed in front of Papa, constantly asking if he was okay. When he asked if the vinyl floor mat was too heavy for me to carry, I told him I could manage. Sweat dripped down my face as ordnances exploded in the distance, reminding each of us to always be careful.

It finally rained on our fifth night. Had the downpour occurred sooner, more lives would have been lost: the rain erased all the markings of safe spots and footprints left by others. The sky rumbled as if it, too, was outraged by our affliction.

Once we felt the raindrops, we unfurled the tent and vinyl mat, held them over our heads, and directed the rainwater into pots and pans. It rained hard enough that we were able to dig into the ground with our hands for muddy water for the next few days. There were twigs on the ground, but they were too wet to start a cooking fire. We shared our last bag of instant noodles and chewed on raw rice for dinner as we camped that night in the rain in the middle of the minefields buried in the mountains.

The next day we walked into night. We trailed from a dense jungle into one even denser and darker. Trees were so tall that their trunks seemed to rise forever and disappear into the heavens above. Branches and foliage spread out like blankets to block the sun. Day beneath the canopy was darker than a new moon night in the open. Light was passable only through small breaks from above. The few rays of light that snuck in through the overreaching foliage produced a muted light like candles in a deep cave.

We hadn't heard any explosions for a few hours now. The ground might be free of mines, but that wasn't certain, for no one dared to be the first to stray off the path? We continued as though we were still bound by the same circumstances as the day before.

Uncle Tek's mind was now weaker than his body. He had accepted that the mountains would be his final resting place. He had malaria and bouts of diarrhea. He even told us to leave him behind, but Mama wouldn't hear of it. She once again became the fierce gatekeeper of his beating heart. She applied the coin-scraping therapy all over his body, massaged his aches to the best of her ability, and boiled herbs she bought with a small piece of gold. She demanded his obedience and he complied, for he had tasted her resolve with the chili peppers and had endured her cruelty with the hitting stick.

When we rested for the day, we built a fire. Each family had to care for itself. Even Uncle Jo and his son never ate with us. Uncle Yi and Aunt Gai stayed with their other families. Aunt Wui's family of six was a stone's throw away from our fire. Papa's sister-in-law Dai and her four children were around, but not within sight. Each family was too busy fending for itself to pay attention to the suffering of others.

One night, a young couple with their parents and infant daughter camped next to us. As we started the cooking fire for dinner preparation, the infant caught my attention. She was a chubby little doll, always laughing and cooing, jostling up and down in her mother's lap. Her smile lit up more brightly than the fire burning in front of them. She was passed around from lap to lap. Four adults lavished all their love and attention on her. For a moment I was envious and sad at the same time: envious because the baby looked extremely healthy and happy and was safely protected in the folds of their embraces; sad because Half-Kilo looked nothing like her. It was a stark lesson in the contrast between the living and the dying.

Any night could have easily been my younger sisters' last. A hacking cough could have fractured Black Ghost's ribs. Half-Kilo had no nourishment other than water and a bit of sugar. Her meek and scrawny frame was grotesque and alarming. Strangers would shake their heads in pity; and when our paths crossed again at some later time, they were surprised that death hadn't claimed either of them. Not one soul reached into their pots to give us a spoon of rice as charity, but occasionally a young mother would take Half-Kilo's hungry mouth to her bosom for milk.

As our fire reduced to embers, the baby camped near us wailed uncontrollably. Something was clearly wrong. All ears followed her distressed cry. The men in their group continued to feed wood to the fire to keep the area lit. Through the leaping flames I saw the baby convulsing with epileptic attacks, her eyes rolling upward, revealing their whiteness. Her body shook as if possessed by a demon. The young mother panicked.

Nearby, people converged to see the distressed baby. Someone suggested the coining therapy, bruising the baby's skin to air out the fever. Another yelled to feed the baby urine from an infant boy. The young mother was desperate and agreed to every suggestion thrown her way.

I watched the scene with strange detachment, but with total clarity. A stranger tapped me on my shoulder and told me to look for a boy to collect his pee. I shook my head to decline the task. I was skeptical about urine being medicinal, but it wasn't the reason why I didn't move: I didn't run because I was in a trance. My mind was reeling in the unfolding crisis. I just stood there, staring deep into the flames dancing in front of the hysterical mother who was trying to save her baby.

The grandmother took the coin and ointment when a stranger offered them. She grabbed the infant from the young mother, placed it on her own lap, and begin disrobing the small trembling body. The baby was turning blue and her cries had turned into a death rattle. Her epileptic attacks suddenly ended and the wailing abruptly ceased. The coin didn't even meet her delicate skin.

Death came for the baby swiftly.

The mother shrieked. She hammered her fists into her chest, beating herself violently as if it were her mortal enemy. She pulled at her own hair and slapped her own face. The old woman quickly passed the dead infant to the father to free her hands. Before the young mother could do more harm to herself, the old lady wrapped her arms around her daughter tightly and cried with her. Their faces were etched with pain. The veins on the young mother's forehead bulged. Her mouth was wide open from her prolonged wail.

"Let me die! I don't want to live anymore!" She tried to free herself from her mother's tight embrace. She wanted to run back to step on a land mine and end her agony.

The grandmother continued to hold her daughter, telling her she was still young and could have many more children in the future. She cried even louder.

Eventually everyone left the scene in a state of shock.

That night the young mother lost herself completely. When dawn broke, she was crazed, her hair disheveled and her eyes staring blankly at her feet. She refused breakfast and was reluctant to depart from the mound of dirt where her baby was buried.

We rolled our mats, packed our things, and solemnly waved goodbye to them.

◆ ◆ ◆

The next day a family with older boys caught a wild dog, a skinny and scraggly thing with ribs protruding through its skin. This forest was truly devoid of wildlife. We hadn't even come upon a bird's nest or a lizard. Perhaps the thousands of people stomping through the jungle had scared everything away. If the dog struggled to procure a meal, there was no way any of us could have done better.

After capturing the dog, they killed it and chopped it into pieces. Mama approached them, asking if she could buy some.

They eyed her with pity but still gently shook their heads. They hadn't eaten meat for several days and weren't willing to part with any of it. Mama pointed her finger in our direction. Their gaze followed her finger to meet ours. We waved at them.

Mama strode back, triumphant. Blood was dripping down her hands. When others saw her carrying a chunk of meat, they rushed over to the supplier, only to be turned away.

While we were making dog stew for dinner, Papa excused himself and took a bowl of water over to squat behind a huge tree trunk. He excavated the gold hidden in his body and used a thin wire to saw off a tiny piece of it to pay for the food.

After we had eaten the delicious meat and sucked the bone marrow dry of nutrients, we still didn't throw the bones away: we saved them for another day to re-boil them with rice, water, and salt. We continued to use the bones until we were certain nothing was left.

We descended a steep cliff, proceeding with extreme caution in our collective effort. Roots reached through the side of the slope, lianas splayed on the ground, and vines dangled off tree branches. The wounded, the sick, and the old were brought down using hammocks suspended from vines obtained in the jungle above.

Vunn and I made it down with little difficulty, giving courage to Nuy and White Ghost to follow suit.

While Papa secured Black Ghost's basket with vines, Uncle Tek came down to direct the lowering of the caged girl. Her eyes burned with fright as the basket swung from side to side. Mama and Papa then worked their way down.

From here the path became more defined, but extremely narrow. Papa could only carry the two baskets front and back, not sideways. I walked in front of him, identifying the potholes, stumps, and stones that could be of danger to him. The path curved, wound to the right, and continued around many bends, boulders, and trees. For the next few days our routine was so mundane that its events were meshed together before we finally saw real daylight.

The path led us to a running stream. The music of waterfalls misting in the sun formed colorful dancing rainbows in front of majestic boulders and lush trees. I ran to it and joined the crowds in washing myself. It had been close to ten days since I last bathed. It was clear and cool, and the beauty of the sunshine lured all my senses into remembering this moment as heavenly and surreal. It was the most gorgeous stream; no waterfall since could compare to its beauty. It was utterly invigorating.

My old life died there. I felt the rebirth of a new self as the grime peeled away from me in the water. I no longer stank like a pig and scratched myself like a monkey. My numbness was slowly ebbing away.

I smiled and laughed. I splashed water at my siblings and strangers. The child in me had landed safely from its long, silent fall.

It was next to this running stream that we encountered the Vietnamese soldiers. They handed out food vouchers that each person could redeem for a few cans of stale rice and stale millet. We cooked and had real meals for the first time since the bus dropped us off at the top of the escarpment.

Those who were well stocked, strong, or able didn't stand in the long queue for food. They traded their vouchers with people such as my family for gold pieces instead. Mama haggled with them for more vouchers, and we continued to eat decently for the next few days.

Mama was shrewd. She cut in line with Half-Kilo in one hand and a dirty cloth diaper in the other. The six-month-old cried hysterically because Mama pinched her thigh. People were too disgusted by the smelly diaper and too sympathetic toward the crying baby to make a fuss. They just stepped aside and let the woman with her dying baby march right up to the front of the line.

Nearly two weeks after the Thai government fired at us, we reached the base of the Dangrek Mountains on Cambodian soil. Papa had to empty the second basket to carry White Ghost, now. We divided the rest of the essentials among us. As we distanced ourselves from the mountains and walked onto the only dirt road, our pace quickened. We were walking into the horizon, away from the jungles and away from death and life's injustice—but not to a new beginning nor a new hope, because we dared not hope as much now as we once had done. The world and its splendor still felt far out of reach. We still lacked a clear sense of direction and purpose. All we could do was pick ourselves up and continue walking.

We had just embarked on a three-month-long journey.

34. THE JOURNEY BACK IN CAMBODIA (JUNE TO SEPT. 1979)

Thousands of us refugees took to the pockmarked, unpaved road at the base of the mountains which meandered slowly southward toward Cambodian civilization.

Papa set the pace since he carried two basketfuls of his own flesh and blood. Black Ghost and White Ghost endured the humiliation as everyone looked at them with wonder and sympathy, as though they were broken animals.

Each family traveled at its own pace. Their speed depended upon the endurance and health of the weakest member in the family, the size of the family, and the age of the children. My family qualified for the trifecta. We were practically the last ones on the road.

My family had adopted a special needs boy along the way. He was a young straggler, an unwanted child whom Mama claimed was our distant cousin, third or fourth removed. His parents had abandoned him alone on the road. We found him around the time we reached the bottom of the mountains. He was no more than eight years old.

He was lost, hungry, and distressed when we found him. We stopped to ask where his parents were and whether he needed help.

It was when he answered our questions that we took pity on him.

"My dad wanted to throw me away, but my mom said, 'What a pity, he's our son.'" That was all he was able to express other than nodding fiercely when asked if he was hungry or thirsty. "My dad wanted to throw me away," he repeated, "but my mom said, 'What a pity, he's our son.'"

Now he walked with us, slept in our tent, and shared our food.

His name was Meer. He was an odd-looking child. His head was lopsided and too big for his scrawny body. His complexion was light, but it was tainted with jaundice. When walking, his right hip thrust forward with his left arm bent at the elbow, making him look somewhat imbalanced or like an old man with a broken arm and an injured leg.

When mealtime rolled around, he received the same rations as the rest of us.

Mama firmly believed that doing good deeds led to good karma. She was convinced some external forces were at play to provide us safe passage out of the mountains and away from the mines. It was our duty to pay it forward with this orphan: should we ignore him, ominous circumstances would subsequently befall us. She resolved to care for him the way she cared for any of us, to continue the cycle of positive karma.

Meer was born beautiful and healthy and an only child, too. His parents had mishandled his fever when he was an infant. Instead of disrobing him and soaking him in a bucket of water, they wrapped him in extra layers of clothes and blankets. The fever spiked too high, resulting in permanent brain damage. When he became a burden to them, they threw him out to fend for himself or die.

Meer was with us a little over a week before his parents returned for him.

♦♦♦

There were neither huts nor houses in sight on the road: only endless trees and glaring sunlight. When the glare abated, it rained. We all walked barefoot except for Mama, who'd borrowed my tiny flip-flops and never given them back— which was alright by me because that was the least I could do for her. My sandals covered only three-quarters of her feet.

Nature seemed untarnished and unaffected by our suffering, always pristine and somewhat primeval. We soon encountered more Vietnamese soldiers. Mama's ears perked up when she overheard the soldiers speak Chinese. She approached them for information. Through them, we learned more about the land mine situation and the precarious predicament we had been in back at the mountains. The Vietnamese had lost a few explosives experts during their attempts to clear a path so we refugees could descend.

The Vietnamese knew we were dying of thirst and hunger, but there wasn't much they could do to help. Parachuting water and food supplies was not an option because of the dense trees and explosive ordnances. The only viable solution was to clear the mines and grenades to minimize the casualties. The group of soldiers we had talked with had been in the vicinity close to three months, long before our arrival at the top of the mountain. They were sent to annihilate the Khmer Rouge and secure the perimeter. The Khmer Rouge were still a threat to them; their presence and shadows were still lurking in these treacherous jungles. For our safety, they told us to remain on the road and not deviate from it.

Because Mama could communicate with them, she seized the opportunity to barter with them. They were eager to make exchanges for a few tiny gold bits. Collectively, they displayed several items on the ground. We all squatted to inspect, but mostly to marvel. I saw an incandescent light bulb and immediately went into a fit of excitement.

I picked up the bulb to feel its smooth and delicate white surface. Wondering at its simplicity, I reminisced about a past where we had all sat at a dinner table together prior to our forced evacuation. We had had a handful of such lights throughout the house. They hummed with a low buzzing noise as they generated heat to warm the immediate space. They brightened up the kitchen where Papa peeled fruit for us. They illuminated the big family room where Vunn, Nuy, and I danced to entertain the adults at night. They lit up the photography studio where people came for family pictures even in broad daylight. I remembered a gentler time, and now I wanted a piece of it back.

"Mama, get the bulb so we can see in the dark." I brought the bulb closer to her face, convinced it would be the best purchase ever.

She brushed my hand away, saying, "It doesn't work like that. It's missing electricity."

Not knowing a thing about electricity and how it worked, I remained quiet while marveling at the bulb the way a child drooled over lollipops, turning it around and imagining how it would light up our tent out here in the wilderness.

In the end, the soldiers sold us a half cup of ground coffee, a few pounds of rice, and a bit of sugar. We immediately made coffee. We boiled the water in a pot, emptied the ground beans into the boiling water, and poured in some sugar.

There was nothing we could use to filter the coffee grounds, so we waited for the sediment to settle to the bottom before pouring it out into bowls to share. The coffee was sweet and bitter and it was slightly crunchy, too; but it was still so good.

Like the dog bones, we didn't throw out the coffee dregs. We saved them and reboiled them a few more times until the brew only tasted like water.

♦♦♦

As we distanced ourselves from the mountains, the monsoon season began to whirl in full force. Trying to gain some ground, we walked in the rain whenever we could, but we often stopped and pitched a tent to stay dry. The surroundings looked the same every day, with tall trees flanking the only paved road, leading us somewhere mysterious. It guided us away from the primeval jungle to lush fields of endless paddies with huts dotting the green landscape.

Upon encountering civilization, we hitchhiked a wagon ride from the natives. The demand far surpassed the supply, as countless people traveled the same road. Those natives who were altruistic allowed the feeble, the old, and the young to ride with no strings attached. Those who were opportunistic always wanted something in exchange, including the shirts off our backs.

Mama successfully solicited an oxcart filled with bales of hay and wood. It barely had enough room for her and Half-Kilo in the back. Both Black Ghost and White Ghost managed to cling to the sides. One was tucked against the left side and one against the right.

This allowed Papa to help us with our loads for the next seven or eight miles, where Mama and the three youngest were to be dropped off at a designated place.

When the oxcart came to a halt, Mama jumped off the wagon with Half-Kilo bouncing on her. She went to Black Ghost's side to lift her off the wagon, then she retrieved her bag of essentials. She thanked the driver and waved goodbye to him.

As the wagon pulled away, she realized White Ghost was missing. She stormed after it, shouting and waving to get the driver's attention. She caught up to the wagon a few minutes later, panting and huffing, with Half-Kilo crying. The three of them came back safely to find Black Ghost sitting patiently and demurely on the side of the road as if the world could pass by without her playing a part in it.

About three hours later, Papa, Uncle Tek, Vunn, Nuy and I caught up to Mama as she recovered from almost losing White Ghost.

The patter of the raindrops lulled and comforted us into a much-needed sense of rest despite the streaks of white lightning zapping through black clouds with thunderous zeal. The air was cool and the ground was wet, but we didn't care. We children kept to ourselves like turtles inside their shells.

Rain was benign and harmless compared to land mines. Everything else seemed inconsequential and non-life threatening, including the claps of thunder. Off to one corner and underneath a tree bough and tarp, the adults conversed about politics and the prospects of Cambodia. They talked mostly of what to make of our own immediate future. There were always questions to go with the uncertainties, and never any definitive answers.

Now that Uncle Tek had somewhat recovered from his illness, it was decided he should forge on with others to deliver the news of our surviving the mines and the mountains at the red brick house where we had slaughtered a cow several months ago.

There were many nights, initially, when we camped among relatives. Vunn and I ventured slightly deeper into the woods a short distance from the road to forage for bamboo shoots, edible leaves, and firewood. We chopped the bamboo shoots to make soup and gathered twigs for fire.

We pitched our tarps next to other people; and it was hard for anyone not to notice the four-inch rectum protruding out of Black Ghost. Everyone was aghast at the sight. Her anus was bright red, as if dripping blood and feces. No matter how often we washed it and pushed it back in, it always fell out again when she coughed or sneezed. Nuy, Papa and I did most of the cleaning and stuffing. I cringed each time at the slimy texture in my palm.

Black Ghost's immune system was shutting down. Her cough was tinged with blood and she complained of painful joints. She couldn't stand on her own and preferred to lie down, as if waiting for death to take her away. Her ribs pushed through her discolored skin like sharp blades. Her eyes retracted deeper into their hollow sockets. The fire and life in her irises were sputtering and slowly fading away into nothing.

We were desperate. When a stranger told us to skewer earthworms with wild gourds to save Black Ghost, Papa immediately dug in the ground, combing it for the wiggly antidote while Mama asked around for a fresh gourd. Black Ghost ate them in blissful ignorance. Nuy and I almost vomited in utter disgust.

When we caught a snake, we boiled it for broth to give Black Ghost energy. We ate the eggs inside it and sucked on its vertebrae.

Black Ghost held on to our realm with every fiber of her soul, but we were slowly losing her. This was a battle that Mama didn't know how to win. Mama might have already resigned herself to defeat.

Along the way, we traded our worldly possessions with the locals. We handed over an article of clothing for fish and rice and a night or two of refuge. We had kept the rubber bands from the water bags given to us by the Thai Samaritans, and we traded those for coconuts. Some locals freely fed our family and allowed us to sleep under their huts. Some provided food and shelter with the understanding that Papa and Vunn would devote a day or two to helping them in the fields and around the hut.

Mama exchanged the flip-flops for a night of comfort and a meal with a family that had a big well in front of their hut. We washed and refreshed our physical appearance and mental well-being there. They even gave us a few cans of rice to take on the journey.

We traipsed through the countryside at our own speed. The eight of us aimed to put ten to twelve miles behind us per day. There were many days when we reached that goal, interspersed with days when we had to take a break because we had no choice but to rest when one of us became ill.

We didn't know where we were headed at first. Mama wanted to head south to Phnom Penh, to start our new lives. Papa insisted on going west to Battambang to plant our roots. We ended up walking south to Mama's preference.

The sun was brutally hot. During our journey, we saw heat waves so intense they could be mistaken for ocean waves. There were days when our feet took a punishing beating from the hot gravel and the melting asphalt. The bottoms of our feet blistered and became tender and raw before forming thick, hard calluses.

It was only when we couldn't go another step that we would search for shelter.

We sought food and shelter from well over twenty families. They would have refused us had it not been for the pitiful states of White Ghost, Black Ghost, and Half-Kilo. More than half of these strangers had asked us, directly or indirectly, if they could help our family by adopting one of us. It never crossed my mind that my parents would be tempted, because we had gone through so much together as a family. Through thick and thin, even to the precipice of death, we were one.

Black Ghost's dying look drew people's attention. For whatever reason, they felt they could do a better job of taking care of her than we had.

"The journey to the city is a long one," they would say.

"This child won't make it. If she stays with us, there's a good chance she'll recover. Please consider our offer."

Mama would jokingly ask Black Ghost if she'd like to stay with them.

Initially, Black Ghost had resolutely shaken her head; but after a few more propositions from other families, she became quiet.

Black Ghost might have come undone by being hauled around and bounced up and down in a basket across the countryside. She was keen and intuitive for her age: a silent observer who would selflessly give all she had to save someone. She might have sensed that her own time was near and probably thought that if she removed herself, she'd spare the rest of us the burden she perceived herself to be.

Papa's baskets reminded me of when we first left our home during the forced evacuation. It was the same scenario, except that he carried the two huge bags of cameras. Now two of my siblings dangled in the baskets like diseased creatures lost in time.

Black Ghost would rather endure her own suffering silently than remind us of her ailment. She seldom complained of her aching and stiff body. She knew Papa was feeble and blind. He had been carrying her in a basket longer than she could remember.

When asked the next time, Black Ghost nodded.

She nodded each time thereafter. Black Ghost wanted to be adopted by a family who had three older sons and no daughters. She was lured by the food they fed her: solid white rice with fish and green mangoes. They also lived in a large, sturdy hut. While the rest of us slept under their hut's floorboards, Black Ghost could sleep and play inside.

Her future with this native family was presented to her on a silver platter. They adored her and invited her into their gentle and caring embraces. She ate well and slept well.

She nodded and said, "I want to stay with them."

Black Ghost recalled us walking away from her. She was fine at first, until she sensed the finality of our departure.

When she realized she would never see us again, she cried. Her adoptive family hugged her tightly, but she was inconsolable.

She cried until she saw Mama running back to her with open arms.

From Mama's recollection, she was only toying with Black Ghost. It was never her intention to leave her baby behind. She would rather die before giving any of her children away.

I truly believed the earth was flat; that somehow our journey would conclude, and we would just stop. It felt like we had been walking since infinity, from one sunrise to its sunset, from a single step to a million strides. It only made sense to me that things had a beginning and an end like a spool of thread eventually reaching the tip. Upon entering the world, life began with brightness; and upon exiting, it ended in a black void. I deduced somehow that our journey would reach the edge of the earth and I would surely be forced to stop or fall off the ledge with my next step.

My mind was always filled with such minutiae. It didn't take much for me to get lost in thought and wander off ahead of my family, especially when Mama was attending to Half-Kilo and when Papa stopped to rest with two children in baskets.

I walked a mile before realizing I should stop to wait for my family to catch up. I sensed something was wrong, so I paused in midstride and moved to the side of the road and watched people go by. After waiting a good hour or so, I retraced my steps. I came to a junction where the road had forked. The road I was on consisted of hot pavement surrounded with rice paddies and huts. The road I assumed my family must have taken was paved and flanked by sidewalks and concrete buildings. I began doubting myself and questioning the timing of our split. I cast so many doubts that they paralyzed me. I decided the best course of action was to wait there at the junction for them to find me.

I waited at the fork for perhaps an hour, to no avail. Passersby asked if I was lost. At first, I said no, telling them I was waiting for my parents; and then later on, I said yes. A few invited me to go home with them. I declined their kind offers. One person gave me food. It was a hairy fruit the size of a tennis ball, orange and red on the outside and yellow on the inside. It was sweet and sour with a noticeable tang. The fruit quenched my thirst while I continued to wait for my family's return.

Finally I decided to take my chances with a stick. Whichever direction it pointed to, I was determined to follow. I bent down to concentrate as I closed my eyes tight. With fond memories of Grandma, I conjured her face in my mind. She smiled at me. I softly asked her to guide my hand. I twirled the stick and held my breath. When I opened my eyes, it pointed straight ahead to the other road. There wasn't much I could do but have faith and follow the path before me.

Once I set off on this new road, an overwhelming feeling of panic assailed me. What if it takes me farther away from my family? The road quickly transitioned from a rural path to a more urban roadway, where the sidewalks were made of concrete and the buildings were of polished stone with glass windows. It felt as though I was walking away from something ancient and familiar, as if I was saying goodbye to the dirt and trees and possibly my family. I was heading straight into something foreign and artificial, and it frightened me. The world felt strangely large and modern as I entered Kampong Tom Province. I felt more lost now than I'd ever felt before. There were so many moments when I wanted to turn back, but I told myself to go a little farther. This feeling went on for a good thirty minutes as I passed countless people scurrying in various directions.

I eventually came upon a crowd of people converged in a concrete plaza looking down at something. I walked over and, sure enough, I saw my family sitting atop a low stone wall, also staring at the attraction.

Mama knew this spot would be the ideal location to find one another. She told Papa that she would wait there until she turned grey if she had to for my eventual return.

Meanwhile, Papa was searching for me. My parents couldn't believe they had worked so hard to keep me alive only to lose me in such an absurd manner. It was like swimming across an open sea only to drown in a backyard swimming pool. They were angry with themselves more than with me, although I couldn't help feeling guilty for not paying attention and for wasting precious time. After all, our goal was still to trek at least ten miles across the land each day.

Everyone had already eaten. I ate my meal by the encased well where everyone congregated. I listened to people telling stories of the alligators in the well below. I looked down and saw four pairs of eyes looking up at me. Someone nearby was telling a story that this area became a ghost city after the Khmer Rouge took over. The only time he heard noises was when the Khmer Rouge tossed people into the well to feed these alligators. I wasn't sure if the story was true, but I wouldn't be surprised if it was, for I knew the Khmer Rouge's cruelty had no bounds.

The images came unbidden as I pictured myself thrown inside this well and ravaged by these alligators. How they would fight each other for my head and limbs! I was rattled at such grim thoughts and quickly backed away to join the rest of my family on the stone wall. We sat idly waiting for Papa's return.

Papa eventually came back to the well. He was relieved to see me, but I felt ashamed: I had needlessly caused everyone anxiety and slowed our progress.

◆◆◆

My parents eventually agreed to head west to Siem Reap, tossing out Phnom Penh from our future; they were entertaining the idea of escaping to Thailand, again. In Siem Reap, we staked our tent on a busy street for two weeks to restore our vitality and make a tiny profit. We pitched our tent next to a busy thoroughfare and opened a food stall business. We sold pickled vegetables and marinated beef skewers. People loved them and came back for more. Some came bearing bananas, mangoes, or fish to barter with us. Some even offered their baskets and wooden chairs. We gladly accepted the baskets and gently declined the chairs. We picked and chose what we absolutely needed; which wasn't much, since we had to continue our journey.

Our initial capital investment came from the same piece of gold hidden in Papa. Since the trek down the mountains, we had used most of it. Papa sawed what was left of the gold into two pieces. He delicately put one piece, no more than the tip of my finger, into a tiny tin container with a few white pills and his foot-long strand of floss, made of sewing thread. He would reuse the floss until it broke, but even then he would tie the two ends together and put it back into the container, saving it for another use.

He gave the other piece of gold to Mama to exchange for two big bags of rice, which weighed about fifty pounds total. We then hauled the rice around to barter for beef and vegetables. Rice was the medium of exchange, an inconvenience for everyone. People walked around carrying bags of rice over their shoulders, saddled by their weight. They paid for our beef skewers with rice.

Mama was able to sell the excess rice for a few bits of gold fragments. She took a bag of rice along with a tiny piece of gold to barter for a bicycle. I rode on the back with her a few times to buy vegetables and beef for the following day.

Gold was a precious commodity, but we didn't have much left: a half an ounce at most.

Papa always kept it in his pocket, extremely mindful of it. I often saw him patting his shirt and pants to make sure it was still there. The essence of our future resided in a tiny container.

As we made our way south, we camped at many more locations and sold more beef and vegetables to make ends meet.

One day Papa took us to scale Angkor Wat, a religious monument with ancient architecture displaying massive cone-like stone towers. As I climbed those huge steps, a sense of wonder and mystery overcame me. The monument was colossal, and its beauty exuded an ingenuity and power that dominated nature. Intricate designs and patterns were woven with symmetry and symbols that seemed to belong to another place and time. Lotuses, elephants, deities, and strange creatures were carved into the stone walls as if they permanently resided there. I could almost hear their voices echoing and calling to me from the past to pull me into their magical realm.

I couldn't believe that such ancient beauty existed in the desolation of my world. Did men build the Angkor Wat temple or did the gods create it themselves? It was hard to imagine that humans could create something this beautiful, magnificent and of a magnitude beyond comprehension, because all I had seen and experienced so far were death and destruction—men were the destroyers of youth and innocence and killers of future and dreams. If I could, I would manifest myself into mist and walk into these sacred stones to live amongst the gods and spirits. With two hands, I rubbed the nose of a giant statue, closed my eyes, and wished with all my might for immortality. I knew it was silly to wish and pray, but I couldn't help wanting to exit my ugly realm and start anew in a magical one. Soon, voices yanked me out of my reverie as my family called for me from below to head home.

The trip to Angkor Wat was pleasant and intriguing, but exhausting.

The next day Papa took White Ghost and me to a swimming pool. It was a large, man-made pool shrouded with trees and foliage. Papa reached into his pocket to place the tin container by the steps as we descended into the water. We all swam in our clothes. It was refreshing and much more fun than swimming in a lake or pond because I didn't have to worry about leeches clinging to my body.

White Ghost held on to Papa as he taught her how to swim. We frolicked in the pool for almost two hours. There were a few other people who came in later as we were about to leave. We climbed out of the pool and left, leaving the tiny container behind, completely forgotten in our merriment. We hopped and sang on the way back.

Just as we approached our tent, Papa panicked. He frantically searched his shirt and pants. He made a beeline for the bike parked next to our tent and rode off in a rush. About twenty minutes later he came back looking like he had waged a war, lost the battle, and didn't have the courage to return home.

My parents fought that night and for many more nights to come.

The next day we worked harder to sell more food and save more of the profits we made. This continued for a couple of weeks as we traveled through various towns. We would pitch the tent next to a running river, on a concrete slab next to a building, under a big tree, or in the sun while selling pickled vegetables and beef skewers for rice.

35. BACK TO THAILAND (SEPTEMBER 1979)

Instead of heading straight to the red brick house to recuperate from our journey for a few weeks, my family pressed on westward. We eventually made it back to Svay Sisophon and chanced once more to escape to Thailand.

Cambodia was a lost cause, a castaway country with no hope for the future. By that point it was clear that if we were to stay, Black Ghost would surely die. Mama knew we had to get out of Cambodia. The only country she was familiar with that was attainable by foot was Thailand. We simply had to hope that if we made it there again, we would be allowed to stay.

We were desperate, not insane.

Only Papa's sister-in-law and Mama's sister Gai didn't attempt a second chance at freedom.

The rest of my family and relatives who survived both the land mines and mountains risked it all again to get to Thailand.

Mama's three sisters (Lan, Hang, and Sing) were too terrified to take such a risk after they learned about our ordeal with the Thai government and how we plunged down from the mountaintop and got trapped in a sea of explosives.

Eventually, Uncle Yi and Uncle Jo were able to convince their second youngest sister Hang to come along and help Mama with the young ones. Aunt Hang came with us out of a deep sense of loyalty and obligation.

Papa's sister Wui and her family of six left for Thailand a day or two after Uncle Tek. Finally, we made our way to the border. This time we didn't need a guide to show us the way. With countless people taking the same risk, the roads and jungles were busy with refugees.

Papa continued to carry Black Ghost in one basket and pots and pans in the other. White Ghost was able to walk on her own, now.

We arrived in 007 Refugee Camp in early September of 1979. I was nine years and nine months old. Just after we arrived, they blocked off the border. We pitched our tent in a sea of tents in an area sprawling and filled with red clouds of dust. I must have breathed in a pound of red dirt each day. My lungs felt heavy and dry and clogged like a blocked filter. Every time I blew my nose, red mucus came out in large masses.

There was no water nearby. We had to walk one mile each way to haul water from a well, and everyone flocked there like bees to a hive. We waited in a long line for our turn, and sometimes it took over an hour to fetch a bucket of water.

◆◆◆

About two months later, we were transferred to Khao-I-Dang, a holding center for displaced people. We jumped in jubilation upon learning that the United Nations and other organizations had intervened to rescue us. It was the greatest feeling in the world to know we would be spared from being dumped and thrown away again at the mountaintop. Despite the smell of landfills and human waste brewing in the refugee camp, it was still as invigorating as clean, fresh air.

We moved from camp to camp and went from breathing red dust in our tent to living in quadrangular units on pure white sand. The sand was so white that it resembled, exactly, both sugar and salt. I even staked out a small corner under the quad to farm a small patch of bean sprouts to sell to the neighbors for a few Thai bahts.

There were buses taking us to a white sandy beach dotted with swaying palm trees. It was heavenly, and my eyes feasted with hunger on its dreamlike serenity. We swam in the warm ocean repeatedly. I have yet to come across a more beautiful beach.

Modern medicine pulled Black Ghost back from death's shroud. We all received immunization shots. Her tuberculosis was somewhat under control, but she didn't fully recover until after we reached our final destination.

Mama's practical skills and talents were put to good use once more. She wrote a sign in both Chinese and Cambodian, simply stating "Hair Cut." Nuy and I took turns being her assistant. She later resumed her role as broker. Bargaining blood coursed through her veins as naturally as a bird is made to soar in the sky. She was always out finding buyers and sellers for precious stones and gold.

My family stayed in Thailand a little over two years, moving from one camp to the next. We stayed in a total of five refugee camps: 007, Khao-I-Dang, Meirut, Chhunbury, and Lumpini. We celebrated two Cambodian New Years and two Chinese New Years, and we welcomed the birth of yet another newborn in our family.

Our latest addition was a beautiful baby boy. My parents named him *Chifong*, or Abundant Knowledge. He weighed over twelve pounds and the doctor had to perform a Cesarean section to deliver him.

Chifong was born on August 31, 1981, in a Thai hospital.

The prophecy came to fruition: nine children. Mama had two miscarriages and five girls sandwiched between two boys. She had nine pregnancies as prophesized, a number she once feared but now was content with; for she had done all she could to keep us alive.

On September 21, 1981, we boarded an airplane and headed to America. We landed in Chicago. The Hillcrest

Church in Hudsonville, Michigan sponsored my family. The church members, the Rusticus and the LePoire families, who were also our sponsors, were there as we disembarked from the plane. I was eleven years and nine months old when I finally arrived in America, which had once seemed as elusive as an oasis in the desert. In my darkest hours, I always desired to be lifted out of the hell of Cambodia and taken anywhere else; and here I was, in America, at last.

♦♦♦

We felt euphoric when we landed. It was as if a beautiful cloud drifted over to me and allowed me to capture it in a jar, where I could place it warmly next to my heart and make my soul soar.

I'm where the sky kisses the grass and where children run and laugh in the park. The trees tango in the wind with birds and butterflies dancing in harmony.

I'm where I no longer dream of food when I sleep.

I'm where my education began at the age of twelve.

I'm home.

(The End)

STATUE OF LIBERTY INSCRIPTION

"Give me your tired, your poor,
Your huddled masses yearning to breathe free,
The wretched refuse of your teeming shore.
Send these, the homeless, tempest-tossed to me."

Photo 3: Thai Refugee Camp– 1981

L to R: Aunt Hang; Nuy; Yook or Yuk, "White Ghost";
Meiyeng, "Beautiful Hero"; Sy, "Half-Kilo"; Ling, "Black Ghost";
Sann; King, "Geng"; and Vunn

Photo 4: Family Mugshots - 1981

EPILOGUE

My family loves the Hillcrest Church people in Hudsonville, Michigan. We are indebted to the church and to countless people who helped us settle in America. There were people who tutored us in English, drove us to school and to doctor's appointments, taught my parents how to drive, and found full-time jobs for the adults and part-time jobs for us children. However, even though we loved the snow in Michigan, we hated the cold. After living nineteen months in Hudsonville, we moved to California.

Meiyeng, Sann, and all seven children are alive and well. Mama and Papa are presently living in La Habra, California. All seven children and an additional nine grandchildren, ages ranging from one month old to fourteen years old, surround them with love and laughter.

We do what many Cambodian families do: we own a donut shop. We don't mind the hard work. It puts food on the table while we pursue our education.

Vunn, who goes by the name of Steve, has a wife and two sons. He now owns Boston Donuts in La Habra.

Nuy (now called Vivian) received her BA in business from Cal State Fullerton and has a daughter and a son.

I am married with one daughter and one son and am currently the president of Topp and Lau Inc., a Certified Public Accounting firm, practicing taxation, financial advisory, and accounting in Orange County.

White Ghost, also known as Cathy, sales insurance and real estate. She lives in Huntington Beach and loves to snowboard and surf.

Black Ghost, or Ling, received her master's degree in physics. She loves teaching math.

Half-Kilo, or Sy, is a registered nurse.

Lastly, there is comfort in knowing my youngest brother Chi Fong is in the U.S. military, defending our freedom. He's married with three adorable girls.

◆ ◆ ◆

If it hadn't been for Beautiful Hero, my mother Meiyeng and her heart of stone, my family wouldn't have lived to tell this story. In retrospect it appears her sole purpose was to save us from the hell of the Khmer Rouge.

Did any of us truly escape the hell that was Cambodia? I believe part of us is still there, held against our will. I still have nightmares, but they are less frequent now after I've committed my memory to paper. I've come to discover and appreciate that writing is therapeutic, like a confession—not just for one person, but for a world waiting to hear it.

Photo 5: Hudsonville, MI (November 1981)

L to R: Cathy, "White Ghost"; Vivian, "Nuy"; Chi Fong, "Baby"; Mom;
Ling, "Black Ghost"; Jenny (center), "Geng"; Aunt Hang;
Sy, "Half-Kilo"; Dad; and Vunn

Photo 6: Family Portrait - 1996

Front: Chi Fong; Mom; Dad; and Syrah, "Half-Kilo"
Back: Ling, "Black Ghost"; Cathy, "White Ghost"
Steve, "Vunn"; Vivian, "Nuy"; and Jenny, "Geng"

Photo 7: Fullerton, CA (2012)

Front L to R: Dad (Sann) and Mom (Meiyeng)

Back L to R: Steve (Vunn), Vivian (Nuy), Jenny (Geng), Cathy, (White Ghost), Ling (Black Ghost), Syrah (Half-Kilo), and Chi (Army Boy)

Photo 8: Book signing event (Dec. 2016)

Front L to R: Mom and Dad

Back L to R: Steve (Vunn), Vivian (Nuy), Jenny (Geng), Ling (Black Ghost), and Sy (Half-Kilo)

ACKNOWLEDGMENTS

I owe this book to my parents, uncles, aunts, and siblings. Their blessings and encouragement propelled me to complete our family memoir.

Special thanks to my husband Kai and daughter Elise for reading and editing the manuscript, creating maps, designing the website, and touching up photos. Their love and devotion have sustained and encouraged me from penning the first word all the way to the very last. Along with my son Ethan, you all are my rock and sunshine.

I am also indebted to many friends who are not only generous with their time but also with their wines. We have enjoyed endless bottles of libations as we discussed the manuscript. Their willingness to edit as I wrote, and re-edit as I re-wrote (countless times), moved me to the core. Lynne Yost, Angela White, Pam Berg, and Anne Solaas, you guys are my angels!

Thank you also to Susan Foy, Lourdes Lejano, Alex Nackoul, Donnie Crevier, Jenny Eng, and Pat Hom for reading and providing constructive criticism with your wise and insightful suggestions for the book. Each of you at various points in time imparted and contributed invaluable advice to me, and I am beyond grateful for it all.

Finally, thank you to the readers of this book for taking a leap of faith to mentally dive into an era the world knows so little about. I truly appreciate you and your time.

AUTHOR'S NOTE

I wrote this book for two reasons: to slay my nightmares and to contribute insight into a dark period in Cambodia, which was marred by many internal conflicts and external forces of mighty nations.

The events that occurred in Cambodia have shaped me forever. I can't seem to forget the faces of my cousins and the Khmer atrocities that I endured and survived. Here in America, living a life so far removed from my past, an empty plastic container can easily take me to Uncle Rain, Big Daughter and Sida's plight of thirst in the jungles. My inner voice often echoes this thought to me: *If they only had their own water container, they might have lived.*

And rice. Rice in abundance often reminds me of its lack during the Khmer Rouge regime. Every time I see rice, I take a spoon and scoop it into my mouth. That first spoonful is a remembrance of those who died of hunger; it is my ritual to honor their deaths and express an overwhelming gratitude for my life.

ABOUT THE AUTHOR

Jennifer H. Lau was born in Cambodia in 1970, the third of seven children. She was only five when the Khmer Rouge forcibly relocated her family, friends and neighbors to live and work in one giant concentration camp. She endured four long years of living in perpetual fear, under constant threat of execution, disease, and starvation. Her daily survival often depended on finding the next drop of water, the next grain of rice.

Finally arriving in America at age twelve, illiterate and traumatized, Jennifer forged on—neither willing to accept these setbacks nor to let her former oppressors dictate her future. In addition to working full-time alongside her family to contribute to a fragile new beginning, she also pursued her education with great fervor, endeavoring to learn how to survive the enigmatic first-world challenges of her new country. Her keen understanding of the harsh realities of a struggling nation served her well in her studies at the University of California, Irvine, where she earned dual degrees in Chinese and Chinese Literature, and Economics.

Today, as a Certified Public Accountant, Jennifer Lau owns and runs Topp and Lau accounting firm, where she is proud to contribute to society by assisting individuals, businesses, and charitable organizations. She lives in Orange County, California with her husband and their two children.

Having early on been deprived of education herself, Jennifer contributes both time and money to her immediate and extended communities to combat illiteracy. She hopes her story of sorrow and survival inspires readers from all walks of life in their own struggles and successes. She provides this firsthand account of the Khmer Rouge atrocities for future generations to study in the hope of shedding light into a dark time. Her greatest fear is that history will repeat itself if we don't learn from it. Revolution everywhere in the world just doesn't happen overnight.

VISIT WEBSITE

www.JenniferLau.net

For more content, photos, and omitted chapters.

Email: JenniferHongLau@gmail.com

BOOK DISCUSSION QUESTIONS

(From easy to difficult)

1. What message do you think *Beautiful Hero* is trying to convey in quoting Edmund Burke: "All that is necessary for the triumph of evil is that good men do nothing"?

2. What are some of the metaphors and symbolism in the story?

3. Would the family have survived without Beautiful Hero? Do you think Sann and Meiyeng complement each other?

4. How credible is the perspective of a five year old? How accurate do you think her recollection is of the events that took place? Did the story develop as the child grew over time?

5. The song quoted in the book appears three times throughout the story. Discuss the three stages of its meanings at these three points.

6. Discuss and provide examples of the extreme duality of Beautiful Hero's compassion and heart of stone. Is she a likable or sympathetic character?

7. If the family were to divide up (if Beautiful Hero and the two smallest children were to remain in District 5, while Sann

and the three oldest children were to escape to District 3), what would the chances have been that the two groups would have survived separately?

8. Besides to scare children from venturing outside the village, why were there stories of monsters in the wood? Did the adults experience a similar kind of fear with darkness?

9. Could the family have done more to save the Vietnamese family (Wonhing and Didi) from walking to their deaths? Would you have acted differently?

10. Genocide and communism are serious topics. What do you think you have learned about them from reading this book? Give examples.

11. Compare bribery and corruption under the monarchist government to the system during the Khmer Rouge era. Is it possible to eradicate 100% of corruption and bribery in any society? How does law keep order?

12. How are the concepts of individual vs. group, tyranny vs. democracy, sacrifice vs. selfishness, and life vs. death portrayed in the book?

13. Do you think the casualties at the top of the Dangrek Mountains would have been much higher had the refugees never experienced and suffered the hardships and starvation under the Khmer Rouge?

14. The author was five years old when the Khmer Rouge took over Cambodia, and her education began at the age of twelve in America.

(A) Had she been any younger, would she have been able to remember those horrendous experiences.

(B) Had she been a couple of years older, would she have had enough time to go to school to gain a good enough command of English to write the book?

15. List other instances of communism and genocides in other parts of the world. How are they different or similar to the one in Cambodia?

16. Almost forty years later, Cambodia is still struggling as a third-world nation. Do you have any suggestions about how Cambodia can heal and move forward as a nation? What can be done to prevent history from repeating itself?

AMAZON REVIEW

If you like the book and have a few minutes to spare, please leave a review on Amazon. I'd be tremendously happy and dance with joy; and I might even hug a stranger for that matter. Thank you so much for your time.

To write a review on Amazon, **go to**:
Amazon.com> *Search* for Beautiful Hero How We Survived the Khmer Rouge> *Click* on Customer Reviews (right below the title)> *Click* on Write a Customer Review

Made in the USA
Middletown, DE
25 March 2019